INTERNATIONAL DEVELOPMENT IN FOCUS

Orders without Borders

Direct Enforcement of Foreign Restraint and Confiscation Decisions

STEFANO BETTI, VLADIMIR KOZIN, AND JEAN-PIERRE BRUN

WORLD BANK GROUP

STAR Stolen Asset Recovery Initiative
The World Bank • UNODC

Contents

Acknowledgments   *vii*
Abbreviations   *xi*

CHAPTER 1 **Introduction**   **1**

1.1 Background   1
1.2 Objectives, Structure, Audience   2
1.3 Methodology   3
Notes   4

CHAPTER 2 **The International Legal Framework on Direct and Indirect Enforcement**   **5**

2.1 UN Convention against Corruption   5
2.2 Enforcement of Foreign Confiscation Orders under Other Legal Instruments   11
2.3 The Enforcement of Foreign NCB Confiscation Orders in the International Legal Framework   14
2.4 Takeaways   14
Notes   15

CHAPTER 3 **Domestic Legal Approaches to Direct Enforcement**   **17**

3.1 Overview   17
3.2 Authorities Involved in Direct Enforcement   23
3.3 Scope of Direct Enforcement Action   24
3.4 Scope of the Examination by Requested Jurisdictions   27
3.5 Existence of a Treaty and Reciprocity   30
3.6 Substantive Conditions and Grounds for Refusal   30
3.7 Direct Enforcement of Freezing and Seizing Orders   35
3.8 Rights of Interested Parties   39
3.9 Takeaways   43
Annex   45
Notes   51

CHAPTER 4 **Challenges and Obstacles to Direct Enforcement Action**   **55**

4.1 Overview   55
4.2 Limited Familiarity with and Use of Direct Enforcement Procedures   55
4.3 Lack of Sufficient, or Sufficiently Precise, Information   58

4.4 Difficulties Stemming from Lack of Non-Conviction-Based (NCB) Procedures   59
4.5 Lack of Understanding of Foreign Procedures   59
4.6 Competing Requests from Different Jurisdictions   60
4.7 Resource Constraints in Requested Jurisdictions   60
4.8 Differences in Legal Systems and Procedures   60
4.9 Slow and Time-Consuming Confiscation Proceedings in Requesting Jurisdictions   61
4.10 Burdens for Requested Jurisdictions in Maintaining Temporary Measures on Perishable or High-Cost Items   62
4.11 Lengthy Processes in the Requested Jurisdiction to Determine Whether the Conditions for Direct Enforcement Have Been Fulfilled   62
4.12 Confiscation Orders Contained in Long and Bulky Documents   63
4.13 Conditionality Placed on the Direct Enforcement of Foreign Confiscation Orders   64
4.14 Takeaways   64
Notes   65

CHAPTER 5   **Recommendations   67**
5.1 Establishing and Enhancing Legal Frameworks   67
5.2 Effectively Applying Existing Legal Frameworks   72
Notes   77
References and Other Readings   78

Appendix A   **UNCAC Provisions (Excerpts)   81**

Appendix B   **Questionnaire for National Experts   87**

Appendix C   **Surveyed Countries' Legal Frameworks (Excerpts)   91**

Boxes

Case Study 3.1:   Nigeria's path toward comprehensive direct enforcement legislation   19
Case Study 3.2:   Use of crime-specific (money-laundering) statutes: the case of Cyprus   20
Case Study 3.3:   Use of general mechanisms for the recognition of foreign criminal judgments: the case of Italy   21
Case Study 3.4:   Authorities involved in direct enforcement in Canada   23
Case Study 3.5:   Value confiscation and recognition of foreign confiscation orders: recent Canadian and UK jurisprudence   24
Case Study 3.6:   Recognition of non-conviction-based (NCB) foreign orders in France and Canada   26
Case Study 3.7:   Hong Kong SAR, China—direct enforcement of non-conviction-based (NCB) foreign confiscation orders   27
Case Study 3.8:   UK jurisprudence on limiting the scope of examination for foreign confiscation orders   29
Case Study 3.9:   British Virgin Islands' Direct Enforcement Procedure and Conditions   31
Case Study 3.10: Singapore's use of the disposal inquiry mechanism in mutual legal assistance (MLA) proceedings   32
Case Study 3.11: New Zealand's procedure for the direct enforcement of foreign restraining orders   35
Case Study 3.12: South Africa's template application for the registration of foreign restraint orders   36
Case Study 3.13: South Africa's template notification to affected parties   40

Case Study 4.1: Statistical information on enforcement action in surveyed
           countries   56
Case Study 4.2: New Zealand's opening of a domestic investigation   57
Case Study 4.3: Non-execution in France of a request for confiscation regarding
           immoveable property   58
Case Study 4.4: Switzerland's evidentiary challenges with common law
           countries   61
Case Study 4.5: Singapore's experience with foreign authorities going "cold"   62
Case Study 4.6: The Lucy case in the United States: corruption and the illegal wildlife
           trade   63

Tables

Table 3.1 Main stages and flow of direct enforcement procedures   42
Table A3.1 Direct and indirect enforcement country comparison,
       by legal system   45

Acknowledgments

This study is the result of special collaborative efforts from colleagues around the world. Their time and expertise were invaluable in developing a tool to familiarize practitioners with the use of direct and indirect enforcement mechanisms to recover proceeds and instrumentalities of corruption through international cooperation.

This publication was written by Stefano Betti (International Security and Criminal Policy Expert), Vladimir Kozin (Crime Prevention and Criminal Justice Officer, United Nations Office on Drugs and Crime), and Jean-Pierre Brun (Senior Financial Specialist, World Bank). The authors are especially grateful to Emile Van der Does (Stolen Asset Recovery Initiative Coordinator) and Jean Pesme (Global Director, World Bank) for their overall guidance and support.

The team benefited from many insightful comments that helped shape the study during the peer review process. Additionally, the views and input of practitioners from 31 jurisdictions were solicited through a written survey and an online Expert Group Meeting held on June 18, 2020. Special thanks go to the Permanent Missions to the United Nations (Vienna) for providing input and supporting the identification of relevant national experts. The authors wish to extend a special thanks to the practitioners who offered their experience, perspectives, and drafting suggestions throughout the process.

JURISDICTION	NAME AND POSITION
Australia	**Sarbjeet Banwait** Senior Litigation Lawyer—VIC Criminal Assets Litigation Australian Federal Police
Brazil	**Cristina Luisa Hedler** Advisor at the General Assets Recovery Coordination—CGRA/DRCI/SENAJUS
Brazil	**Duílio Mocelin Cardoso** General Coordinator of the General Assets Recovery Coordination—CGRA/DRCI/SENAJUS
Brazil	**Edson Fabio Garutti Moreira** General Coordinator of the General Institutional Articulation Coordination—CGAI/DRCI/SENAJUS

JURISDICTION	NAME AND POSITION
Canada	**Ivan Nault** Counsel International Assistance Group Criminal Law Operations Section National Litigation Sector Department of Justice Canada
China	**Mei Fen** Official Department of International Cooperation Central Commission of Discipline Inspection (CCDI) Commissioner of the National Commission of Supervision (NCS)
China	**Huang Er** Official Department of International Cooperation Central Commission of Discipline Inspection (CCDI) Commissioner of the National Commission of Supervision (NCS)
China	**Szeto Ying Lok** Senior Government Counsel Department of Justice Hong Kong SAR, China
China	**Lin Zeyu** Permanent Mission of China, Vienna
Cyprus	**Maria Kyrmizi Antoniou** Senior Counsel Republic Unit for Combating Money Laundering MOKAS FIU, ARO Cyprus
Egypt, Arab Rep.	**Ahmed Mohamed Abdelaziz Osman** Office of the Prosecutor-General
France	**Sophie Verneret-Lamour** MLA team Ministry of Justice
France	**Anne Haller** Head of the Legal Division French Agency for the Management and Recovery of Forfeited and Confiscated Assets (Agrasc)
India	**Amit Dua** IRS Joint Director Enforcement Directorate, New Delhi
Indonesia	**Yusfidli Adhyaksana** Legal/Attorney-General's Office Attaché Indonesian Embassy, Singapore
Italy	**Michele Fini** Office for International AffairsDirectorate General for International Affairs and Judicial CooperationMinistry of Justice
Kazakhstan	**Issatay Jahanger** Senior Assistant to the Prosecutor General Prosecutor General's Office
Latvia	**Dace Sauša** Lawyer Department of the International Cooperation Ministry of Justice
Lebanon	**Judge Rana Akoum** Focal Point on Anti-Corruption Cooperation Ministry of Justice

JURISDICTION	NAME AND POSITION
New Zealand	**Craig Hamilton** Detective Inspector/Manager Asset Recovery Units Asset Recovery Unit Financial Crime Group New Zealand Police
Nigeria	**Aliyu Wali** Senior Project Officer External Cooperation Unit EFCC
Nigeria	**Barr Abba Muhammed** Senior Legal Analyst EFCC
Nigeria	**Emmanuel Ikechukwu Nweke** Permanent Mission of Nigeria, Vienna
Nigeria	**Chisom Aghadinuno** Federal Ministry of Justice
Russian Federation	**Victor Baldin** Head Department for Supervision of the Enforcement of Anti-Corruption Legislation General Prosecutor's Office
Russian Federation	**Aslan Yusufov** Deputy Head Department for Supervision of the Enforcement of Anti-Corruption Legislation General Prosecutor's Office
Russian Federation	**Vadim Tarkin** Deputy Director Department for International Legal Cooperation Ministry of Justice
Russian Federation	**Olga Mokhova** Chief Prosecutor Department for Supervision of the Enforcement of Anti-Corruption Legislation General Prosecutor's Office
Russian Federation	**Natalia Primakova** Second Secretary Department for New Challenges and Threats Ministry of Foreign Affairs
Russian Federation	**Sergey Plokhov,** Head, Department for Institutional and Legal Cooperation - Deputy Head, Directorate-General for International Legal Cooperation, General Prosecutor's Office
Singapore	**Teo Yu Chou** Deputy Senior State Counsel Attorney-General's Chambers
Singapore	**Muhammad Faiz Khafidz** Case Manager Attorney-General's Chambers
South Africa	**Adv. Dianne Willman** Deputy Director of Public Prosecutions
Spain	**Pedro Perez Enciso** Senior Prosecutor at International Cooperation Unit
Switzerland	**Julia Volken** Deputy Head Mutual Legal Assistance Unit I Federal Office of Justice

JURISDICTION	NAME AND POSITION
United States	**Teresa C. Turner-Jones** Sr. Trial Attorney U.S. Department of Justice Criminal Division Money Laundering Asset Recovery Section
StAR Initiative	**Emile Van Der Does De Willebois** Lead Financial Sector Specialist and Global Lead for Financial Market Integrity, World Bank, Coordinator of the StAR Initiative
StAR Initiative	**Badr El Banna** Crime Prevention and Criminal Justice Officer Corruption and Economic Crimes Branch United Nations Office on Drugs and Crime (UNODC), Stolen Asset Recovery Initiative

Abbreviations

CARIN	Camden Assets Recovery Inter-Agency Network
CoSP	Conference of the States Parties
EGM	Expert Group Meeting
EU	European Union
FATF	Financial Action Task Force on Money Laundering
GRECO	Group of States Against Corruption
NCB	non-conviction-based
OECD	Organisation for Economic Co-operation and Development
MLA	mutual legal assistance
MLACMA	Mutual Legal Assistance in Criminal Matters Act
StAR	Stolen Asset Recovery Initiative
UNCAC	United Nations Convention against Corruption
UNODC	United Nations Office on Drugs and Crime
UNTOC	United Nations Convention against Transnational Organized Crime

1 Introduction

1.1 BACKGROUND

Despite the growing number of grand corruption cases causing worldwide outrage and the vast amounts of stolen assets moved to foreign jurisdictions, global recovery efforts are still struggling with severe institutional, legal, and practical challenges. The proportion of successful procedures leading to the return of looted assets to rightful owners is still inadequate when compared with the estimated value of proceeds of corruption circulating worldwide.

In various international settings, countries emphasize challenges created by excessive procedural requirements and related delays in the asset recovery process, practitioners' poor familiarity with foreign legal procedures, lack of trust between jurisdictions, and, crucially, differences in confiscation regimes.[1] In its Resolution 7/1, "Strengthening mutual legal assistance for international cooperation and asset recovery," the Conference of States Parties to the United Nations Convention against Corruption (UNCAC) specifically called for the enactment of adequate mechanisms to, among other things, allow or expand cooperation in the enforcement of foreign seizure and restraint orders and confiscation judgments, including through raising awareness for judicial authorities and through permitting, where possible under national law, recognition of non-conviction-based seizure and freezing orders and of confiscation judgments.[2]

This study is part of the World Bank and the United Nations Office on Drugs and Crime (UNODC) Stolen Asset Recovery (StAR) Initiative.[3] Since its inception, the StAR Initiative has provided a global platform (a) to enhance countries' ability to trace and return tainted property and (b) to prevent the laundering of proceeds from corruption offenses. It has contributed a series of publications aimed to raise awareness about the problem, examine current trends, challenges, and shortcomings in asset recovery as well as shed light on promising policy and legal tools, including those aimed to ensure seizure and confiscation of corruption proceeds in transnational cases.

Among the tools aimed at facilitating the recovery of assets illicitly moved or transferred abroad, attention has recently been directed to a legal mechanism enabling the processing of mutual legal assistance (MLA) requests through the direct enforcement of foreign confiscation orders. The concept of *direct enforcement* stands in contrast to *indirect enforcement*, which is predicated on the need for the requested jurisdiction to issue its own confiscation order as a prerequisite for executing the foreign request.

Crucially, whereas there is growing recognition of the value of direct enforcement as an international cooperation tool, this legal mechanism is not fully used or understood despite its advantages in speeding up and streamlining asset recovery proceedings. Also, countries are often unaware that adopting domestic direct enforcement mechanisms is not optional, but a requirement for UNCAC States Parties.

1.2 OBJECTIVES, STRUCTURE, AUDIENCE

The objective of the present study is to offer an in-depth analysis of the notion of direct enforcement, existing legal approaches, and related challenges, thereby building on the initial findings of previous publications of the StAR Initiative. Among these, the manual *Barriers to Asset Recovery* identified the inability to recognize and enforce foreign confiscation and restraint orders as one of the major legal barriers to the recovery of the proceeds of corruption (Stephenson and others 2011, 76). Also, the *Asset Recovery Handbook* touched on the issue by identifying typical conditions necessary to directly enforce a foreign confiscation order in requested jurisdictions (Brun and others 2021). However, apart from examples drawn from a few countries, these publications were not intended to provide a comprehensive illustration of how direct enforcement works worldwide.

This study seeks to fill this gap by doing as follows:

- Examine the meaning and scope of direct enforcement and indirect enforcement models in the international legal framework, notably UNCAC, which addresses the issue in chapter V of the convention among other possible channels for asset recovery. Whereas UNCAC is used as the international reference instrument, its provisions on direct and indirect enforcement are compared with those found in many other treaty frameworks, including regional conventions.
- Map the institutional approaches to direct and indirect enforcement in force in 31 selected jurisdictions. Chapter 3 of this study discusses which of these jurisdictions rely on direct enforcement and which do not, how they incorporate treaty requirements into domestic laws, what the competent authorities are, and what types of procedures are used. Chapter 3 also includes an analysis of jurisdictions that are not able to directly enforce confiscation orders and asks why this is the case, what level of awareness practitioners have of direct enforcement models, and whether policy-making bodies have taken any step to introduce this legal mechanism.
- Understand what specific challenges countries face in implementing a direct enforcement model. On the basis of extensive contributions by practitioners from the selected jurisdictions, this study's chapter 4 provides an overview of the practical, institutional, and legal obstacles encountered in having stolen assets confiscated by direct enforcement mechanisms. The inquiry also seeks to determine the extent to which reported critical qualities are specific to this particular type of MLA as opposed to common problems associated with the handling of general MLA or asset recovery requests.

- Suggest a series of practical steps and good practices for consideration by (a) countries exploring the possibility to introduce a direct enforcement mechanism into their domestic legal frameworks and (b) countries already in a position to directly enforce foreign confiscation orders, but that are considering options to streamline processes and maximize results obtainable via direct enforcement approaches (chapter 5).

In view of its structure and objectives, this study is addressed to a broad range of law enforcement, justice, and asset recovery practitioners as well as bodies involved in legislative and regulatory processes, such as the following:

- Officials of the offices of state attorneys general and prosecutors general, ministries of justice, and prosecutorial and judicial authorities with responsibilities in asset recovery proceedings;
- Central authorities in charge of processing outgoing and incoming MLA requests, including for asset recovery; and
- Policy makers in charge of preparing and drafting normative instruments in asset recovery, money laundering, corruption, MLA, and other related fields.

1.3 METHODOLOGY

This study focuses on 31 jurisdictions selected to ensure balanced geographical distribution among different United Nations Regional Groups and representation of different legal systems including civil law, common law, and mixed systems.[4] Some of them are major financial centers receiving a significant amount of MLA requests related to asset recovery. Overall, the selected jurisdictions appear to constitute a representative sample providing an overview of the situation worldwide and from which guidance could be drawn. The choice of not showcasing more countries was a deliberate one owing to practical and time considerations. Future editions of this study may benefit from geographical expansion and fresh information on progress obtained in the review of countries examined under UNCAC's Implementation Review Mechanism. Such an updated edition would allow for fine-tuning current findings and a more granular illustration of the associated challenges.

The initial phase of the study has been conducted through desk research. Information about domestic legal structures and procedures was extracted from several official sources, including national legislative databases, country-specific asset-recovery guides, and publicly available peer-review assessments. Those assessments were conducted by organizations such as (a) the Financial Action Task Force (FATF) or FATF-style bodies, (b) the Council of Europe's Group of States Against Corruption and (the Committee of Experts on the Evaluation of Anti-Money Laundering Measures and the Financing of Terrorism, and (c) the Organisation for Economic Co-operation and Development (OECD) in its review of the implementation of the OECD Convention on Combating Bribery of Foreign Public Officials in International Business Transactions. The Mechanism for the Review of Implementation of UNCAC also featured as an important source of information. In this context, the bulk of the information was collected from evaluations conducted during the first review cycle (dealing with criminalization, law enforcement, and international cooperation). In a few cases, country information was available from this current (second) review cycle, with its specific focus on countries' implementation of chapter V (Asset Recovery) of UNCAC in addition to its chapter II (Preventive Measures).

The desk research phase was complemented by information obtained through a questionnaire (see Appendix B) sent to asset recovery governmental practitioners in the 31 selected jurisdictions.[5] Answers to the questionnaire allowed for a more in-depth understanding of how domestic legal provisions and procedures work and are implemented in practice. Moreover, the answers provided first-hand knowledge of practical challenges. In some cases, information received from the questionnaire had to be clarified or needed additional input. In these cases, the drafters engaged in direct exchanges with the respondents or other practitioners from the same country.

The recommendation section of the study is derived from the best available data as well as responses to questionnaires received from 29 surveyed countries. Note that the featured recommendations focus on the theme of this study. As such, and in an effort to avoid duplications, they add to existing bodies of recommendations, notably those contained in manuals published under the aegis of the StAR Initiative. Readers are encouraged to refer to those manuals for general guidance on the development of sound legal and institutional frameworks for asset recovery and associated good practices.

Finally, an advanced draft of this study was submitted for final review to practitioners from the selected jurisdictions. An online Expert Group Meeting (EGM) that took place June 18, 2020, refined the text and verified the relevance and accuracy of information processed in the previous phases. Participants to the EGM included practitioners and experts from Australia, Brazil, Canada, China, Cyprus, Arab Republic of Egypt, France, India, Indonesia, Italy, Kazakhstan, Latvia, Lebanon, New Zealand, Nigeria, Russian Federation, Singapore, South Africa, Spain, Switzerland, and United States.

NOTES

1. See, for example, United Nations Convention against Corruption, "Report of the 10th Meeting of the Open-ended Intergovernmental Working Group on Asset Recovery Held in Vienna on 25 and 26 August 2016," CAC/COSP/WG.2/2016/4, ¶ 17 (September 2016), www.unodc.org/documents/treaties/UNCAC/WorkingGroups/workinggroup2 /2016-August-25-26/V1605555e.pdf.
2. See Conference of the States Parties to the United Nations Convention against Corruption, Resolution 7/1, Strengthening Mutual Legal Assistance for International Cooperation and Asset Recovery (November 2017), www.unodc.org/unodc/en/corruption/COSP/session7 -resolutions.html.
3. For information about StAR, see https://star.worldbank.org/.
4. These jurisdictions are Australia; Brazil; British Virgin Islands; Canada; China; Cyprus; Arab Republic of Egypt; France; Germany; Hong Kong SAR, China; India; Indonesia; Italy; Japan; Kazakhstan; Republic of Korea; Latvia; Lebanon; New Zealand; Nigeria; Panama; Peru; Russian Federation; Seychelles; Singapore; South Africa; Spain; Switzerland; United Arab Emirates; United Kingdom; and United States.
5. The questionnaire was responded to by practitioners from 29 countries. Data about countries that did not respond to the survey has been collected through open sources, including official government reports available through several international peer-review mechanisms.

2 The International Legal Framework on Direct and Indirect Enforcement

2.1 UN CONVENTION AGAINST CORRUPTION

2.1.1 Overview of UNCAC asset recovery provisions

Whereas various multilateral treaties such as the United Nations Convention against Illicit Traffic in Narcotic Drugs and Psychotropic Substances (1988 Drug Trafficking Convention) and the UN Convention against Transnational Organized Crime (UNTOC) feature provisions on international cooperation related to asset recovery, the UN Convention against Corruption (UNCAC) vastly expands the arsenal of legal tools, options, and channels available to its States Parties.

The return of proceeds from corruption to their countries of origin is considered a "fundamental principle."[1] (UNCAC devotes an entire chapter of its text to asset recovery.[2]) At the initial stages of the negotiating process, there was substantial agreement among delegations that "maintaining a separate chapter on the question of asset recovery had a considerable political significance, because the subject matter had been identified by the General Assembly as a key component of the Convention. That political significance could not be neglected in examining the architecture and contents of the draft convention" (United Nations 2010, 435).

UNCAC's chapter V sets the convention apart from all other international instruments in criminal matters. Its provisions, however, should not be examined in isolation. Instead, they should be read and interpreted in conjunction with key provisions found in other chapters. These provisions outline the prerequisites for effective asset recovery actions. In particular, note the following:

- Article 2 (Definition of key terms, for example, property, proceeds of crime, freezing and seizing, confiscation)
- Article 14 (Measures to prevent money laundering)
- Article 31 (Establishment of domestic legal frameworks for freezing and confiscation of proceeds from corruption offenses)
- Article 46 (Procedures, authorities, and requirements for mutual legal assistance, MLA)

2.1.2 What are the legal avenues for asset recovery?

No legal mechanism is, in abstract, better suited than others to recover stolen assets moved abroad. Whereas UNCAC sets forth a menu of possible channels, the decision over which avenue to pursue is eventually a strategic investigative and prosecutorial choice. The decision is, in turn, influenced by a variety of factors, including the ability of the requesting or requested jurisdiction to pursue or enforce conviction-based or non-conviction-based confiscation (NCB) orders, considerations involving standards of proof in force in the foreign jurisdiction, the availability of MLA treaties, and so forth.

The legal avenues envisaged by UNCAC to recover assets associated with corruption offenses are grouped under two categories:

- Measures for the direct recovery of property (article 53)
- Measures for recovery of property through international cooperation in confiscation (articles 54 and 55)

These are illustrated in the next two sections.

2.1.3 Measures for the direct recovery of property (article 53)

These measures can be sought by a country before the civil or criminal courts of another country—depending on the legal system—to regain ownership of stolen assets or be awarded compensation or damages. Because this route does not involve action by the government of the country where the civil proceedings take place, associated costs are born entirely by the plaintiff. At the same time, the establishment and pursuit of a civil action may interfere with criminal proceedings initiated in the same country. For this reason, some governments request that they be kept informed of any privately pursued proceedings taking place in their territory.

2.1.4 Measures for recovery of property through international cooperation in confiscation (articles 54 and 55)

Under this category, UNCAC outlines two mechanisms that States Parties need to have in place to respond to a request for confiscation stemming from another party. For ease of reference, these two proceedings are designated in this study as mechanisms for direct and indirect enforcement. Unlike the previously mentioned avenues (measures for the direct recovery of property), both direct and indirect enforcement entail the active involvement of governments' institutions in recovering assets in their own territories following an MLA request. Whether proceeds of crime are recovered by direct or indirect action, they need to be returned to the requesting jurisdiction on the basis of procedures in force in the requested jurisdiction and applicable international arrangements.

2.1.4.1 Direct enforcement of foreign confiscation orders

According to article 55(1)(b) of UNCAC, a requested party shall, to the greatest extent possible within its domestic legal system, "submit to its competent authorities, *with a view to giving effect to it* to the extent requested, an order of confiscation issued by a court in the territory of the requesting State Party [...] insofar as it relates to proceeds of crime, property, equipment or other instrumentalities [...] situated in the territory of the requested State Party." (Emphasis added.)

The requirement set forth in article 55(1)(b) reflects what is commonly understood as direct enforcement of foreign confiscation orders. Article 54(1)(a) of UNCAC specifically requires States Parties to introduce domestic measures as may be necessary to permit its competent authorities to give effect to an order of confiscation issued by a court of another State Party, to enable the implementation of article 55(1)(b) in practice.

The term "direct enforcement" used in this study is not employed by UNCAC. In written exchanges with practitioners from the surveyed jurisdictions, sometimes there was uncertainty about its exact meaning. In this regard, it should be emphasized that the word "direct" in this study should not be read as a synonym of "automatic." It does not imply that the requested jurisdiction will as an inevitable result recognize a foreign order. In countries adopting a direct enforcement model, it is widely accepted that the foreign order will be scrutinized against a set of conditions including that the foreign order is final or that the person affected received a fair trial in the requesting country and so forth. The term "direct" used in this study thus refers to the fact that the competent authorities in the requested jurisdiction are able to recognize and provide enforcement power to the foreign order (or reject recognition if the set conditions are not fulfilled) without investigating and adjudicating again the merits of the case. Therefore, the term "direct enforcement" in this study is an equivalent of giving effect to an order of confiscation issued by a court of a requesting state under article 54(1)(a) of UNCAC. Direct enforcement thus could involve additional steps including a court process to decide on the recognition and enforcement of the foreign confiscation order. But these additional steps should be on an expedited and streamlined process compared with the usual procedure as applied in the domestic confiscation proceedings of the requested state. Direct enforcement is broader than just automatically registering the foreign confiscation order. Even the registration may be conditioned on the verification of basic conditions that may include due process, rights of defendants, and, in some jurisdictions, dual criminality.

Crucially, under direct enforcement proceedings, requested jurisdictions need to have provisions and procedures in place to ensure that their authorities can enforce foreign confiscation orders without reopening their own full domestic asset recovery case and without conducting a new investigation or a new trial on the merits of the case, subject to a review of the acceptability of the foreign order (due process, competence, public order, and so forth). A major practical advantage of excluding the case from relitigation in the requested jurisdiction is that it shields the case from delaying tactics, avoids duplication of efforts, and expedites proceedings. It also contributes to limiting confiscation enforcement cases from requiring too many resources for requested jurisdictions.

The procedure to enforce, or give effect to, a foreign order may be contained in a dedicated legislative act, in procedures established for the execution of MLA requests, in procedures for registering foreign orders, or in giving various types of exequatur or execution of foreign judgments, and so forth. Importantly, this procedure shall be different from and more straightforward compared with the standard domestic confiscation procedure.

2.1.4.2 Indirect enforcement of foreign confiscation orders

For parties to trigger direct enforcement proceedings, a basic condition is that a valid order of confiscation has been issued by the foreign jurisdiction. This is obviously not possible (a) when the foreign jurisdiction has requested the confiscation of property without having issued a corresponding confiscation order or (b) where a confiscation order does exist but is not deemed valid or in any other way recognizable by the requested jurisdiction. In such events, some jurisdictions may only be able to execute the foreign request by issuing a domestic confiscation order through a full reexamination of the merits of the case. In this study, this scenario is understood as indirect enforcement. In practice, under such an approach, evidence submitted by the requesting jurisdiction is used to support an application for a domestic confiscation order. The requesting jurisdiction is thus expected to provide information satisfying the evidentiary standards in force in the requested jurisdiction.[3]

The indirect enforcement scenario is reflected in article 54(1)(b) and article 55(1)(a). According to this latter provision, in particular, a requested party "shall, to the greatest extent possible within its domestic legal system, submit the request to its competent authorities for the purpose of obtaining an order of confiscation and, if such order is granted, give effect to it."

2.1.5 UNCAC requirements on the enforcement of foreign confiscation orders

Under articles 55(1)(a) and (b) of UNCAC, a State Party that has received a request from another State Party for confiscation of proceeds of crime, property, or equipment of other instrumentalities referred to in article 31(1) of UNCAC situated in its territory shall, to the greatest extent possible within its domestic legal system, do as follows:

- Submit to its competent authorities, with a view to giving effect to it to the extent requested, foreign confiscation orders issued by another party (direct enforcement).
- Submit the request to their competent authorities to obtain an order of confiscation and, if such order is granted, give effect to it (indirect enforcement).

By demanding that parties introduce legal proceedings to enable both direct and indirect enforcement actions, UNCAC seeks to ensure that requested jurisdictions have the legal tools to provide the most effective and expeditious degree of MLA on the basis of the circumstances and needs of each case.[4]

The next few sections highlight other requirements set forth by UNCAC in this area. For all other issues, UNCAC States Parties have discretion in determining the procedures and modalities for introducing both direct and indirect enforcement mechanisms in their own legal systems.

2.1.5.1 Proceeds and instrumentalities

UNCAC States Parties shall ensure that their domestic legal framework dealing with the enforcement of foreign confiscation orders is broad enough to cover requests for the confiscation of "proceeds of crime, property, equipment or other instrumentalities" located in their territory.[5]

Some of these terms are defined in article 2 of UNCAC, notably, as follows:

- "'Property' shall mean assets of every kind, whether corporeal or incorporeal, moveable or immoveable, tangible or intangible, and legal documents evidencing title to or interest in such assets"[6]

- "'Proceeds of crime' shall mean any property derived from or obtained, directly or indirectly, through the commission of an offence"[7]

Whereas UNCAC seeks to ensure that requested parties are able to enforce foreign orders covering property in the broadest sense, an interpretative note to article 55(1)(b) clarifies that "the term 'instrumentalities' should not be interpreted in an overly broad manner" (United Nations 2010, 488).

2.1.5.2 Property of a de minimis value

According to article 55(7), "cooperation [...] may also be refused or provisional measures lifted if the requested State Party does not receive sufficient and timely evidence or if the property is of a *de minimis* value." The rationale is that procedures for the enforcement of foreign confiscation orders are often costly and time consuming and therefore should not be triggered (at least not as a matter of priority) in cases where the costs associated with the recovery of the assets outweigh their value.

On this specific issue, an interpretative note to article 55(7) demands that "the requested State Party [...] consult with the requesting State Party on whether the property is of de minimis value or on ways and means of respecting any deadline for the provision of additional evidence."[8]

2.1.5.3 Applicability of general MLA provisions

Because the direct and indirect enforcement of foreign confiscation orders is a type of MLA, article 55 clarifies that the general provisions of MLA contained in UNCAC article 46 apply once the necessary changes have been made. This entails, notably, that grounds for refusal, rules on the confidentiality of the request, identification of channels for transmitting the request, costs relating to its execution, and so forth, are implicitly applicable to requests in this domain unless the State Party in question is bound by a specific MLA treaty, in which case the latter would prevail.[9]

Recall that under article 46(3), MLA may be specifically requested for, among other things, "(j) Identifying, freezing and tracing proceeds of crime in accordance with the provisions of chapter V of this Convention; [and] (k) The recovery of assets, in accordance with the provisions of chapter V of this Convention."

2.1.5.4 Information to be included in MLA requests for direct or indirect enforcement

Article 46(15) spells out information generally to be included in an MLA request—whether for the purpose of taking evidence, executing searches, or any other type of assistance that is not contrary to the domestic law of the requested party. Accordingly, a request for MLA shall contain the following:

- The identity of the authority making the request
- The subject matter and nature of the investigation, prosecution, or judicial proceeding to which the request relates and the name and functions of the authority conducting the investigation, prosecution, or judicial proceeding
- A summary of the relevant facts, except in relation to requests for the purpose of service of judicial documents
- A description of the assistance sought and details of any particular procedure that the requesting State Party wishes to be followed

- Where possible, the identity, location, and nationality of any person concerned
- The purpose for which the evidence, information, or action is sought

More specifically, concerning requests for the direct enforcement of foreign confiscation orders, the following pieces of information shall also be included under article 55(3)(b):

- Legally admissible copy of an order of confiscation upon which the request is based issued by the requesting State Party
- Statement of the facts and information as to the extent to which execution of the order is requested
- Statement specifying the measures taken by the requesting State Party to provide adequate notification to bona fide third parties and to ensure due process
- Statement that the confiscation order is final

For requests dealing with indirect enforcement, under article 55(3)(a), the following information is required:

- Description of the property to be confiscated
- To the extent possible, the location of the property
- When relevant, the estimated value of the property
- Statement of the facts the requesting State Party relied upon that are sufficient to enable the requested party to seek the order under its domestic law

2.1.5.5 UNCAC as a legal basis

Under article 55(6), "if a State Party elects to make the taking of the measures referred to in paragraphs 1 [enforcement of foreign confiscation orders] and 2 [enforcement of foreign freezing and seizing orders] of this article conditional on the existence of a relevant treaty, that State Party shall consider this Convention the necessary and sufficient treaty basis."

This provision echoes the one set by UNCAC in extradition. According to article 44(5), "If a State Party that makes extradition conditional on the existence of a treaty receives a request for extradition from another State Party with which it has no extradition treaty, it *may* consider this Convention the legal basis for extradition in respect of any offence to which this article applies." (Emphasis added.)

The major difference between the two articles is that in the case of a request for the enforcement of foreign freezing, seizing, or confiscation order, requested states *shall* consider UNCAC as a valid legal basis, whereas they are only encouraged to do so in the case of extradition. In the absence of a treaty, therefore, UNCAC does provide a legal basis for enforcement of foreign confiscation orders in case the requested State Party requires a treaty to that effect.

2.1.6 Enforcement of foreign requests for asset freezing and seizing

The regime envisaged by UNCAC for the enforcement of foreign requests for provisional measures is different from the one established for confiscation-related requests. The main point of divergence with UNCAC requirements concerning requests for enforcement of foreign confiscation orders (article 54(1)(a)) lies in the discretion left to States Parties to establish either a direct or an indirect mechanism to enforce foreign freezing and seizing orders (article 54(2)(a)).

In practice, when a party receives a request for the enforcement of a freezing and seizing order, according to article 54(2)(a), it "may choose to establish procedures either for recognizing and enforcing [it] or for using [it] as the basis for seeking the issuance of its own freezing or seizure order" (United Nations 2010, 216). When, instead, the request is not backed up by a freezing and seizing order, the requested party will obviously have no choice but to trigger its own domestic procedure to issue a freezing and seizing order (article 54(2)(b)).

Whether the request for provisional measures is accompanied by a freezing and seizing order, the requesting party must satisfy the requested party that "there are sufficient grounds for taking such actions and that the property would eventually be subject to an order of confiscation [...]."[10]

Also, before lifting any provisional measure, the requested party shall, "wherever possible, give the requesting State Party an opportunity to present its reasons in favor of continuing the measure."[11]

The legislation and practice of a number of surveyed jurisdictions (although not the majority of them) confirm that the direct enforcement of foreign provisional measures, although not technically compulsory under UNCAC, is indeed available and used.

2.2 ENFORCEMENT OF FOREIGN CONFISCATION ORDERS UNDER OTHER LEGAL INSTRUMENTS

Whereas UNCAC provisions cover proceeds and instrumentalities of corruption-related offenses, identical or similar language is found in other multilateral instruments with overlapping (or partially overlapping) geographical or substantive scopes of application.

2.2.1 The 1998 drug convention and UNTOC

Both the United Nations Convention against Illicit Traffic in Narcotic Drugs and Psychotropic Substances, 1998 (1998 Drug Convention) and the United Nations Convention against Transnational Organized Crime envisage mechanisms for international cooperation in confiscation covering a broad range of drug trafficking and organized crime–related offenses. The 1988 Drug Convention, in particular, represents the original source of several articles, including on confiscation matters, that were subsequently introduced into more recent criminal justice treaties and used as inspiring text for UNCAC.[12]

2.2.2 Regional instruments

Various regional instruments request that parties establish enforcement mechanisms to recover tainted assets using MLA procedures. These include the following:

- 2005 Council of Europe Convention on Laundering, Search, Seizure and Confiscation of the Proceeds from Crime and on the Financing of Terrorism

- EU (European Union) Regulation on the Mutual Recognition of Freezing and Confiscation Orders[13]
- 2002 SADC (South African Development Community) Protocol on Mutual Legal Assistance in Criminal Matters
- Commonwealth Scheme relating to Mutual Legal Assistance

2.2.2.1 Council of Europe Convention on laundering, search, seizure and confiscation of the proceeds from crime and on the financing of terrorism (2005 Warsaw Convention)

The Warsaw Convention applies to requests for the enforcement of orders dealing specifically with money-laundering offenses. It states, in particular, that "a Party which has received a request made by another Party for confiscation concerning instrumentalities or proceeds, situated in its territory, shall: a) enforce a confiscation order made by a court of a requesting Party in relation to such instrumentalities or proceeds; or b) submit the request to its competent authorities for the purpose of obtaining an order of confiscation and, if such order is granted, enforce it."[14]

2.2.2.2. The EU Regulation on the mutual recognition of freezing and confiscation orders

In the EU, the mutual recognition principle has become a cornerstone of judicial cooperation in criminal matters. Its core proposition, predicated on the relative homogeneity and reciprocal confidence in member states' processes and fundamental values, is that decisions made in one EU country are executed in another EU country in the same way as if they were issued in the latter.

The principle has also been applied to confiscation and freezing orders. Regulation 2018/1805, which 25 EU member states[15] were mandated to apply starting on December 19, 2020, is the latest in a series of successive legal instruments aimed to apply the principle of mutual recognition in this field. The 2018 Regulation is now a single instrument that was merged from two separate regimes dealing with the mutual recognition of freezing orders and confiscation orders.[16] Currently, the EU's legal regime represents the most sophisticated international framework binding 25 member states to implement a regionwide system for the cross-border execution of freezing and confiscation orders.

Under the 2018 Regulation, when a competent authority in one EU member state needs to freeze or confiscate assets that are located in another member state, it submits the request by filling in a standard form for the freezing order or a standard certificate for the confiscation order. The authority in the requested state is bound to execute the freezing or confiscation order within a short time. It can only refuse the request based on a limited number of grounds set out in the regulation. For example, according to article 3, freezing or confiscation orders are to be executed without verification of the double criminality of the acts giving rise to such orders, where those acts are punishable in the issuing state by a custodial sentence of a maximum of at least three years and constitute a criminal offense under a predetermined list (which features, among others, corruption and laundering of proceeds of crime).

In comparison with the previous regime, the 2018 Regulation includes the following:

- A wider scope for the mutual recognition of freezing and confiscation orders, including extended and third-party confiscation as well as NCB confiscation issued by a criminal court
- Specific time limits for the recognition or execution of freezing and confiscation orders[17]
- A standard certificate and a standard form containing all relevant information on the order, designed to streamline the process, to support the executing authorities in identifying the targeted property, and to facilitate speedy action
- Reinforced communication channels between the issuing (requesting) and the executing (requested) authorities, for example, in the form of consultations before applying any ground for refusal or postponing action

For the 25 EU member states to which the 2018 Regulation applies, one practical consequence is the need to implement at least three parallel legal regimes (a) to execute requests for mutual recognition vis-à-vis other regulation-bound member states; (b) to execute the same type of requests compared with Denmark and Ireland, based on Council Framework Decisions 2003/577/JHA and 2006/783/JHA; and (c) to enforce requests from non-EU member states.[18]

2.2.2.3 SADC Protocol on mutual legal assistance in criminal matters (2002)

Under this instrument adopted within the SADC, "the requested State shall, to the extent permitted by its laws, give effect to or permit enforcement of a final order forfeiting or confiscating the proceeds of crime made by a court of the requesting State or take other appropriate action to secure or transfer of the proceeds following a request by the requesting State."[19]

2.2.2.4 The Commonwealth scheme relating to mutual legal assistance (Harare Scheme)

The Harare Scheme represents an informal arrangement covering international cooperation in criminal matters. Whereas its provisions are not legally binding, the Harare Scheme, which was revised in 2011, commands widespread support and legitimacy across the Commonwealth legal space.

Under the Harare Scheme's part VI (3)(a) on "Asset Recovery," "[e]ach country is encouraged to take such measures as may be necessary to: give effect to an order of confiscation or forfeiture issued by a court of a requesting country."

2.2.3 The relationship between UNCAC and other treaties

According to article 46(7) of UNCAC, the provisions of this latter covering MLA shall apply whenever the requesting and requested jurisdictions are not bound by an MLA treaty. When such a treaty exists, this latter shall in principle prevail unless the States Parties in question agree to apply UNCAC provisions. In any case, States Parties are strongly encouraged to apply UNCAC's provisions if these facilitate cooperation.[20]

In general, treaties covering the same subject matter can support each other for interpretative purposes, especially when they do not contradict each other and one instrument contains more detailed provisions on specific topics. For example, the 2005 Warsaw Convention makes it clear that "the requested Party shall be bound by the findings as to the facts in so far as they are stated in a conviction or judicial decision of the requesting Party or in so far as such conviction or judicial decision is implicitly based on them."[21] Whereas UNCAC is silent on this point, the Warsaw Convention might be usefully invoked in the event that an interpretative doubt arises between countries having ratified both treaties.

2.3 THE ENFORCEMENT OF FOREIGN NCB CONFISCATION ORDERS IN THE INTERNATIONAL LEGAL FRAMEWORK

Under UNCAC, to provide MLA for asset confiscation purposes, "each State Party shall [...] consider taking such measures as may be necessary to allow confiscation of such property without a criminal conviction in cases in which the offender cannot be prosecuted by reason of death, flight, or absence or in other appropriate cases."[22]

Under the 2005 Warsaw Convention, "the Parties shall co-operate to the widest extent possible under their domestic law with those Parties which request the execution of measures equivalent to confiscation leading to the deprivation of property, which are not criminal sanctions, in so far as such measures are ordered by a judicial authority of the requesting Party in relation to a criminal offence [...]."[23] An explanatory note to the Warsaw Convention clarifies that such types of proceedings "include, for instance, the so called '*in rem* proceedings.'"

By defining "confiscation order" as a "final penalty or measure, imposed by a court following proceedings in relation to a criminal offence, resulting in the final deprivation of property of a natural or legal person,"[24] the EU's 2018 Regulation ensures that the principle of mutual recognition also covers proceedings that did not end up in a criminal conviction. Moreover, the 2018 Regulation specifies that the ground for nonrecognition or nonexecution of a foreign confiscation order, consisting in the circumstance that the person in question did not appear in person at the trial in the requesting country, does not apply "where proceedings [in the requesting country] result in non-conviction-based confiscation orders."[25]

2.4 TAKEAWAYS

- Under UNCAC, States Parties shall be able to provide the most effective and expeditious degree of assistance to other parties based on the circumstances and needs of each case. A key mechanism envisaged by UNCAC for international asset recovery is the enforcement of foreign freezing and seizing and confiscation orders through MLA channels.
- Domestic legal frameworks covering the enforcement of foreign freezing and seizing and confiscation orders need to be wide enough to encompass "proceeds of crime, property, equipment or other instrumentalities" located in their territory.[26]

- UNCAC States Parties shall be in a position to trigger both procedures: (a) recognize and enforce foreign confiscation orders issued by another party (direct enforcement) and (b) submit a foreign request to their competent authorities for the purpose of obtaining an order of confiscation and, if such order is granted, give effect to it (indirect enforcement). See Recommendation 5.1.2 in this study.
- In relation to foreign (provisional) freezing and seizing orders, States Parties can choose to enforce them directly or indirectly. In practice, the legislation of some surveyed jurisdictions allows for the direct enforcement of such orders.
- States Parties should determine, also based on their constitutional requirements on incorporating treaty provisions into their legal systems, the extent to which legislative action is needed to ensure that UNCAC requirements on direct and indirect enforcement are properly introduced and effectively available as part of domestic MLA proceedings. See Recommendation 5.1.1 of this study.
- In addition to UNCAC, other multilateral treaty frameworks require parties to enforce foreign freezing and seizing and confiscation orders. States Parties to both UNCAC and one or more such treaties are expected to apply provisions stemming from all of them. Treaties covering the same subject matter can support each other, especially when one instrument contains more detailed provisions. See Recommendation 5.1.5 of this study.
- In some cases, domestic authorities and procedures already in place to implement treaty frameworks other than UNCAC may automatically serve to implement UNCAC requirements. In other cases, however, procedures and authorities only may have been established for specific treaty-based offenses such as money laundering. UNCAC States Parties need to ensure that the scope of implementing legislation extends to the full range of UNCAC-based offenses. See Recommendation 5.1.5 of this study.
- Ideally, countries should adopt a single legal framework allowing for direct enforcement action to be taken in relation to a broad range of criminal offense reflecting all their treaty-based commitments. It is important to avoid a fragmented approach whereby different procedures or authorities come into play depending on whether the foreign request concerns property involved in corruption or other offenses. See Recommendation 5.1.5 of this study.
- The Mechanism for the Review of Implementation of UNCAC, particularly its current review cycle focusing on the implementation of chapter V of the Convention (Asset Recovery), may be leveraged to obtain guidance and exchange good practices to implement UNCAC requirements on direct and indirect enforcement. See Recommendation 5.2.1 of this study.

NOTES

1. UNCAC, Measures and Provisions of the Convention, ch. V, art. 51.
2. UNCAC, Measures and Provisions of the Convention, ch. V, art. 51–9.
3. For example, in many countries where hearsay rules of evidence are relaxed, out-of-court statements are admissible. In others, however, the live testimony of civilian witnesses or law enforcement officers may be required in the courtroom or by sworn recorded testimony.

4. The approach outlined here represents the yardstick against which States Parties' compliance with UNCAC's chapter V is being assessed in the framework of UNCAC's Implementation Review Mechanism.

5. UNCAC, arts. 55(1)(b) and 31(1).

6. UNCAC, art. 2(d).

7. UNCAC, art. 2(e).

8. United Nations Office on Drugs and Crime, *Travaux Préparatoires of the Negotiations for the Elaboration of the United Nations Convention against Corruption* (New York: United Nations, 2010), p. 492.

9. Even when States Parties are indeed bound by a specific MLA treaty, UNCAC strongly encourages them to apply article 46 provisions if "they facilitate cooperation," UNCAC, art. 46(7).

10. UNCAC, art. 54(2)(a)(b).

11. UNCAC, art. 55(8).

12. See, in particular UNTOC, art. 5(4), "Confiscation" and UNTOC, art. 13, "International Cooperation for Purposes of Confiscation."

13. Regulation (EU) 2018/1805 of the European Parliament and of the Council of 14 November 2018 on the Mutual Recognition of Freezing Orders and Confiscation Orders, PE/38/2018?REV/1, https://eur-lex.europa.eu/legal-content/EN/TXT/?uri=CELEX %3A32018R1805.

14. 2005 Warsaw Convention, art. 23, "Obligation to Confiscate."

15. The regulation is not applicable to Denmark and Ireland.

16. Council of European Union, Council Framework Decisions 2003/577/JHA of 22 July 2003 on the Execution in the European Union of Orders Freezing Property or Evidence; Council of European Union, Council Framework Decision 2006/783/JHA of 6 October 2006 on the Application of the Principle of Mutual Recognition to Confiscation Orders.

17. Concerning freezing orders "where the issuing authority has stated in the freezing certificate that immediate freezing is necessary since there are legitimate grounds to believe that the property in question will imminently be removed or destroyed, or in view of any investigative or procedural needs in the issuing State, the executing authority shall decide on the recognition of the freezing order no later than 48 hours after it has been received by the executing authority. No later than 48 hours after such a decision has been taken, the executing authority shall take the concrete measures necessary to execute the order," Regulation (EU) 2018/1805, art. 9(3). Concerning confiscation orders, "the executing authority shall take the decision on the recognition and execution of the confiscation order without delay and, without prejudice to paragraph 4, no later than 45 days after the executing authority has received the confiscation certificate," Regulation (EU) 2018/1805, art. 20(1).

18. Starting on December 19, 2020, there was to be a transitional period during which freezing and confiscation certificates transmitted before this date would continue to be governed by Framework Decisions 2003/577/JHA and 2006/783/JHA.

19. South African Development Community (SADC), Protocol on Mutual Legal Assistance in Criminal Matters (2002), art. 22(1).

20. UNCAC, art. 46(7).

21. 2005 Warsaw Convention, art. 24(2). NCB confiscation orders should not be confused with restitution orders or judgments based on administrative violations. Even among countries with NCB confiscation enforcement authority, there may be no ability to enforce foreign restitution orders or other judgments based on no-forfeiture related proceedings.

22. UNCAC, art. 54(1)(c). Most jurisdictions under examination in this study allow for foreign NCB orders to be enforced through MLA channels (section 3.3.2 of this study).

23. 2005 Warsaw Convention, art. 23(5).

24. Regulation (EU) 2018/1805, art. 2(2).

25. Regulation (EU) 2018/1805, pmbl. pt. (32).

26. UNCAC, arts. 55(1)(b) and 31(1).

3 Domestic Legal Approaches to Direct Enforcement

3.1 OVERVIEW

The majority of the surveyed jurisdictions can rely on basic legal mechanisms to directly enforce foreign confiscation orders. Some countries, however, (for example, China,[1] Indonesia, and Panama) have adopted no legal framework for direct enforcement. For example, the concept has not been debated during Indonesia's recent elaboration of a draft law dealing with non-conviction-based (NCB) confiscation. A practitioner from this country who was interviewed, however, thought that its introduction into domestic law would help cooperation efforts and, crucially, provide Indonesia with increased leverage to ensure that foreign countries directly enforce an Indonesian confiscation order.

Other countries do have some basic legal framework but lack the necessary implementing legislation. Under article 20 of the Egyptian Anti-Money Laundering law, for example, the "competent Egyptian judicial entities may order the enforcement of final criminal rulings issued by competent foreign judicial authorities, concerning the confiscation of the funds resulting from money laundering and terrorism financing crimes or proceeds thereof, in accordance with the rules and procedures stipulated in bilateral or multilateral treaties to which Egypt is a party."[2] However, confronted with a foreign request and in the absence of more detailed legislation, Egyptian authorities have no choice but to launch a domestic money-laundering investigation where the facts are examined and a domestic order of confiscation is ordered.

Jurisdictions belonging to both common law and civil law legal systems employ direct enforcement mechanisms. Common law countries, however, tend to provide more detailed provisions on procedural matters such as document authentication, third-party notifications, and criteria for calculating property value.

3.1.1 Choice between direct and indirect enforcement channels

Resorting to direct enforcement modalities for implementing foreign orders may in some cases be an "obliged route" for technical reasons. In the United States, direct enforcement of foreign orders may be the only way to provisionally restrain assets that are not criminal proceeds (that is, value confiscation orders or substitute assets up to the value of criminally derived profits).[3] Similarly, in Canada the ability to confiscate assets on behalf of a foreign country as part of foreign criminal proceedings is typically not available by a domestic confiscation order. Specifically, obtaining such an order under Canadian criminal legislation depends on the existence of a related Canadian criminal investigation to obtain a domestic order. Whereas there will be some situations where obtaining a domestic order is possible, in the vast majority of cases this would not be possible because Canadian law enforcement and prosecuting authorities lack jurisdiction.

As to foreign freezing orders, Cyprus would usually pursue the direct enforcement route unless the recognition of such orders was not possible because, for instance, the conditions set out in the legislation for registering the orders could not be met.

On one hand, some jurisdictions[4] indicate a preference for direct enforcement as the most cost-effective model. On the other hand, indirect enforcement is favored when, in the execution of the request, additional assets are discovered that are not accounted for in the foreign order. South African officials would first ask the requesting country to amend the order, failing which they would consider taking indirect action. In Switzerland, indirect enforcement is used in practice to enforce foreign orders pertaining to compensation claims with countries that have not ratified the Council of Europe Convention on Money Laundering.

Overall, the simultaneous availability of both models (direct and indirect) is seen as injecting an important element of flexibility for determining the best course of action.

3.1.2 Mutual legal assistance (MLA) statutes, criminal procedure codes, and asset recovery legislation

Most jurisdictions regulate direct enforcement through MLA or asset recovery statutes. Others include special provisions in the sections of their criminal procedure codes dealing with international judicial cooperation.[5]

The structure, depth, and level of detail of domestic laws dealing with direct enforcement vary. Some legislative acts go to a great length to cover all issues that can potentially emerge, ranging from the effects of foreign confiscation orders to the entitlements of affected people.[6] In South Africa, for example, the 1996 International Cooperation in Criminal Matters Act contains the main legal framework on the registration of foreign restraint and confiscation orders. It is accompanied by a set of implementing regulations setting forth detailed criteria for notifying interested parties as well as the period and the manner in which a person may apply to the competent authorities to set aside the registration of foreign restraint and confiscation orders. In Singapore, the MLA Act is complemented with a Third Schedule that applies to matters in relation to which the attorney general has authorized the enforcement of foreign confiscation orders. These matters range from the criteria for calculating interest on the amounts to be recovered under the foreign order to the appointment of a public trustee or other persons as receivers to deal with realizable property.

In other cases, direct enforcement issues are the object of only a few provisions, thus leaving room for interpretation.[7] In some statutes, the general provisions of criminal codes and criminal procedure codes (for example, dealing with the rights of third parties to challenge the act with which the foreign order has been recognized) are declared applicable once the necessary changes have been made. Also, as a type of MLA, the direct enforcement of foreign confiscation orders is subject to the conditions set forth by requested countries for executing MLA requests in general (for example, dual criminality, requirements for reciprocity, general grounds for refusal, and so forth).

3.1.3 Direct enforcement by crime-specific statutes (money laundering, organized crime)

In some jurisdictions, procedures for direct enforcement are spelled out in legislation dealing with specific crime categories. Japan, for example, handles the control of crime proceeds in the same legislative act devoted to the suppression of organized crime. The Republic of Korea's detailed procedure on the direct enforcement of foreign confiscation orders is contained in its legislative act on the prevention of illegal trafficking in narcotics. Such a procedure is then made applicable—once the necessary changes have been made—to foreign orders related to corruption and other crimes.

Case Study 3.1: Nigeria's path toward comprehensive direct enforcement legislation

Nigeria offers an interesting example of a legal system where direct enforcement action is potentially available only in limited circumstances and via different statutes.

One relevant piece of legislation is the Foreign Judgment (Reciprocal Enforcement) Act, whose chapter 175 permits the registration and enforcement of judgments obtained in other jurisdictions. Under this act, enforcing judgments taken in foreign criminal proceedings is only allowed in respect of payment of compensation or damages to an injured party. This leaves the possibility that, at least in theory, the act be used for the direct enforcement of foreign non-conviction confiscation-based orders taken in civil proceedings. The state practice in support of this hypothesis, however, could not be determined.

The other relevant statute is the Mutual Assistance in Criminal Matters within the Commonwealth (Enactment and Enforcement) Act (Mutual Legal Assistance (MLA) Act), whose section 22(1) states that "[a] request under this Part of the Act may seek assistance in invoking procedures in the requested country leading to the recognition or review and confirmation and the enforcement of an order for the forfeiture of the proceeds of criminal activities made by a court or other authority in the requesting country." Under section 22(3), "[t]he law of the requested country shall apply to determine the circumstances and manner in which an order may be recognized, confirmed or enforced." However, it appears that no implementing laws have yet been adopted for the competent authorities to carry out direct enforcement action under the MLA Act.

In its recent publicly available self-assessment report (31.08.2016) related to the Second Phase of the Mechanism for the Review of Implementation of the United Nations Convention against Corruption (UNCAC), Nigeria has stated that an amendment to the MLA Act is currently pending within its National Assembly. The amendment will seek, among others, to make the MLA Act applicable generally to all UNCAC States Parties as its scope of application is currently limited to 53 Commonwealth member countries.

Case Study 3.2: Use of crime-specific (money-laundering) statutes: the case of Cyprus

In Cyprus, although direct enforcement procedures are set forth in anti-money-laundering legislation, these procedures relate to proceeds in general. In turn, proceeds are defined as any economic advantage derived from "illegal activities," which are all predicate offenses. Thus, the anti-money-laundering statute enables the authorities to directly recognize foreign confiscation orders whether they include or do not include money-laundering offenses.

In particular, according to The Prevention and Suppression of Money Laundering and Terrorist Financing Activities Laws of 2007–2018 (Anti-Money Laundering and Combatting Financial Terrorism (AML/CFT) Law), mutual legal assistance requests in this area are submitted to the Cyprus Ministry of Justice and Public Order Central. That ministry acts as the central authority on the basis of one of the international treaties mentioned in section 37 of the AML/CFT Law, including the United Nations Convention against Corruption. The central authority transmits the requests to the Unit for Combating Money Laundering (MOKAS, the Cypriot Financial

Intelligence Unit) for execution. The lawyers of MOKAS prepare the relevant application for the court for the purpose of obtaining a court order for the registration and enforcement of the foreign confiscation order.

Section 38 of the AML/CFT Law sets out the conditions that must be satisfied for the court to register a foreign order. When a foreign order is registered by the court, it becomes enforceable as if the order had been made by a competent domestic court under the AML/CFT Law.

Section 39 calls for the procedure to be followed after the court registers the foreign order. Specifically, when the confiscation order is registered, it is enforced by MOKAS under the following conditions: (a) if within six weeks from when the persons affected by the order received notification of the registration order, the persons took no action to cancel or to set aside the registration order and (b) if it is not possible to notify, or if the accused or the third person in the possession of the proceeds cannot be located, despite making reasonable efforts.

In the Arab Republic of Egypt,[8] India,[9] and United Arab Emirates, the legal framework for direct enforcement purposes is contained in anti-money-laundering statutes. In United Arab Emirates, in particular, the anti-money-laundering law provides that "any court injunction or court decision providing for the confiscation of funds, proceeds or instrumentalities relating to money laundering, terrorist financing or financing of illegal organizations may be recognized if issued by a court or judicial authority of another state with which the State has entered into a ratified Convention."[10]

The choice to provide direct enforcement exclusively in anti-money-laundering statutes may raise problems over whether such procedures can be applied by analogy to recognize foreign orders that have been made in criminal proceedings other than those for money-laundering offenses (for example, when foreign proceedings in the requesting jurisdiction relate to corruption offenses and the request for asset recovery does not stem from a money-laundering conviction).

3.1.4 Reliance on general mechanisms for the recognition of foreign judgments

Sometimes the direct enforcement of foreign confiscation orders is made possible through the same provisions broadly applicable to recognizing foreign judgments in criminal matters.[11] In Latvia, for example, the execution of a punishment imposed in a foreign state "shall be applied to the assessment of a request of a foreign State regarding the execution of a confiscation of property, if it has not been specified otherwise [...]."[12]

Similarly, for enforcing foreign confiscation orders, Germany uses the procedure generally applicable to the "enforcement of a penalty or any other sanction imposed with final and binding force in a foreign country."[13] This action is known as exequatur procedure. In this procedure, a competent court examines whether the foreign order is admissible as well. The court needs to find a comparable German order to the foreign order. Only then can the court declare the foreign judgment to be enforceable in Germany.

In Brazil, an exequatur procedure is used to enforce foreign court decisions in general, thus also confiscation orders. The Superior Court of Justice examines whether the execution of such orders is admissible according to the country's constitution.[14]

In Lebanon, the president of the Civil Court of Appeal gives foreign orders (including confiscation) enforceable power on the basis of the Code of Civil Procedure. The use of civil procedures appears justified because the recovery of assets acquired through the commission of corruption acts is not considered as a criminal sanction, but rather a form of compensation.

However, in various countries, general exequatur procedures cannot be used to enforce foreign confiscation orders; such procedures are explicitly designed to give effect to foreign civil or arbitral judgments. In Egypt, for example, the possibility to directly enforce foreign judgments through the Civil Procedure Code is limited to compensation orders benefiting the victim of a crime.[15] This is the case in Panama, where the application of article 1419 of the Judicial Code ("Judgments of foreign courts") is limited to cases where the "judgment has been handed down following the exercise of a personal right."[16] In Nigeria, the enforcement of orders made in foreign criminal proceedings is limited to those related to the payment of compensation or damages to an injured party.[17]

Case Study 3.3: Use of general mechanisms for the recognition of foreign criminal judgments: the case of Italy

Italy's ability to provide international cooperation in asset recovery measures in conviction and non-conviction-based (NCB) proceedings has been identified as a good practice in the country report related to the second cycle of the Mechanism for the Review of Implementation of the United Nations Convention against Corruption (UNCAC). In particular, for the direct enforcement of foreign confiscation orders, Italy relies on provisions contained in the Code of Criminal Procedure generally aimed at the recognition of foreign criminal judgments. To dissipate any doubt that foreign confiscation orders (including those stemming from NCB proceedings) are also covered, article 731(1-bis) states the applicability of those provisions to "cases of execution of confiscation and when the relevant measure has been adopted by the foreign judicial authority by means of a decision other than a judgment of conviction." (See Appendix C for more information.)

After receiving a request for executing a confiscation order issued by foreign judicial authorities, the Minister of Justice, acting as the central authority in the field of judicial cooperation, forwards the request to the public prosecutor attached to the competent Court of Appeal (Procuratore Generale della Repubblica). The Minister of Justice does so in cases where there is an international instrument (bilateral or multilateral treaties or agreements) between Italy and the requesting state that provides for this type of mutual legal assistance (MLA). In this regard, UNCAC is considered as "the necessary and sufficient treaty basis" to carry out the procedure of direct recognition and enforcement of confiscation orders in compliance with article 55(6) of UNCAC. Also, Italy is party to a number of multilateral and bilateral treaties in the field of MLA that Italian courts regard as sufficient basis for directly recognizing and enforcing foreign confiscation orders.

Once the request for recognition and enforcement has been forwarded to the prosecutor attached to the Court of Appeal, the prosecutor lodges a written request for recognition and enforcement accompanied by a copy of the confiscation order and its translation into Italian and any other supporting documents transmitted by the requesting jurisdiction.

According to article 734 of the Code of Criminal Procedure, the Court of Appeal shall decide on the request for recognition without delay and not later than 90 days from the receipt of the prosecutor's request. The decision of the Court of Appeal can be challenged by the prosecutor, the interested person, and his or her defense counsel before the Court of Cassation for infringement of the law. The Court of Cassation shall decide within 60 days from the receipt of the appeal.

As to the requirements for recognition and enforcement, according to article 733 of the Code of Criminal Procedure, the Court of Appeal shall reject the request for recognition and enforcement in the following cases:

- If the judgment or confiscation order is not final according to the law of the requesting jurisdiction
- If the judgment or confiscation order includes provisions that are contrary to the fundamental principles of the Italian legal system
- If the judgment or confiscation order has been issued by a judge who is not independent and impartial
- If the defendant or interested party was not summoned to appear before the foreign court or was not permitted to defend himself or herself
- If there are grounded reasons to believe that the defendant or interested person was discriminated against for reasons related to his or her nationality, race, religion, sex, language, political opinions or other personal or social conditions
- If the fact for which the judgment or confiscation order was rendered is not provided for by Italian law as a criminal offense
- If a final judgment was rendered by Italian judicial authorities against the same person for the same criminal offense
- If in Italy a criminal proceeding is pending against the same person for the same criminal offense

The procedure outlined here is not applicable in cases where the requesting jurisdiction is a European Union member state. In such cases, the EU regime on the mutual recognition of freezing and confiscation orders applies (section 2.2.2.2 of this study).

Whether the Nigerian legislation is applicable to recognizing and enforcing foreign confiscation orders taken in civil proceedings remains unconfirmed.

3.1.5 Direct enforcement through the EU legal framework

As highlighted in section 2.2.2.2 of this study, once the new procedure set forth in the EU 2018 Regulation of the Mutual Recognition of Freezing and Confiscation Orders comes into force, EU Member States will recognize and enforce foreign orders based on three separate procedural tracks: (a) under the old EU procedure for cases opened before the entry into force of the 2018 Regulation and in relation to Denmark and Ireland; (b) under the new procedure for cases opened after the entry into force of the 2018 Regulation (except in relation to Denmark and Ireland); and (c) under separate procedures, applicable to requests from non-EU countries.

3.2 AUTHORITIES INVOLVED IN DIRECT ENFORCEMENT

Typically, the process leading to the direct enforcement of foreign confiscation orders involves three main entities:

- The requested jurisdiction's central authority for MLA in charge of receiving and processing the foreign request[18]
- A prosecutorial or other law enforcement authority[19] acting on behalf of the requesting jurisdiction and mandated to file an application for a court order
- A judicial authority in charge of determining whether the foreign order shall be registered and recognized and enforced

Domestic legislation varies in prerogatives assigned to each of those bodies, including the extent of the assessment that each carries out to verify the foreign request's compliance with the applicable formal and substantive requirements.

In a number of cases, the central authority performs a summary evaluation. In Latvia, for example, the Ministry of Justice is tasked with verifying that the necessary documentation has been received before sending it to the competent district court. The latter is thus in charge of examining the request in light of all the applicable conditions.[20] In New Zealand, the bulk of the formal and substantive evaluation is carried out by the attorney general acting as the central authority, with the role of the High Court limited to making the order for the registration of the foreign order upon being satisfied that it is in force in the foreign country.[21] In Australia, the competent court restricts itself to registering the foreign order unless it is satisfied that doing so would be contrary to the interests of justice.[22]

Case Study 3.4: Authorities involved in direct enforcement in Canada

In Canada, the Minister of Justice is responsible for implementing the Mutual Legal Assistance in Criminal Matters Act. The minister's authority is exercised by delegates in the form of Counsel at the International Assistance Group of the Department of Justice Canada, Canada's central authority responsible for international cooperation in criminal matters.

The process is triggered when a written request is presented to the minister by a state or entity for the enforcement of an order of forfeiture of property situated in Canada issued by a criminal court. On receipt of the request, the minister may authorize the Attorney General of Canada, or an attorney general of a province, to make arrangements for the enforcement of the order. In practice, as a matter of operational policy, all such requests are referred to the Attorney General of Canada for enforcement to ensure consistency of practice.

The Attorney General of Canada then files a copy of the order with the superior court of criminal jurisdiction of the province in which all or part of the property that is the subject of the order is believed to be located. On being filed, the order shall be entered as a judgment of that court and may be executed anywhere in Canada. No separate domestic court order is required.

In several cases, the judicial authority in charge of recognizing (or rejecting an application to recognize) foreign confiscation orders is the country's superior jurisdiction (for example, the High Court in New Zealand and Singapore, the Supreme Court in the Seychelles). Some other jurisdictions do not vest this power in a single authority. Instead, they set the criteria for identifying the competent court such as (a) the place of residence of the person in relation to whom the decision on confiscation was made or (b) the place in which the property subject to confiscation is located.[23] In Lebanon, the authority to provide enforceable power to foreign confiscation orders is vested with the president of the Civil Court of Appeal.

3.3 SCOPE OF DIRECT ENFORCEMENT ACTION

3.3.1 Property of corresponding value

When national laws provide for the confiscation of property of corresponding value in domestic cases, this possibility normally extends to the direct enforcement of foreign confiscation orders.

Case Study 3.5: Value confiscation and recognition of foreign confiscation orders: recent Canadian and UK jurisprudence

Canada

The decision of the Ontario Court of Appeal in *Canada (Attorney General) v. Georgiou* in 2018 reflects a success story of Canada directly enforcing a foreign order for asset freezing. In *Georgiou*, the court upheld under the Mutual Legal Assistance in Criminal Matters Act (MLACMA) the direct enforcement in Canada of a restraint order made as part of US criminal proceedings directed at a bank account in Canada. The court held that Canada has the ability under MLACMA to enforce foreign orders for restraint of proceeds of crime against property of equivalent value or substitute assets as permitted under foreign law even though there is no corresponding ability under Canadian criminal law to enforce domestic restraint orders against property of equivalent value or substitute assets. In Canada, if a restraint or forfeiture order cannot be realized against proceeds of crime or offense-related property, there is no ability to restrain or forfeit substitute assets or property of equivalent value

in lieu of the proceeds of crime or offense-related property. Rather, a fine can be imposed in the amount of the restraint or forfeiture.

The court in *Georgiou* reached this conclusion for three reasons. First, as domestic legislation enacted to implement Canada's international obligations, MLACMA should be interpreted broadly and purposively with the aim of fulfilling those obligations. Thus, where a court is faced with two possible interpretations of a statute implementing Canada's international obligations, the interpretation that allows Canada to fulfill those obligations will be preferred. Second, in transnational law, due regard must be paid to differences in foreign legal concepts. The phrase "proceeds of crime" should be interpreted in a manner that respects differences in legal systems. Third, imposing the limits of the Canadian criminal code definition of foreign orders would undermine Canada's ability to cooperate with other states and prevent the government from honoring its treaty obligations.

Source: Canada (Attorney General) v. Georgiou, 2018 ONCA 320, www.canlii.org/en/on/onca/doc/2018/2018onca320/2018onca320 .html?resultIndex=3).

United Kingdom

In *R v. Moss* [2019] EWCA Crim 501, the court held that confiscation orders could extend to property that did not directly represent the proceeds of crime where the defendant had benefited from general criminal conduct. The Criminal Justice and Data Protection (Protocol No. 36) Regulations 2014 were to be read purposively so as to give effect to Framework Decision 2006/783 on the application of the principle of mutual recognition to confiscation orders.

In 2005, the appellant pleaded guilty to a significant number of drug offenses. The judge found that he had a criminal lifestyle and that the assumptions in section 10 of the Proceeds of Crime Act 2002 (POCA) were to be applied. (Such assumptions include, for example, that any property held by or transferred to the defendant at any time after the relevant day was obtained by him as a result of his general criminal conduct.) The recoverable amount was assessed as £1,433,753 and a confiscation order was made in that sum. Among the assets listed in the order was a property in Spain, valued at £350,000. In 2018, the prosecution obtained a certificate to enforce the confiscation order over the appellant's Spanish property. The matter proceeded on the basis that it was not to be regarded as derived from criminality, as there was no evidence as to the date or circumstances of the appellant's purchase of that property. The appellant appealed against a certificate issued under the Criminal Justice and Data Protection (Protocol No. 36) Regulations 2014 (the Regulations) for the enforcement of the confiscation order, submitting that a certificate could only be issued in respect of property shown to represent the proceeds of crime.

The court dismissed the appeal. The recoverable amount could extend to the value of assets that might have nothing to do with crime; the general scheme of the confiscation process operated in personam. However, the scheme had a wider, European context derived from Framework Decision 2006/783, which was implemented by the Regulations and which emphasized the principle of mutual recognition as the cornerstone of judicial cooperation with the European Union. The Regulations were to be read purposively so as to give effect to the Framework Decision.

It was obvious from the wording and purpose of the Framework Decision that the whole scheme was designed to extend to both value confiscation and property confiscation systems. The available amount under POCA could include property that might have no taint of criminality but where there was a link to the benefit obtained by the defendant through general or particular criminal conduct. A confiscation order for the recoverable amount was not to exceed the amount of the benefit. Accordingly, the Framework Decision respected value-based schemes. Because the Regulations gave effect to the Framework Decision, they were to be interpreted accordingly.

Source: 6KBW College Hill, Weekly Digest, April 1, 2019, https://blog.6kbw.com/posts/weekly-digest-1-april-2019.

3.3.2 Non-conviction-based (NCB) foreign orders

Most of the surveyed jurisdictions can directly enforce foreign confiscation orders rendered in NCB judicial proceedings.[24] Among those jurisdictions, two main legislative drafting approaches are used.

The first approach is to make the legal framework dealing with direct enforcement explicitly applicable to both conviction-based and NCB foreign orders.[25] Italian legislation on the recognition of foreign criminal judgments, for example, clarifies its applicability to cases where "the relevant measure has been adopted by the foreign judicial authority by means of a decision other than a judgment of conviction."[26] In Cyprus, the foreign orders that can be registered and enforced include "a confiscation order without conviction, issued by a court within the framework of the procedure relating to a criminal offence [...] Provided that, for the purpose of the present paragraph, 'confiscation order without conviction' includes an order without conviction [...] from a court of a foreign country which leads to the deprivation of property and does not constitute a criminal sanction, to the extent that it is ordered by the court of a foreign country in relation to a criminal offence, provided it has been proven that the property relating to the order constitutes proceeds."[27]

Under the second approach, the direct enforceability of NCB foreign orders is inferred in the absence of any indication to the contrary.[28] In Singapore, for example, a "foreign confiscation order" is defined broadly as "an order made by a court in a foreign country," thus encompassing both in rem and conviction-based foreign orders.[29] Similarly, Republic of Korea's legal framework on the direct enforcement of foreign confiscation orders refers generally to a "final and conclusive judgment" rendered by a foreign court.[30] Peruvian legislation broadly covers "confiscation orders, expiration of ownership (extinción de dominio) or similar legal orders made by foreign courts."[31]

Case Study 3.6: Recognition of non-conviction-based (NCB) foreign orders in France and Canada

France

Whereas France's domestic legal system does not contemplate non-conviction-based confiscation, it has nonetheless been able to recognize and enforce foreign NCB orders. A watershed judgment was a decision by the French Court of Cassation in 2003, which allowed the direct execution of an Italian confiscation order issued as a preventive measure. The Court of Cassation relied on the argument that neither French law nor the applicable international treaties binding the two countries required that the respective confiscation systems be identical; it required that the confiscation order in the requesting state be final and enforceable, that the confiscated asset would also be susceptible to confiscation in analogous circumstances under French law, and that its execution did not endanger public order (Affaire Crisafulli, Cour de Cassation, 2003, Arrêt n° 5848 du 13 novembre 2003).

This case law, which was confirmed by a judgment of the Civil Chamber of the Court of Cassation on June 4, 2009, opens up interesting prospects for cooperation between France and the countries that envisage NCB confiscation. Based on the previously mentioned jurisprudence, it is possible to have a seizure carried out by an investigating judge or a confiscation by a criminal court (tribunal correctionnel) on the basis of a request for seizure or confiscation issued by a foreign judicial authority in an NCB procedure.

Canada

The mutual legal assistance channel, which supposes that foreign requests be addressed to the Minister of Justice, cannot be used to request the recognition and enforcement of an NCB forfeiture order. This does not mean, however, that assistance cannot be granted in the recognition of NCB orders. Because of Canada's constitutional division of power, such requests fall within the jurisdiction of the country's provinces. As most of the provinces have adopted legislation on a civil confiscation regime, requesting states intent on recovering assets through NCB orders need to hire private counsel to act on their behalf in the province where the assets are located.

Case Study 3.7: Hong Kong SAR, China—direct enforcement of non-conviction-based (NCB) foreign confiscation orders

Hong Kong SAR, China, may directly enforce foreign NCB orders as these fall within the notion of "external confiscation order" as defined in section 2 of the Mutual Legal Assistance in Criminal Matters Ordinance, chapter 525, Laws of Hong Kong SAR, China (MLAO). An order may be made for confiscating or forfeiting property derived directly or indirectly from the commission of a crime, the instrument used or intended to be used in the commission of a crime, or the corresponding value of the property. Such an order may be made against a person or property in both civil and criminal proceedings.

Section 2 of the MLAO defines "external confiscation order" to mean an order, made under the law of a place outside Hong Kong SAR, China, for the purpose of the following:

(a) recovering (including forfeiting and confiscating)

i. payments or other rewards received in connection with an external serious offense or their value;

ii. property derived or realized, directly or indirectly, from payments or other rewards received in connection with an external serious offense or the value of such property; or

iii. property used or intended to be used in connection with an external serious offense or the value of such property; or

(b) depriving a person of a pecuniary advantage obtained in connection with an external serious offense, whether the proceedings that gave rise to that order are criminal or civil in nature and whether those proceedings are in the form of proceedings against a person or property.

3.4 SCOPE OF THE EXAMINATION BY REQUESTED JURISDICTIONS

A major advantage of direct enforcement mechanisms compared with indirect ones is to bar the possibility to relitigate the case on its merits before the authorities of the requested jurisdiction. This entails, crucially, that the defendant cannot argue before the courts of the requested jurisdiction that the judges in the requesting state did not give proper consideration to the evidence that was brought for their consideration.

For example, the courts of the requesting jurisdiction may have found a person guilty of giving a US$100,000 bribe to a public official. As a consequence, property equal to this exact amount was confiscated. In proceedings for direct enforcement brought before the authorities of the requested jurisdiction, the public official cannot argue that he had been bribed for a lesser amount. The authorities of the requested jurisdiction would be bound by the findings of the authorities of the requesting one. This implies, notably, that the court of the requested jurisdiction would not be able to examine new evidence in respect to facts already ascertained by the requesting state.[32]

Among the jurisdictions that are able to directly enforce foreign confiscation orders, some do not make this rule explicit in their legal frameworks. This may be because its application is considered to be implicit in judicial practice. In other cases, expressing it may simply appear to be superfluous as the claims that can be made in direct enforcement proceedings are exhaustively listed in domestic legislation. In the United States, for example, other than claims alleging lack of jurisdiction by the foreign court, absence of substantive or procedural due process, or that the restraining order or judgment was obtained by fraud or, in the case of final confiscation orders, is not final and non-appealable, any other arguments would fall outside the scope of 28 U.S.C. § 2467 and thus would have to be rejected.

However, several jurisdictions do articulate the point in an explicit manner—albeit using different formulations—which suggests that the issue may not always be self-evident to practitioners. For example, Cyprus' courts in charge of determining if a foreign order shall be registered, "shall be bound by the findings as to the facts in so far as they are stated in the conviction or decision of a court of the foreign country or in so far as such conviction or judicial decision is implicitly based on them."[33] Using similar language, Latvia's Criminal Procedure Law provides that "the factual circumstances established in a court adjudication of a foreign State and the guilt of a person shall be binding to a court of Latvia."[34] Under Japan's legislation, "the court may not review whether the finally-binding adjudication concerned is justifiable or not."[35] In Peru, those who wish to object to the request for the enforcement of a foreign confiscation order "can only provide or request the evidence that is pertinent and conductive in relation to the fulfillment of the requirements for the execution of a foreign order in Peru."[36]

In the EU mutual recognition legal framework (see section 2.2.2.2 of this study), the prohibition to reexamine the case on its merits is inherent in the mutual recognition principle itself. In this regard, both the 2003 and the 2006 framework decisions[37] provide that, once transmitted in accordance with the specified procedure, freezing or confiscation orders shall be recognized in the executing state without any further formality being required and shall be immediately executed (unless one of the specifically listed grounds for nonrecognition or nonexecution applies). The 2018/1805 Regulation,[38] whose application will be mandatory from December 19, 2020, is predicated on the exact same principle.

As highlighted in section 2.1.4.1 of this study, direct enforcement should not be confused with automatic enforcement. Under all direct enforcement models, with the exception of the EU mutual recognition legal framework, the competent authorities in requested jurisdictions are in a position to request supplementary information needed to determine the fulfilment of the conditions set in domestic laws for the direct enforcement of foreign confiscation orders (for example, that the order is final and that the concerned person had the opportunity to defend himself or herself). In the Russian Federation, for example, if the court has any doubts about the incompleteness or absence of required information, the judge may request in the prescribed manner additional clarifications, additional information, and materials from the competent authority of the foreign state, as well as from other persons participating in the consideration of the request.[39]

Likewise, short of requesting a reexamination of the case on its merits, the person subject to the order and other interested parties is normally given the chance to claim that the conditions for the registration of the foreign order have not been fulfilled.

Case Study 3.8: UK jurisprudence on limiting the scope of examination for foreign confiscation orders

In *A v. DPP* [2017] 1 W.L.R. 713; [2017] 1 Cr. App. R. 6, an English Court of Appeal ruled that a challenge to the substantive reasons for the making of an overseas restraint order may be made only in the courts of the issuing state.

The applicant argued that an English judge of first instance did not correctly apply the 2014 Regulations, which transposed into domestic law European Union (EU) Council Framework Decision 2003/577/JHA on the execution in the EU of orders freezing property or evidence.

The case involved a French criminal investigation that began in 2006, alleging that A, a French citizen, had committed money laundering, aggrieved fraud, and other offenses involving the sale of real estate in southern France.

In 2006, a criminal investigation against A was also opened in Switzerland, but was abandoned because of lack of conclusive information, which, under Swiss law, equals to a formal acquittal. (However, since dropping the charge is made in a summary procedure, the criminal procedure may be reopened if new facts are discovered.) The French investigation, however, continued and led to a French court making a restrained order relative to assets held by A with a London-based financial institution. Application was then made for that order to be registered in England under the 2014 Regulations. The order was registered.

The main argument raised by A's defense lawyers was that, because the facts of the case had already been the object of a judicial decision by the Swiss authorities, the French proceedings had violated the principle of ne bis in idem (not twice in the same thing). Hence, the French restraint order should not continue to be registered in England.

This argument was rejected by the English court. According to it, the conclusive objection to the applicant's argument was found in the relevant EU legal instrument as domesticated by the 2014 Regulations. Under Regulation 10.6, in particular, a challenge to the

substantive reason for making an overseas restraint order may be made only in the courts of the issuing state. The courts of the executing state shall not themselves consider such a challenge.

The English court also did not accept the applicant's argument that substantive reasons did not extend to a consideration of the fundamental rights of an affected citizen. The fact that the ne bis in idem principle had already been considered by the competent French courts (and, in this specific case, considered not to have been violated) was necessarily to be regarded as a substantive reason for making and continuing an overseas order by the issuing state.

According to the court, following the applicant's faulty reasoning would have led to a situation where, had the French authorities sought to have the order recognized not only in England but also in, say, Belgium, Germany, Italy, and Spain, the same challenge could have been substantively brought in each of these jurisdictions, with the potential for different outcomes in each of them. This possible outcome was considered unacceptable in a "scheme designed to be operated speedily and on the basis of mutual recognition and of confidence on the legality of decisions of fellow member States."

Moreover, if the courts of the executing state were able to consider the substantive reasons already evaluated by the issuing state, the restraint order would potentially continue to bind A in personam (against a particular person) in France, but would cease to bind the assets of A in rem in England.

The English court concluded in the sense that "the circumstances in which registration may be refused or challenged in an executing State (for good practical reasons of making the scheme efficacious) are closely circumscribed [....] If a wider challenge is to be made as to the substantive reasons for making the restraint order, then that challenge is to be made, and made only, in the courts of the issuing State" as the appropriate forum.

Source: A v. Director of Prosecution at Casemine, www.casemine.com/judgement/uk/5a8ff7a560d03e7f57eb0bff.

3.5 EXISTENCE OF A TREATY AND RECIPROCITY

Most of the surveyed jurisdictions do not require a treaty as a precondition for directly enforcing foreign confiscation orders.[40] In the absence of applicable treaties, they normally require an offer of reciprocity by requesting jurisdictions whereby the latter provide assurances that a future request for similar assistance addressed to them will be complied with. In France, an exception to the application of the reciprocity rule is when a non-EU country submits a request for extended confiscation.[41] In this case, the request can only be enforced on the basis of explicit provisions in a bilateral or multilateral treaty.

There seems to be little awareness, instead, that article 55(6) UNCAC may constitute a sufficient legal basis for enforcement purposes. This may not be a problem to jurisdictions that do not need a treaty to execute a request for asset recovery. However, knowledge of this fact may be relevant for those where the existence of a treaty is strictly required, lacking an alternative legal basis. In this sense, interviewed practitioners from Italy and the United States confirmed that UNCAC is considered an adequate mechanism for cooperation, with their respective governments being able to provide assistance to requests made under this treaty.

3.6 SUBSTANTIVE CONDITIONS AND GROUNDS FOR REFUSAL

3.6.1 Overview

Although direct enforcement arguably offers a quicker and more straightforward channel to achieve asset recovery than indirect enforcement, it remains subject to a degree of control by the requested jurisdiction.

Requests for direct enforcement of foreign confiscation orders are subject to the conditions and requirements applicable to MLA requests in general (for example, the provision of assurances of reciprocity, respect for prescribed forms and channels of communication, and document authentication requirements). They are also commonly examined against generally applicable grounds for refusal such as lack of dual criminality, incompatibility with the requested jurisdiction's fundamental principles, discriminatory nature of the request, and so forth.

Additionally, as a discrete type of MLA, the direct enforcement of foreign confiscation orders is subject to several specific requirements. Sections 3.6.2 and 3.6.3 of this study examine two conditions that consistently appear in all domestic legal frameworks:

- That the foreign confiscation order is final and not subject to appeal
- That the persons in relation to whom the confiscation order was made were given the opportunity to appear and assert defenses to cover either criminal or NCB cases in proceeding in the requesting jurisdiction

Sections 3.6.4 to 3.6.11 in this study provide an overview of further conditions and substantive requirements found in surveyed jurisdictions for requests for direct enforcement. Some of these requirements are only present in a few legal frameworks. The information in those sections is presented to illustrate the variety of approaches to the subject.

Case Study 3.9: British Virgin Islands' Direct Enforcement Procedure and Conditions

For a foreign order to be enforced in the British Virgin Islands, the attorney general in its capacity as the central authority would make the relevant application to the High Court for the order's registration. Once the application is granted, the foreign order will become enforceable.

However, a number of legislative requirements must be met before any registration application can be granted. In particular, the High Court must be of the opinion that enforcing the order in the British Virgin Islands would not be contrary to the interests of justice. In addition, it must be satisfied with the following:

- At the time of registration, the order is in force and not subject to appeal.
- If the person against whom the order is made did not appear in the proceedings, he or she needed to have received notice of the proceedings in sufficient time to enable him or her to defend himself or herself.

Sources: Criminal Justice (International Co-operation) (Enforcement of Overseas Forfeiture Orders) Order, § 10 (2017); Proceeds of Criminal Conduct (Enforcement of External Confiscation Orders) Order, § 33 (2017), provide for the enforcement of External Orders.

3.6.2 Non-appealability of the foreign order

Surveyed jurisdictions invariably establish that foreign confiscation orders shall be in force and no longer subject to appeal as prerequisites for their enforcement.

To dissipate any doubts and avoid terminological issues, a few jurisdictions[42] define the meaning of "appeal" broadly as including any proceedings by way of discharging or setting aside the order or an application for a new trial or stay of execution. The legislation of Hong Kong SAR, China, further clarifies that "an external confiscation order is subject to appeal so long as an appeal, further appeal or review is pending against the order; and for this purpose an appeal, further appeal or review shall be treated as pending until the expiration of the time prescribed for instituting the appeal, further appeal or review under the law of the place outside [Hong Kong SAR, China] concerned."[43]

In some cases,[44] legislation specifies that the non-appealability requirement must be assessed at the time when the foreign order is being registered. This clarification suggests that, at least in theory, countries may submit a formal request for the direct enforcement of a confiscation order that is still formally subject to appeal. This possibility might be interesting for saving time, potentially allowing countries to request assistance even when a confiscation order is not yet final, but when it is expected to become final shortly.

Some jurisdictions[45] require that both the foreign judgment convicting the offender and the confiscation order be final. This reflects the fact that in several countries, particularly those belonging to the common law legal tradition, the two decisions are contained in separate legal instruments and thus each of them is subject to its own time frame and conditions for appeal. The question would not arise in countries where the confiscation order is an integral part of the conviction judgment.

3.6.3 Fair trial in requesting jurisdictions

In all surveyed jurisdictions, the enforcement of foreign confiscation orders is conditional on the verification that the rights of the defense were respected in the proceeding that took place in the requesting country. Most requested jurisdictions[46] are satisfied with the factual determination that the defendants were duly notified of the relevant proceedings in sufficient time to defend themselves, even when they did not appear in such proceedings. In Italy, an additional requirement is that the defendant was granted the right to be questioned in a language that he or she can understand and be assisted by a lawyer.[47]

Other jurisdictions envisage a broader examination that looks into whether the foreign judgment was made under a system with procedures compatible with due process requirements[48] or whether the court in the requesting country possessed the necessary requisites of independence and impartiality.[49] The United States poses the additional requirement that the judgment was not obtained by fraud. Without further guidelines on how to interpret broad and undefined notions such as due process, extended litigation could occur at court hearings in the requested jurisdiction.

Unless reliable information exists on the violation of the procedural rights of defendants in the requesting jurisdiction, the authorities of that jurisdiction would normally consider the fair trial requirement fulfilled in the absence of arguments raised by defendants at the court hearing in the requested jurisdiction.

Case Study 3.10: Singapore's use of the disposal inquiry mechanism in mutual legal assistance (MLA) proceedings

This case concerned an influential businessman who was found to have collected bribes in awarding telecommunications and construction contracts. The proceeds originating from the bribery scheme were moved from two foreign states in the amounts of SGD2,000,000 and US$900,000 respectively, and deposited in Singapore bank accounts held by two shell companies.

With information from the two foreign states, domestic money-laundering investigations began, which led to the discovery and domestic seizure by police of SGD2,000,000 and US$900,000 deposited in accounts held by the two shell companies. Following domestic seizure, a joint MLA request was received from the two states for enforcement of state A's confiscation order for approximately SGD2,000,000 and state B's confiscation order for approximately US$900,000.

The confiscation order from state A for the SGD2,000,000 had fulfilled the requisite legal requirements under the Mutual Legal Assistance in Criminal Matters Act and the money was confiscated without much difficulty. State A did not request repatriation of funds.

However, there were problems with state B's request; state B had not given the defendant adequate notice of its confiscation proceedings. Therefore, a fundamental principle of justice—the opportunity to be heard—which is a condition to enforcement of state B's confiscation order, was not met.

As the accounts were seized by the police according to domestic investigations, Singapore authorities used the domestic Disposal Inquiry Mechanism (DIM) for cross-border asset recovery.

Such mechanism is typically employed under Singapore's domestic criminal procedure to return items seized by police in investigations to its rightful owners. All persons with interests in the asset are notified and invited to make claims to them. Generally, the DIM is intended for things such as a computer, tools, and jewelry.

The DIM had never been used before in mutual legal assistance. However, in this case, there were no other claimants to the proceeds (state B was the only real prospective claimant); but there was sufficient evidence of state B's claim to ownership, and the defendant was very unlikely to challenge proceedings. Given that Singapore courts use the common law adversarial process, the Singapore authorities were confident the disposal inquiry would achieve return of the assets to state B. The full amount of recovered funds of US$932,000 was returned to state B.

3.6.4 Penalty thresholds

In some jurisdictions, the underlying offense needs to satisfy a minimum penalty requirement as a condition for the enforcement of related foreign confiscation orders. Australia and the Seychelles outline it by demanding that the offence be a serious offense. In Australia, a serious offense is defined as an offense for which the maximum penalty is death, imprisonment for at least 12 months, or a substantial fine of legislated value.[50]

This requirement should not be confused with article 55(7) of the UNCAC, according to which, "Cooperation [...] may also be refused or provisional measures lifted if the requested State Party does not receive sufficient and timely evidence or if the property is of a *de minimis* value" (section 2.1.5.2 of this study). In the latter case, the rationale for refusing cooperation lies in the low value of the assets whose confiscation is requested. Instead, in the case under consideration, the rationale is to ensure that MLA procedures are only triggered where the cost of executing them (normally borne by the requested country) is commensurate to the gravity of the conduct at stake, regardless of the value of the assets at stake. At the same time, the setting of penalty threshold conditions may lead to a situation where an offense that is punished too lightly has nonetheless generated high-value proceeds, and these cannot be confiscated abroad.

3.6.5 Location of the property subject to the foreign order

Under some legal frameworks, requesting jurisdictions need to confirm,[51] or at least indicate a reasonable suspicion,[52] that the property needed to satisfy the confiscation order is located in the requested jurisdiction.

The legislation of Russia further draws a distinction between property located in its territory and property that, whereas geographically in its territory, is not subject to its jurisdiction (potentially, thus, on diplomatic premises or other assets belonging to a foreign state).[53] In relation to the latter, a foreign confiscation order may not be recognized and enforced.

3.6.6 Jurisdiction of the issuing authority

Some jurisdictions must be satisfied that the foreign confiscation order was issued by a competent authority according to the laws of the requesting jurisdiction.[54] When enforcing conviction-based confiscation orders, legislation in the United States explicitly extends the scope of the inquiry into whether the foreign court had personal as well as subject-matter jurisdiction.[55]

3.6.7 Dual criminality

For dual criminality, surveyed jurisdictions reveal a fragmented landscape with four main approaches at play:

a. Compliance with the dual criminal principle is not required in relation to any type of MLA, including asset recovery related requests.[56]
b. Dual criminality is in principle not required, with the exception of asset recovery requests or, more broadly, measures requiring coercion.[57]
c. Compliance with the dual criminality requirement is always necessary in relation to all forms of MLA. In some cases, the requirement is made explicitly applicable for actions aimed at the direct enforcement of foreign confiscation orders.[58]

d. All MLA requests are examined against dual criminality, although this is framed as a discretionary as opposed to compulsory ground for refusal.[59]

3.6.8 Dual confiscability

In addition to dual criminality, some jurisdictions subordinate the direct enforcement of foreign confiscation orders to what may be called as dual confiscability. In other words, the authorities of the requested jurisdiction need to be satisfied that the property in question could have been the object of an equivalent measure in a purely domestic case.[60]

In some cases, the dual confiscability requirement receives a specific treatment. The United States, for example, does not limit enforcement to situations where the property sought to be provisionally restrained could be forfeited under US law if the offense had occurred in the United States, but it is necessary that the dual confiscability requirement be met for entry of a final confiscation order. However, if the foreign provisional restraint order is enforced, even in the absence of dual confiscability, it may still be possible for the parties to reach an agreement to be sanctioned by the US court under which the property holder consents to final forfeiture.[61]

3.6.9 Compatibility with the essential interests and principles of the state

Most surveyed jurisdictions examine whether direct enforcement action would negatively affect their national interests, sovereignty, fundamental legal principles, public order, and so forth.[62] Under some legislative acts, the competent authorities are also mandated to establish that the execution of the request would not be contrary to the interests of justice.[63]

These provisions are standard ones found in many MLA laws. Whether contained in general MLA-related statutes or specific asset-confiscation provisions, similar provisions aim to equip requested jurisdictions with a safety valve and a degree of flexibility to refuse the execution of a foreign request on grounds that have not been specifically listed in domestic statutes. At the same time, their broad and undetermined nature may lend them to abuse.

3.6.10 Interference with domestic proceedings

Under some legal frameworks, the direct enforcement of foreign confiscation orders may be refused under the following conditions:

- Judicial proceedings are taking place in the requested jurisdiction for the same facts or against the same person.[64]
- Confiscation orders have already been issued regarding the property that is the object of the foreign request.[65]
- Enforcement would be in contradiction with international commitments vis-à-vis another state.[66]

3.6.11 Financial burdens on the requested jurisdiction

Some jurisdictions make direct enforcement action conditional on a determination that it would not be excessively expensive. Under Canada's legislation, for example, the minister must refuse an asset confiscation request if they are "of the opinion that enforcement of the order would impose an excessive burden on the resources of federal, provincial or territorial authorities."[67] In Latvia, the request may be refused if the expenses that would be incurred are not considered to be commensurate with the seriousness of and harm caused by the criminal offence.[68]

3.7 DIRECT ENFORCEMENT OF FREEZING AND SEIZING ORDERS

3.7.1 Overview

The fact that some jurisdictions are able to directly enforce foreign confiscation orders does not necessarily mean that they can also take direct action vis-à-vis foreign provisional orders.[69] Whereas they can respond to foreign requests through the enactment of domestic provisional measures, freezing and seizing orders rendered by a foreign authority cannot always be directly enforced. In these cases, foreign requests are examined against a set of conditions and, if deemed acceptable, are enforced after issuance of an order taken in application of procedures required for an equivalent domestic measure.

In some jurisdictions, the inability to directly enforce provisional measures is justified by their temporary nature.[70] Instead, other countries consider that freezing and seizing orders may well be directly enforceable in much the same way as confiscation orders once all the possible appeals have been exhausted. Various surveyed countries indeed see no legal or practical obstacles in achieving this result.[71] In these jurisdictions, a few conditions that are applicable to foreign confiscation orders also apply to provisional orders. This includes, notably, the requirement that the foreign restraint order is not subject to appeal.[72]

Case Study 3.11: New Zealand's procedure for the direct enforcement of foreign restraining orders

Under the Mutual Assistance in Criminal Matters Act 1992 (MACMA), requests are received by the attorney general's office in its capacity as central authority for mutual legal assistance (MLA). Once the attorney general is satisfied that there are reasonable grounds to believe some or all of the property that is able to be restrained under the foreign restraining order is located in New Zealand, it may authorize the commissioner of police to apply to the High Court to register the foreign forfeiture order in New Zealand.

In practice, formal MLA requests are received by the Crown Law Office (CLO) on behalf of the attorney general. Within the criminal team established within the CLO, specially trained counsels assess incoming requests. There may be communication between the CLO and the foreign jurisdiction to finalize the material to meet the required legal standards. In processing the request, the CLO takes note of the time framework and time constraints of the requesting jurisdiction. It gives priority to requests that have been marked as urgent and where there is a risk that the assets may be dissipated. Following a positive assessment, the request is referred to the deputy solicitor general (criminal team) who, according to delegations from the attorney general, consents to the request being actioned.

The hearing before the High Court can occur, if necessary, on an ex parte basis.[a] If the High Court is satisfied that the foreign restraining order is in force in a foreign country, it makes an order that it be registered in New Zealand.

Significantly, MACMA allows for foreign restraining orders to be registered in New Zealand initially on

a. Ex parte, that is, without notifying interested parties.

the basis of only a facsimile copy of the foreign order. This fact reduces delays in waiting for the original of the order arriving by the mail.

Once registered, the order is assigned to the local asset recovery unit where the assets are situated. The asset recovery unit will enact the order and have the assets restrained. It will serve documents on local parties named and have the assets transferred to the official assignee. The official assignee is a government agency working under the umbrella of New Zealand's Ministry of Business, Innovation, and Employment. The official assignee's role is to deal with proceeds of crime or insolvency and bankruptcy matters.

Case Study 3.12: South Africa's template application for the registration of foreign restraint orders

In South Africa, a foreign restraint order may be registered in terms of section 24 of the International Cooperation in Criminal Matters Act. The order is received by the competent authority and, if it is not subject to review or appeal, it is sent to the High Court for registration. In practice, registration is handled by

the asset forfeiture unit, which belongs to the National Prosecuting Authority. Next is an example of a notice to the registrar concerning a foreign restraint order. A certified copy of the foreign order is required for registration.

IN THE HIGH COURT OF SOUTH AFRICA

GAUTENG DIVISION, PRETORIA

CASE REGISTRATION NO:...............................

In re: Registration of a foreign restraint order: Mr. X

NOTICE TO THE REGISTRAR IN TERMS OF SECTION 24 OF THE SOUTH AFRICAN INTERNATIONAL CO-OPERATION IN CRIMINAL MATTERS ACT 75 OF 1996

1. I am an adult, female/male advocate in the employ of the Asset Forfeiture Unit of the National Prosecuting Authority and I have been duly authorised to make this official request to the Registrar of the Gauteng Division of the High Court (**the Registrar**) on behalf of the Director General of the Department of Justice and Constitutional Development.

2. I annex hereto a certified copy of a foreign restraint order made against Mr. X **(restraint order)**.

3. In terms of section 24 of the **International Co-Operation in Criminal Matters Act 75 of 1996 (the ICCMA)** and the Regulations under the ICCMA, I hereby request the Registrar to open a file/case cover in which this request and a copy of the restraint order is to be filed.

4. The Registrar is further requested to register the lodged restraint order by

    4.1 numbering the restraint order with a consecutive case number for the year during which it is lodged;

    4.2 recording the restraint order in respect of the property which is specified therein and full particulars of that property, in so far as the particulars are available on the case file.

5. You are also requested to forthwith give notice, in writing and in accordance with [the applicable regulations and forms], to Mr. X to the effect that

5.1 the foreign restraint order has been registered at this division of the High Court; and

5.2 Mr. X may within the prescribed period and in terms of the Rules of the Court, apply to the honourable Court of this Division for the setting aside of the registration of the restraint order.

6. To the best of my knowledge, Mr. X is currently present within/outside the Republic of South Africa. His current address is: [....]

7. Copies of the following documents are annexed

    7.1 Letter of request from the International Criminality Unit in London;

    7.2 Letter of request from the Serious Fraud Office in London;

    7.3 A letter from the Director-General: Department of Justice and Constitutional Development;

    7.4 The relevant sections of the ICCMA;

    7.5 The relevant Regulations under the ICCMA.

Dated at Pretoria on [date].

———————————————

[Signature]

On behalf of the Director-General: Department of Justice and Constitutional Development

In comparison with domestic procedures in place for the direct enforcement of foreign confiscation orders, those that are used to recognize freezing and seizing orders envisage fewer conditions. The scrutiny exercised by requested jurisdictions is generally of a lower intensity. In Canada, for example, several grounds for refusal are spelled out in relation to foreign confiscation orders, but not to foreign restraint orders. In the Seychelles, the requirement that the foreign order not be subject to appeal is explicitly set forth only in relation to confiscation orders.

Some jurisdictions set a number of conditions that are specific to the recognition of foreign restraint orders. A critical one is that they may be obtained in ex parte proceedings where the government can show a risk of dissipation or flight.[73]

In relation to the direct enforcement of foreign restraint orders, major areas deserving regulation are as follows:

- The extent of the validity of the domestic order through which a foreign restraint order has been registered
- The stage of the procedure (in the requesting jurisdiction) in which a foreign restraint order must have been issued for this order to be registered in the requested jurisdiction

- The probability that a final confiscation order will eventually be issued in the requesting jurisdiction

Each of these issues are examined separately in the sections that follow.

3.7.2 Extent of the validity of the registration order

The question arises in practice when the validity of the preventive measure according to the law of the requested country is shorter than the validity of a similar measure according to the law of the requesting country or when the requesting jurisdiction, after having obtained the registration of a provisional order, does not act to request the enforcement of the subsequent confiscation order, or when it makes no confiscation order at all (for example, because related proceedings result in an acquittal).

The general rule is that the laws of the requested jurisdiction applicable to the validity, duration, renewal, and so forth of domestic restraint orders are applicable—once the necessary changes have been made—to foreign orders. In the Seychelles, for example, a foreign restraining order registered in the Supreme Court has effect, and may be enforced, as if it was a restraining order made by the Supreme Court under any written law of Seychelles relating to the tracing, seizure, confiscation, or forfeiture of proceeds of crime.[74]

According to interviewed practitioners, based on the Mutual Assistance Act, Swiss authorities are in a position to keep foreign assets seized for several years. However, the account holders have the right to appeal against the maintenance of the seizure. If the foreign jurisdiction does not issue a confiscation order or lengthy procedures last several years without progress and thus is not pursuing the criminal proceeding swiftly enough, the seizure will have to be lifted.

In Italy, the deadlines are set in legislation, with provisional measures being revoked if the requesting jurisdiction does not forward the confiscation order within one year of the execution of the seizure. This term can be prolonged up to six months.[75]

By contrast, under US law there are no statute-imposed time limits for keeping in place provisional orders requested by a foreign jurisdiction. In theory, it is possible that if a property owner claimed that the enforcement of the foreign order was time barred under foreign law, the competent US court may direct the government to inquire about the issue with the foreign authorities and report back to the court for further consideration. Whereas this situation has not occurred yet, US courts on their own initiative often request the government to find out why no final confiscation order has been entered in the foreign jurisdiction.

3.7.3 Procedural stage in the requesting jurisdiction

Whereas a few jurisdictions make the direct enforcement of foreign restraint orders conditional on the requirement that the person in question be officially charged, most do not provide for such condition. In New Zealand and South Africa, for example, direct enforcement action can occur at any stage of the criminal proceeding in the requesting jurisdiction, thus even before charges have been raised.[76]

In the Seychelles, where the direct enforcement of foreign restraint orders is also possible, the legislation does not specify at which stage of the criminal proceedings those orders must have been made. Some guidance may be inferred, however, from a separate set of provisions dealing with the indirect enforcement of foreign restraining orders. In this case, the MLA law makes the enforcement conditional on the fact that "a criminal proceeding has commenced in a foreign country in respect of a serious offence."[77] Crucially, in both countries foreign restraining orders are considered those made under the law of a foreign country by a court or other judicial authority. By referring to orders made by a judicial authority in general, such formulation ensures that direct enforcement action can also be taken in relation to provisional orders issued in NCB proceedings.

3.7.4 Probability that a foreign order will be issued or be enforceable

In Hong Kong SAR, China, there must be, as a minimum, reasonable grounds for believing that an external confiscation order may be made in the proceedings instituted in the requesting jurisdiction.[78]

In Italy, the enforcement of the foreign order for asset freezing and seizure shall be refused "if there are reasons to believe that the conditions for the recognition of the subsequent confiscation order will not be met."[79]

3.8 RIGHTS OF INTERESTED PARTIES

3.8.1 Main approaches

Interested parties are all those with a reason to claim that the enforcement of the foreign order would unfairly prejudice them. In direct enforcement procedures, they include the person against whom the foreign order was made as well as other parties such as those claiming to be bona fide holders and owners.[80] In New Zealand, the commissioner of police must serve notice of the court application to every person who, to his or her knowledge, has an interest in the property to which the order relates.[81]

The examination of domestic laws specifically dealing with the direct enforcement of foreign orders reveal three main legislative approaches on the issue of protecting the rights of interested parties:

- Some jurisdictions spell out the detailed rights and prerogatives of affected (or potentially affected) parties. These countries often set forth procedures about the timing and the modalities with which these rights shall be exercised.[82]
- Other jurisdictions[83] do not have any ad hoc provisions to protect third parties' interests in the context of MLA procedures for the enforcement of confiscation orders. However, they refer to the general rules applicable to domestic orders, which include general provisions for protecting affected parties.
- In other cases, there are neither dedicated provisions nor an explicit reference to the applicability of rules dealing with domestic confiscation and restraint orders. Whereas this might sometimes reveal a legislative gap, in other cases it might simply suggest that legislators considered the application of the general domestic regime implicitly applicable to foreign confiscation and restraint orders and thus not worth stating in legislative terms.

3.8.2 Right to be notified and take part in the hearing

The protection of the rights of interested parties normally starts with a notification to them that an application for the registration of a confiscation or restraining order has been filed. In direct enforcement procedures, in particular, the goal of notification aims to enable interested parties to make their representations at the court hearing within the limits already highlighted, that is, enable them to claim that the conditions for the recognition of the foreign order have not been fulfilled, short of requesting the reexamination of the merits of the case.

Some jurisdictions set forth strict time requirements for the notice to be served. In Italy, it is communicated at least 10 days before the hearing date to enable the interested parties to take part in the hearing leading to the recognition of the foreign confiscation order.[84]

In other cases,[85] interested parties are only allowed to make representations after the court has already registered the foreign order, but before the decision has become enforceable. In Cyprus, "a registered confiscation order is executed if, within six weeks from notification given to affected parties, these persons took no action for the cancellation or the setting aside of the registration order. If notification is impossible or the accused or the third person in the possession of whom the proceeds are held cannot be located, despite making reasonable efforts, the confiscation order is executed immediately."[86]

Case Study 3.13: South Africa's template notification to affected parties

Upon registration of the foreign order, according to the Regulations to the International Cooperation in Criminal Matters Act, a notice is to be sent to the person against whom the order is made. The following is an example of a notice sent out by the registrar of the High Court.

IN THE HIGH COURT OF SOUTH AFRICA
GAUTENG DIVISION, PRETORIA

Case No: ....
NOTICE OF REGISTRATION OF A FOREIGN RESTRAINT ORDER

To: Mr. Z

Residential address: [...]

Business/employment address: [...]

You are hereby notified that a foreign restraint order (attached hereto as Annexure A) has been registered at the High Court of South Africa, Gauteng Division, Pretoria on [date] in respect of the following property/interests in property:

1. Any interest, including shares by Mr. Z in ABC Investments (Pty) Ltd (Registration number [...]);

2. The business registered in accordance with the laws of the Republic of South Africa and located at [...];

3. Any interest in the property located at [...]; and

4. Any interest in a Standard Bank account with account number [...] held in the name of ABC Investments (Pty) Ltd which account is held at the Fourways Branch of Standard Bank.

The registration of the foreign restraint order has the effect of a restraint order made by the above-mentioned High Court.

In terms of section 24(3)(b) of the **International Co-operation in Criminal Matters Act 75 of 1996** read with regulation 16 of the Regulations for International Co-operation in Criminal Matters, 1997, you may within 20 court days from the date on which such registration came to your knowledge, and in terms of the rules of court, apply for the setting aside of the registration of the order to the above-mentioned High Court. If the notice was not served on you personally it is presumed that registration came to your knowledge within 10 days after the date of service of the notice.

Signed at Pretoria on ....
REGISTRAR OF THE HIGH COURT

PRETORIA

Because of the transnational nature of cases underlying MLA requests, interested parties are often not physically present in the territory of the requested jurisdiction. This situation may severely complicate the task of reaching out to them. Some jurisdictions take this aspect into consideration. In Russia, interested persons shall be notified of the place, date, and time of the hearing not later than 30 days before the hearing if they are present in the territory of Russia. The time limit is extended to six months for those who are not present in the territory.[87]

In Brazil, interested parties have 10 days to present their arguments (*deduzir* [to deduct] embargos) if they reside in the federal district where the Supreme Court in charge of homologating the foreign (provisional or confiscation) decision is established, or 30 days if they reside elsewhere.[88]

3.8.3 Ex parte applications

To limit the risk of asset dissipation, some of the jurisdictions under examination explicitly foresee the possibility to apply for a court order ex parte, without notifying interested parties.[89] For example, in New Zealand a court that receives an application for the registration of a foreign restraining order may, on the request of the applicant, consider the application without giving notice to any or all of the interested persons if it is satisfied that there is a risk of the proposed restrained property being destroyed, disposed of, altered, or concealed if notice were given to those persons.[90]

3.8.4 Right of appeal

Some jurisdictions provide for the right of appeal to a higher court against the decision with which the court (in the requested jurisdiction) has granted enforcement power to a foreign confiscation order.[91]

In the United Kingdom, for example, if on an application for the Crown Court to give effect to an external restraint or confiscation order by registering it, the court decides not to do so, the decision may be appealed to the court of appeal, which may either (a) confirm or set aside the decision to register or (b) direct the Crown Court to register the external order.[92] The legislation of Kazakhstan makes it clear that "the decision of the court may be appealed or protested in the manner and terms established by this Code."[93]

In some cases, domestic legislation sets forth the possibility to lodge a further appeal to the highest judicial body in the country.[94]

3.8.5 Forms and modalities of the court hearing

A number of legal frameworks dealing with the direct enforcement of foreign confiscation orders provide for a further layer of protection for intervening parties by outlining the forms and modalities of the court hearing. In Japan, the court shall hold the hearing at a public courtroom.[95] Russian legislation requires that the foreign request be considered by a single judge in open court.

Some laws aim to make the exercise of the right of defense effective.[96] This issue appears to be of particular relevance where intervening parties are not familiar with the language and the legal system of the country in which the hearing for the registration of a foreign confiscation order takes place. In Germany, for example, "in respect of requests for enforcement of foreign orders for confiscation or deprivation, the convicted person as well as third parties who could, depending on the circumstances of the case, claim rights to the object, may avail themselves of the assistance of counsel at any stage of the proceedings. If the convicted person did not privately appoint counsel, he shall be assigned counsel if: because of the complexity of the factual and legal situation, the assistance of counsel appears necessary; it is apparent that the convicted person cannot

TABLE 3.1 Main stages and flow of direct enforcement procedures

Stage 1: Request sent

The restraint or confiscation order is sent to the requested jurisdiction for enforcement purposes through mutual legal assistance (MLA) channels.

Stage 2: Request evaluated by the central authority

The MLA central authority of the requested jurisdiction verifies that the request complies with the formal requirements in place for MLA requests in general and those specifically set for the enforcement of foreign restraint or confiscation orders.

(Depending on domestic laws, the central authority may also be in charge of verifying compliance with all or some of the conditions prescribed for the enforcement of foreign orders. For example, if the order is not subject to appeal, if the persons against whom the order was made had the opportunity to defend themselves in the requesting jurisdictions, and so forth.)

Stage 3: Foreign order transmitted to court for registration or recognition

The central authority applies to the competent court for the registration and recognition of the foreign freezing or confiscation order. (Alternatively, depending on domestic laws, the central authority transmits the documentation to another authority who makes the formal court application. (For example, a law enforcement or prosecutorial authority.)

Interested parties are notified of the application and given the opportunity to make representations before the court. In the case of restraint orders, the application to the court may be done ex parte to prevent the risk of asset dissipation.

Stage 4: Foreign order registered or recognized

The competent court registers or recognizes the foreign order if it is satisfied that the conditions prescribed for the enforcement of the foreign restraint or confiscation order have been fulfilled (except when this assessment has already been made in Stage 2, depending on domestic laws). The court is bound by the findings related to the facts of the case as they are stated in the foreign request. The case is not reassessed on its merits.

Interested parties are heard at the court hearing. (In some jurisdictions, they are only allowed to make representations after the court has registered the order, but before the order is enforced.)

Stage 5: Foreign order enforced

The foreign restraint or confiscation order is enforced by the requested jurisdiction as if it were a domestic order.

Note: Table 3.1 gives an overview of the main procedural steps generally followed in surveyed countries. Procedures in force in individual jurisdictions may differ from the proposed model.

himself adequately protect his rights or; the convicted person is in detention outside German territory and there are doubts whether he himself can adequately protect his rights."[97]

In Russia, persons held in custody whose property was confiscated through, among other things, a foreign confiscation order, shall be given the right to participate in the hearing directly or through a video conference as well as the right to inform the court of their positions through their representative or in writing. At the same time, failure to appear in the court of persons, timely notified of the place, date, and time of the hearing (except those whose participation in the hearing is recognized by the court as compulsory), shall not preclude the consideration of the request.[98]

3.9 TAKEAWAYS

- The vast majority of the surveyed jurisdictions has adopted at least basic legal mechanisms for the purpose of directly enforcing foreign confiscation and—less commonly—freezing and seizing orders. Not all of them, however, appear to be in a position to use such mechanisms in practice because they lack implementing legislation on procedural matters.
- Direct enforcement mechanisms are employed by jurisdictions belonging to both common law and civil law legal systems.
- The structure and level of detail of domestic laws dealing with direct enforcement issues varies considerably. Most jurisdictions regulate the matter through specific sections of MLA and asset recovery statutes or within legislation generally dealing with the recognition of foreign judgments in criminal matters.
- In some jurisdictions, procedures for direct enforcement are spelled out in legislation dealing with specific crime categories, notably in anti-money-laundering statutes. However, this choice raises the question of whether such procedures can be applied by analogy to recognize foreign orders that have been made in criminal proceedings other than for money-laundering offenses.
- Countries should be cautious before concluding that their general exequatur procedures can be used to enforce foreign confiscation orders as these procedures are often only designed to give effect to foreign civil or arbitral judgments.
- The availability of both direct and indirect enforcement mechanisms in domestic legal frameworks is regarded as providing an important degree of flexibility as requested jurisdictions can often choose the most effective channel to execute the request based on the circumstances of each case.
- Legislation on direct enforcement usually scrutinizes the request against conditions and requirements applicable to MLA requests in general (for example, reciprocity, dual criminality, document authentication). Also, foreign requests are consistently examined against the following two conditions: (a) the foreign order is final or not subject to appeal and (b) the persons in relation to whom the order was made were given a fair trial.
- Under direct enforcement models, whereas requested jurisdictions retain the ability to review the request against a number of conditions, they do not have to reopen a full domestic asset recovery case nor conduct a new investigation

or a new trial on the merits of the case. In practice, this helps shielding the case from delaying tactics, avoids duplication of efforts, and expedites proceedings. It also contributes to limiting confiscation enforcement cases from becoming too resource-intensive for requested jurisdictions.

- For the sake of clarity and to avoid interpretative doubts, legislation enabling the direct enforcement of foreign freezing and seizing or confiscation orders should explicitly provide that the requested jurisdiction is bound by the findings related to the facts of the case as they are stated in the foreign request (no reexamination of the merits of the case). See Recommendation 5.1.3 of this study.
- Although it is technically not a compulsory action under UNCAC, States Parties should consider introducing the ability to directly enforce foreign freezing and seizing orders. When such orders are no longer subject to appeals in the requesting jurisdiction, the possibility to subject them to direct enforcement offers the same advantages observed in confiscation orders, notably the exclusion of case relitigation before the authorities of the requested jurisdiction. See Recommendation 5.1.9 of this study.
- Legislation enabling the direct enforcement of foreign confiscation orders should provide fair opportunities for affected parties to make representations at proceedings set up in requested jurisdictions. They should also make regulations to ensure the possibility of directly enforcing foreign freezing and seizing orders through ex parte proceedings (that is, without notice being given to affected parties). See Recommendation 5.1.7 of this study.

TABLE A3.1 **Direct and indirect enforcement country comparison, by legal system[a]**

COUNTRY	CIVIL LAW SYSTEMS	COMMON LAW SYSTEMS	MIXED SYSTEMS	DIRECT ENFORCEMENT OF FOREIGN FREEZING AND SEIZING ORDERS AND RELEVANT LEGISLATIVE BASIS	DIRECT ENFORCEMENT OF FOREIGN CONFISCATION ORDERS AND RELEVANT LEGISLATIVE BASIS	IF DIRECT ENFORCEMENT, BAR TO CONDUCT REVIEW ON MERITS (EXPLICIT/IMPLICIT/ CANNOT BE INFERRED FROM LEGISLATION)
Australia		X		Yes Mutual Assistance in Criminal Matters Act, section 34, Requests for enforcement of foreign orders	Yes Mutual Assistance in Criminal Matters Act, section 34, Requests for enforcement of foreign orders	Implicit (Exhaustive list of grounds for nonrecognition and registration of foreign orders)
Brazil	X			Yes Criminal Procedure Code, chapter III, Homologation of foreign orders	Yes Criminal Procedure Code, chapter III, Homologation of foreign orders	Implicit (Exhaustive list of grounds for nonrecognition and registration of foreign orders)
British Virgin Islands		X		No	Yes Criminal Justice (International Co-operation) (Enforcement of Overseas Forfeiture Orders) Order, section 10 Proceeds of Criminal Conduct (Enforcement of External Confiscation Orders) Order, section 33	Implicit (Exhaustive list of grounds for nonrecognition and registration of foreign orders)
Canada		X		Yes Mutual Legal Assistance in Criminal Matters Act, section 9.3	Yes Mutual Legal Assistance in Criminal Matters Act, section 9.4	Implicit (Exhaustive list of grounds for nonrecognition and registration of foreign orders)
China			X	No	No	
Cyprus		X		Yes Prevention and Suppression of Money Laundering and Terrorist Financing Activities Laws, part IV, International Cooperation	Yes Prevention and Suppression of Money Laundering and Terrorist Financing Activities Laws, part IV, International Cooperation	Explicit "The Court [...] shall be bound by the findings as to the facts in so far as they are stated in the conviction or decision of a court of the foreign country or in so far as such conviction or judicial decision is implicitly based on them." (Prevention and Suppression of Money Laundering and Terrorist Financing Activities Laws, section 41(2))
Egypt, Arab Rep.			X	No	No	

continued

TABLE A3.1, *continued*

COUNTRY	CIVIL LAW SYSTEMS	COMMON LAW SYSTEMS	MIXED SYSTEMS	DIRECT ENFORCEMENT OF FOREIGN FREEZING AND SEIZING ORDERS AND RELEVANT LEGISLATIVE BASIS	DIRECT ENFORCEMENT OF FOREIGN CONFISCATION ORDERS AND RELEVANT LEGISLATIVE BASIS	IF DIRECT ENFORCEMENT, BAR TO CONDUCT REVIEW ON MERITS (EXPLICIT/IMPLICIT/ CANNOT BE INFERRED FROM LEGISLATION)
France	X			**No (except EU)** Criminal Procedure Code, section 3, titre X, chapitre 1er, section 3, (articles 694-10 à 694-13) Assistance aimed at restraining proceeds of crime with a view to subsequent confiscation	**Yes** Since 19 December 2020 direct application of EU Regulation 2018/1805 vis-à-vis EU Member States (except Ireland and Denmark): Cooperation with Denmark and Ireland: (EU Framework Decision 2006/783): Criminal Procedure Code, chapter III: International Cooperation for the enforcement of confiscation orders, section 1: Transmission and execution of confiscation orders pursuant to EU Framework Decision 2006/783, articles 713-12 to 713-35 Cooperation with the United-Kingdom:[c] (Non-EU countries or countries): Criminal Procedure Code, livre V title I, chapter III Execution of criminal judgments, section 2 (articles 713-36 to 713-41)	Implicit (Exhaustive list of grounds for nonrecognition and registration of foreign orders)
Germany	X			**No (except EU)** Act on International Cooperation in Criminal Matters, sections 94 to 96	**Yes** (EU countries): Act on International Cooperation in Criminal Matters, sections 88 to 90 (Non-EU countries): Act on International Cooperation in Criminal Matters, part IV, Assistance through Enforcement of Foreign Judgments	Implicit (Exhaustive list of grounds for nonrecognition and registration of foreign orders)

continued

TABLE A3.1, *continued*

COUNTRY	CIVIL LAW SYSTEMS	COMMON LAW SYSTEMS	MIXED SYSTEMS	DIRECT ENFORCEMENT OF FOREIGN FREEZING AND SEIZING ORDERS AND RELEVANT LEGISLATIVE BASIS	DIRECT ENFORCEMENT OF FOREIGN CONFISCATION ORDERS AND RELEVANT LEGISLATIVE BASIS	IF DIRECT ENFORCEMENT, BAR TO CONDUCT REVIEW ON MERITS (EXPLICIT/IMPLICIT/ CANNOT BE INFERRED FROM LEGISLATION)
Hong Kong SAR, China		X		No	Yes Mutual Legal Assistance in Criminal Matters Ordinance, part VI, Assistance in Relation to Confiscation, etc. of Proceeds of Crime	Implicit (Exhaustive list of grounds for nonrecognition and registration of foreign orders)
India		X		No	Yes[b] Prevention of Money Laundering Act, section 60(2A)	Implicit (Exhaustive list of grounds for nonrecognition and registration of foreign orders)
Indonesia			X	No	No	
Italy	X			Yes (Non-EU countries): Code of Criminal Procedure, title V, Effects of foreign criminal judgments. Enforcement of Italian criminal judgments abroad, section I, Effects of foreign criminal judgments, article 737-bis (EU countries): Legislative Decree n. 35/2016, Implementation of Framework Decision 2003/577 on the execution in the EU of orders freezing property or evidence	Yes (Non-EU countries): Code of Criminal Procedure, title V, Effects of foreign criminal judgments. Enforcement of Italian criminal judgments abroad, section I, Effects of foreign criminal judgments, articles 731 to 738 (EU countries): Legislative Decree n. 137/2015 on the implementation of Framework Decision 2006/78 on the application of the principle of mutual recognition of confiscation orders	Implicit (Exhaustive list of grounds for nonrecognition and registration of foreign orders)
Japan	X			No	Yes Act on Punishment of Organized Crimes, Control of Crime Proceeds and Other Matters, chapter VI, Procedures for International Mutual Assistance in the Execution of Adjudication of Confiscation and Collection of Equivalent Value and in the securance thereof and Other Matters	Explicit "In making the examination [. .] the court may not review whether the finally-binding adjudication concerned is justifiable or not." Act on Punishment of Organized Crimes, article 62(5)

continued

TABLE A3.1, *continued*

COUNTRY	CIVIL LAW SYSTEMS	COMMON LAW SYSTEMS	MIXED SYSTEMS	DIRECT ENFORCEMENT OF FOREIGN FREEZING AND SEIZING ORDERS AND RELEVANT LEGISLATIVE BASIS	DIRECT ENFORCEMENT OF FOREIGN CONFISCATION ORDERS AND RELEVANT LEGISLATIVE BASIS	IF DIRECT ENFORCEMENT, BAR TO CONDUCT REVIEW ON MERITS (EXPLICIT/IMPLICIT/ CANNOT BE INFERRED FROM LEGISLATION)
Kazakhstan	X			**No**	**Yes** Criminal Procedure Code, chapter 62, Recognition and enforcement of judgments and decisions of foreign courts	Implicit (Exhaustive list of grounds for nonrecognition and registration of foreign orders)
Korea, Rep.			X	**No**	**Yes** Act on Special Cases Concerning the Prevention of Illegal Trafficking in Narcotics, etc., article 64 Act on Regulation and Punishment of Criminal Proceeds Concealment, article 11 Act on Special Cases Concerning the Confiscation and Return of Property Acquired through Corrupt Practices, article 7	Implicit (Exhaustive list of grounds for nonrecognition and registration of foreign orders)
Latvia	X			**No (except EU)** Criminal Procedure Law chapter 82, sections 860 to 865	**Yes** (Non-EU countries): Criminal Procedure Law, Division Sixteen, Recognition of Judgments of a Foreign State and Execution of Punishment, chapter 69, General Provisions for the Execution in Latvia of a Punishment Imposed in a Foreign State (EU countries): Criminal Procedure Law, chapter 75	Explicit "The factual circumstances established in a court adjudication of a foreign state and the guilt of a person shall be binding to a court of Latvia." (Criminal Procedure Law, section 760(2))
Lebanon			X	**Yes** Penal Code, article 29 Ccode of Civil Procedure, articles 1009 to 1022	**Yes** Penal Code, article 29 Code of Civil Procedure, articles 1009 to 1022	Implicit (Exhaustive list of grounds for nonrecognition and registration of foreign orders)
New Zealand		X		**Yes** Mutual Assistance in Criminal Matters Act, section 54 Request to enforce foreign restraining order Criminal Proceeds (Recovery) Act, sections 128 to 139	**Yes** Mutual Assistance in Criminal Matters Act, section 55 Request to enforce foreign forfeiture order Criminal Proceeds (Recovery) Act, sections 140 to 149	Implicit (Exhaustive list of grounds for nonrecognition and registration of foreign orders)

continued

TABLE A3.1, *continued*

COUNTRY	CIVIL LAW SYSTEMS	COMMON LAW SYSTEMS	MIXED SYSTEMS	DIRECT ENFORCEMENT OF FOREIGN FREEZING AND SEIZING ORDERS AND RELEVANT LEGISLATIVE BASIS	DIRECT ENFORCEMENT OF FOREIGN CONFISCATION ORDERS AND RELEVANT LEGISLATIVE BASIS	IF DIRECT ENFORCEMENT, BAR TO CONDUCT REVIEW ON MERITS (EXPLICIT/IMPLICIT/ CANNOT BE INFERRED FROM LEGISLATION)
Nigeria			X	No	Yes (partly) Mutual Legal Assistance Act, section 22(1)	Cannot be inferred from legislation
Panama	X			No	No	
Peru	X			No	Yes Regulation of Legislative Decree N.1373 on the Extinction of Ownership, article 75	Explicit "[Those who oppose the request to execute the confiscation order] can only provide or request the evidence that is pertinent and conductive in relation to the fulfillment of the requirements for the execution of a foreign order in Peru." (article 78(5), Regulation of the Legislative Decree 1373)
Russian Federation	X			No	Yes Criminal Procedure Code, chapter 55.1, Procedure for Consideration and Resolution of Issues Related to the Recognition and Enforcement of the Verdict, Foreign Court Order in Part of Confiscation on the Territory of the Russian Federation of the Proceeds of Crime	Implicit (Exhaustive list of grounds for nonrecognition and registration of foreign orders)
Seychelles		X		Yes Mutual Assistance in Criminal Matters Act, part VI—Proceeds of Crime—Division 2—Requests by Foreign Countries	Yes Mutual Assistance in Criminal Matters Act, part VI—Proceeds of Crime—Division Requests by Foreign Countries	Implicit (Exhaustive list of grounds for nonrecognition and registration of foreign orders)
Singapore		X		No	Yes Mutual Assistance in Criminal Matters Act, sections 29 to 32 and Third Schedule	Implicit (Exhaustive list of grounds for nonrecognition and registration of foreign orders)
South Africa			X	Yes International Co-operation in Criminal Matters Act, section 24, Registration of foreign restraint order Regulations under the International Co-Operation in Criminal Matters Act, chapter 5	Yes International Co-operation in Criminal Matters Act, section 20, Registration of foreign confiscation order Regulations under the International Co-Operation in Criminal Matters Act, chapter 4	Implicit (Exhaustive list of grounds for nonrecognition and registration of foreign orders)

continued

TABLE A3.1, *continued*

COUNTRY	CIVIL LAW SYSTEMS	COMMON LAW SYSTEMS	MIXED SYSTEMS	DIRECT ENFORCEMENT OF FOREIGN FREEZING AND SEIZING ORDERS AND RELEVANT LEGISLATIVE BASIS	DIRECT ENFORCEMENT OF FOREIGN CONFISCATION ORDERS AND RELEVANT LEGISLATIVE BASIS	IF DIRECT ENFORCEMENT, BAR TO CONDUCT REVIEW ON MERITS (EXPLICIT/IMPLICIT/CANNOT BE INFERRED FROM LEGISLATION)
Spain	X			**No (except EU)** Law 18/2006 on the implementation in the EU of orders freezing property or evidence	**No (except EU)** Law 4/2010, on the implementation in the EU of judicial orders for confiscation	Implicit (Exhaustive list of grounds for nonrecognition and registration of foreign orders)
Switzerland	X			**Yes** Federal Law on International Assistance in Criminal Matters, article 18	**Yes** Federal Law on International Assistance in Criminal Matters, article 74a	Implicit (Exhaustive list of grounds for nonrecognition and registration of foreign orders)
United Arab Emirates			X	**No**	**Yes**[b] Federal Decree-law no. (20) of 2018 on Anti-Money Laundering and Combating the Financing of Terrorism and Financing of Illegal Organisations, art. 20	Cannot be inferred from legislation
United Kingdom		X		**No**	**Yes**[c] Proceeds of Crime Act 2002 (External Requests and Orders) Order 2005, sections 20–27 and 142	Implicit (Exhaustive list of grounds for nonrecognition and registration of foreign orders)
United States		X		**Yes** 28 U.S.C. § 2467	**Yes** 28 U.S.C. § 2467	Implicit (Exhaustive list of grounds for nonrecognition and registration of foreign orders)

Note: EU = European Union; SAR = Special Administrative Region.

a. To the extent possible, data were collected on the basis of desk research and confirmed by interviewed practitioners. In some cases, data reflect best estimates obtained through the analysis of domestic laws, but could not be officially confirmed.

b. Limited to confiscation orders dealing with proceeds of money-laundering offenses, terrorist financing, or financing of illegal organizations and issued by a court or judicial authority of a state with which the United Arab Emirates has entered into a ratified convention.

c. Mutual legal assistance for asset recovery is covered by Title XI (freezing and confiscation) of Part Three (law enforcement and judicial cooperation in criminal matters) of the "Trade and Cooperation Agreement Between the European Union and the European Atomic Energy Community, of the one part, and the United Kingdom of Great Britain and Northern Ireland, of the other part."

The United Kingdom will no longer be bound by the EU legal framework on the mutual recognition of foreign freezing and confiscation orders. Unless a new arrangement is negotiated with the EU, the United Kingdom will thus have to rely on indirect enforcement for freezing and seizing orders issued in EU member states.

NOTES

1. The competent authority of China will review the State Parties' confiscation requests and may arrange for their execution if the legal conditions are met.

2. Law no. 80 for 2002 Promulgating the Anti-Money Laundering Law and Its Amendments (Arab Republic of Egypt).

3. In US domestic public corruption cases, restraining measures can only be taken in relation to proceeds. However, there is the possibility to criminally confiscate—albeit not restrain—substitute assets. The foreign order enforcement authority is interpreted more broadly than the corresponding domestic one, partly out of the need to meet treaty obligations.

4. South Africa and United States.

5. For example, France and Italy.

6. For example, Russia and South Africa.

7. For example, India, Nigeria, and United Arab Emirates.

8. As mentioned in section 3.1 of this study, whereas the Arab Republic of Egypt has the possibility to directly enforce foreign confiscation orders through the anti-money laundering statute, resort to indirect enforcement through the adoption of a domestic confiscation order is inevitable owing to a lack of implementing legislation.

9. The Prevention of Money-Laundering Act, 2002, § 60(2A) (India).

10. Federal Decree Law no. (20) of 2018 on Anti-Money Laundering and Combating the Financing of Terrorism and Financing of Illegal Organisations, art. 20 (United Arab Emirates).

11. For example, Germany, Italy, Kazakhstan, and Latvia.

12. Criminal Procedure Law, ch. 60, § 790 (Latvia).

13. Act on International Cooperation in Criminal Matters, pt. IV, Assistance through Enforcement of Foreign Judgments (Germany).

14. Constitution of Brazil, art. 105.

15. Civil Procedure Code, ch. 4, art. 296 (Arab Republic of Egypt).

16. In this regard, a decision by Panama's Supreme Court of Justice (February 9, 2015) clarified that "the claim is a declaration of will made before the judge and against the counterpart; it is the act by which the judge seeks to recognize something with respect to a certain legal relationship. It is 'personal' when the basis or cause for the request rests on the affirmation of a relative or credit-related right." General Decision of the Supreme Court of Panama, "Request for Recognition and Enforcement of Foreign Divorce Judgment rendered by the Circuit Court for Genesee County," https://vlex.com.pa/vid/divorcio-corte-suprema -justicia-592789138).

17. Foreign Judgment (Reciprocal and Enforcement) Act, ch. 175 (Nigeria).

18. In the case of Kazakhstan, Latvia, and Russia, the central authority is directly tasked with applying to the competent court.

19. In Cyprus, the competent law enforcement entity is the Unit for Combating Money Laundering (MOKAS), established in the attorney general's office and composed of representatives of the attorney general, the chief of police, and the director of the Department of Customs and Excise. In New Zealand, it is the commissioner of the police.

20. Criminal Procedure Law, § 754 (Latvia).

21. Mutual Legal Assistance in Criminal Matters Act 1992, § 56 (New Zealand).

22. Mutual Assistance in Criminal Matters Act, § 34A(1) (Australia).

23. For example, Canada, Russia, and United States.

24. UNCAC, art. 54(1)(c) encourages parties to introduce proceedings "to allow confiscation of [...] property without a criminal conviction in cases in which the offender cannot be prosecuted by reason of death, flight or absence or in other appropriate cases." Depending on the country under consideration, NCB proceedings can take place within both criminal and civil proceedings. In common law jurisdictions, in particular, NCB forfeiture laws typically

establish proof on a "balance of probability" standard, which is in contrast to the "beyond any reasonable doubt" standard applicable in the context of conviction-based proceedings. For a detailed analysis of the features and advantages of introducing NCB systems in national legislation as well as the illustration of related good practices, see Greenberg and others (2009).

25. For example, Italy, Latvia, New Zealand, and South Africa.

26. Code of Criminal Procedure, art. 731, ¶ 1 bis (Italy).

27. The Prevention and Suppression of Money Laundering and Terrorist Financing Law, § 37 (Cyprus).

28. For example, Hong Kong SAR, China; Korea; Russia; and Singapore.

29. Mutual Assistance in Criminal Matters Act, § 2 (Singapore).

30. Act on Special Cases Concerning the Prevention of Illegal Trafficking in Narcotics, Psychotropic Substances and Hemp, art. 64(1) (Korea).

31. Regulation of Legislative Decree 1973 on the expiration of ownership, art. 75 (Peru).

32. By contrast, if the public official in question argued that new facts have occurred since the rendering of the decision in the requesting jurisdiction, or that certain facts existed at that time but were not brought to the attention of the competent authorities, the requested jurisdiction would arguably assess them anew. Most likely, though, it would refer them back to the requesting jurisdiction for fresh examination.

33. Law on the Prevention and Suppression of Money Laundering and Terrorist Financing, art. 41(2) (Cyprus).

34. Criminal Procedure Law, § 760(2) (Latvia).

35. Act on Punishment of Organized Crime, Control of Crime Proceeds and Other Matters, art. 62 (Japan).

36. Regulation of the Legislative Decree 1373 on the Expiration of Ownership, art. 78(5) (Peru).

37. Council Framework Decisions 2003/577/JHA on the Execution in the European Union of Orders Freezing Property or Evidence, art. 5; Council Framework Decision 2006/783/JHA on the Application of the Principle of Mutual Recognition to Confiscation Orders, art. 7.

38. Regulation 2018/1805 on the Mutual Recognition of Freezing Orders and Confiscation Orders, arts. 7 and 18.

39. Procedure for Consideration and Resolution of Issues Related to the Recognition and Enforcement of the Verdict, Foreign Court Order in Part of Confiscation on the Territory of the Russian Federation of the Proceeds of Crime, Criminal Procedure Code, art. 473.4(7), ch. 55.1.

40. Notable exceptions include Canada, Cyprus, Italy, and Latvia. In Latvia, the lack of an agreement with a foreign state can be a specific ground for refusing the execution of a foreign judgment, including a confiscation order (Criminal Procedure Law of Latvia, § 751). In Italy, under article 731 of the Code of Criminal Procedure, the direct enforcement of foreign confiscation orders requires the existence of an international instrument (bilateral or multilateral treaty or agreement). In Canada, the direct enforcement of foreign restraint or confiscation orders requires the existence of a bilateral or international instrument that contains reciprocal MLA provisions. This instrument does not have to be technically a treaty under international law as it can also take the form of an administrative arrangement. However, in the absence of such an agreement, reciprocity alone does not offer a sufficient basis.

41. The notion of extended confiscation refers to the ability to confiscate assets that are not necessarily direct proceeds of a crime so that there is no need to establish a connection between suspected criminal assets and a specific criminal conduct.

42. For example, British Virgin Islands; Hong Kong SAR, China; Singapore; and United Kingdom.

43. Mutual Legal Assistance in Criminal Matters Ordinance, Laws of Hong Kong SAR, China, §28(3), ch. 525.

44. British Virgin Islands; Cyprus; and Hong Kong SAR, China.

45. Canada and Seychelles.

46. For example, British Virgin Islands; Cyprus; Germany; Hong Kong SAR, China; Russia; Singapore; and South Africa.

47. Criminal Procedure Code, art. 733 (Italy).

48. Peru and United States.

49. For example, Germany and Italy.

50. Including offenses punishable only by fines is particularly important in corporate offending, as imprisonment is not a readily enforceable punishment against a corporation.

51. For example, the Russian Federation.

52. For example, Australia and New Zealand.

53. Procedure for Consideration and Resolution of Issues Related to the Recognition and Enforcement of the Verdict, Foreign Court Order in Part of Confiscation on the Territory of the Russian Federation of the Proceeds of Crime, Criminal Procedure Code, art. 473.5, ch. 55.1.

54. Brazil, Lebanon, and South Africa.

55. Enforcement of Foreign Judgment, 28 U.S.C. § 2467, (d)(1)(B)(C).

56. For example, South Africa.

57. For example, the British Virgin Islands, Canada, France, Spain, and the United Kingdom. Kazakhstan only requires dual criminality when assistance is provided based on reciprocity, not when the request is based on UNCAC.

58. For example, Canada, Germany, Italy, Japan, and Korea. In Hong Kong SAR, China, dual criminality is a mandatory ground for refusal under Section 5(1)(g) of Chapter 525 of the Mutual Legal Assistance in Criminal Matters Ordinance (MLAO) and is required for coercive measures, such as the enforcement of foreign confiscation orders. For assistance that does not involve coercive measures, assistance may be rendered under other forms of international cooperation outside MLAO and dual criminality may not be necessary.

59. For example, Australia, New Zealand, and United Arab Emirates.

60. For example, Germany, Italy, and Korea.

61. See Enforcement of Foreign Judgment, 28 U.S.C. , pt. VI, ch. 163, § 2467.

62. For example, Italy, Latvia, Lebanon, Peru, Russia, and Singapore.

63. For example, British Virgin Islands; Cyprus; and Hong Kong SAR, China.

64. For example, Italy, Japan, and Korea.

65. Peru and Korea.

66. Criminal Procedure Law, § 751.9 (Latvia).

67. Orders of Forfeiture, Mutual Legal Assistance in Criminal Matters Act, § 9.4.2(c) (Canada).

68. Code of Criminal Procedure, § 751(9) (Latvia).

69. For example, British Virgin Islands, Germany, Japan, Kazakhstan, Korea, Singapore, and United Kingdom.

70. British Virgin Islands and Singapore.

71. For example, Italy.

72. For example, Brazil, Cyprus, and South Africa.

73. For example, the United States.

74. Mutual Assistance in Criminal Matters Act, §27(7) (Seychelles).

75. Criminal Procedure Code, art. 737-bis (Italy).

76. In New Zealand, criminal proceedings need simply to have commenced in the requesting jurisdiction for the attorney general to authorize an application for direct enforcement of an interim foreign restraining order (Mutual Assistance in Criminal Matters Act, § 60).

77. Mutual Assistance in Criminal Matters Act, § 29(a) (Seychelles).

78. Mutual Legal Assistance in Criminal Matters Ordinance, Laws of Hong Kong SAR, China (MLAO), ch. 525, § 6 of schedule 2.

79. Criminal Procedure Code, art. 737-bis-1 (Italy).

80. Australia refers to any person who is suspected of having an interest in the property.

81. In relation to foreign restraint orders, New Zealand makes a distinction between persons subject to a restraining order and other persons that have an interest in the property. The former's right of appearance at the court hearing is conditioned on him or her not having been granted the possibility to properly defend himself in proceedings in the requesting country, or in any other case where he obtains the leave of the court to appear at the hearing of the application. Instead, the other persons who have a severable interest in the property may apply to the court to have their interest excluded from a restraining order that the court may make.

82. For example, South Africa has enacted detailed regulations under its 1996 International Cooperation in Criminal Matters Act. Peru's legal framework gives notified people a period of eight days to challenge a foreign request for direct enforcement.

83. For example, Canada, Cyprus, Korea, and Seychelles.

84. Criminal Procedure Code, art. 127 (Italy).

85. For example, Canada, Cyprus, and South Africa.

86. The Prevention and Suppression of Money Laundering and Terrorist Financing Laws of 2007–Updated 2018, §39(4) (Cyprus).

87. Federal Law "On Amendments to the Code of Criminal Procedure of The Russian Federation," Criminal Procedure Code, art. 473.4(2).

88. Homologation of foreign orders, Criminal Procedure Code of Brazil, ch. III.

89. For example, Australia, New Zealand, United Kingdom, and United States.

90. Criminal Proceeds (Recovery) Act, 2009, § 22 (New Zealand).

91. For example, Italy, Japan, Kazakhstan, and United Kingdom.

92. The Proceeds of Crime Act 2002 (External Requests and Orders) Order, § 23, ch. 2, External Orders, pt. 2, (United Kingdom).

93. Recognition and enforcement of judgments and decisions of foreign courts, Code of Criminal Procedure, art. 608(8), ch. 62 (Kazakhstan).

94. In the United Kingdom, the ultimate appellate court is the Supreme Court. In Japan, a special "kokoku" appeal may be lodged with the Supreme Court against a decision by a kokoku appeal court.

95. Examination by the Court, ch. VI: Procedures for International Mutual Assistance in the Execution of Adjudication of Confiscation and Collection of Equivalent Value and in the Securance Thereof and Other Matters, Act on Punishment of Organized Crimes, Control of Crime Proceeds and Other Matters, art. 62(8) (Japan).

96. For example, Germany, Japan, and Russia.

97. Assistance of Counsel, pt. IV, Assistance through Enforcement of Foreign Judgments, Act on International Cooperation in Criminal Matters, § 53 (1) and (2) (Germany).

98. Federal Law on Amendments to the Code of Criminal Procedure of the Russian Federation, arts. 473(4)(3 and 5).

4 Challenges and Obstacles to Direct Enforcement Action

4.1 OVERVIEW

Surveyed jurisdictions face a variety of challenges in either directly enforcing foreign confiscation orders or in having their domestic orders enforced abroad. Of these challenges, only a few appear to be linked to intrinsic difficulties in activating and applying procedures for directly enforcing foreign confiscation orders. Indeed, most challenges are of a general nature and appear to be commonly found in mutual legal assistance (MLA) in general (for example, cumbersome MLA procedures, lack of knowledge of foreign legal systems, requests based on dated information where the assets have already been dissipated, poorly drafted or overly vague requests, and so forth).[1]

Such challenges suggest that although direct enforcement mechanisms may be faster and more straightforward channels for confiscation orders to be executed abroad compared with indirect mechanisms, in practice their higher performance may be thwarted by drawbacks and inefficiencies affecting international judicial cooperation in criminal matters.

The following sections provide an overview of the main difficulties highlighted by practitioners belonging to surveyed jurisdictions.

4.2 LIMITED FAMILIARITY WITH AND USE OF DIRECT ENFORCEMENT PROCEDURES

Practitioners from several jurisdictions indicate that, at least in theory, they are well acquainted with the procedures in place to directly enforce foreign confiscation orders. Some countries, such as France, indicate that certain courts are often dealing with MLA requests for purposes of real estate seizure or confiscation, owing in particular to the location of the assets that are often found in areas where real estate prices are high.[2]

However, experts from other jurisdictions point out that such procedures are rarely used in practice as few or no requests for the registration of foreign confiscation orders are received. In South Africa, whereas direct enforcement requests are reported to be well-known and easily processed by the central authority, a degree of unfamiliarity might be present at the court level (although generally this would not prevent or delay registration).[3] Experts from Spain report that incoming MLA requests from non-EU states remain very low at roughly 9 percent. Within that 9 percent, requests for asset freezing or confiscation are even rarer. According to Canadian experts, domestic and foreign law enforcement and prosecuting authorities are not always aware of the existence of the MLA processes for directly enforcing foreign confiscation orders.[4] At the same time, there is a perception that the number of requests in this area, although not pursued as a routine practice, are growing.

Whereas some countries can, at least on paper, take direct enforcement action, they have not had the opportunity yet to apply the relevant legal framework. The British Virgin Islands suggested that it would rely on existing standard operating procedures to obtain guidance if and when such requests would be made. In Peru, where the possibility of directly enforcing foreign confiscation orders has only been introduced recently, the central authority for MLA has not yet received any request. France practitioners mention that so far they have had limited occasions to have their confiscation orders executed outside of the EU.

In short, the landscape appears to be polarized, with some jurisdictions having a relatively high degree of familiarity and practical experience with direct enforcement mechanisms, while others being much less accustomed to them, even when such mechanisms are formally envisaged in their domestic laws.

Case Study 4.1: Statistical information on enforcement action in surveyed countries

Since 2010, Australia has received 47 mutual legal assistance (MLA) requests seeking the direct enforcement of foreign freezing and seizure or confiscation orders. Eight of these requests relate to orders issued in investigations in corruption and related offenses. Moreover, Australian practitioners reported an increase in the number of enquiries and requests from foreign jurisdictions seeking the direct enforcement of foreign orders over the past few years.

In New Zealand, 17 foreign jurisdiction orders have been received since 2008, of which 11 have been registered and 1 is still under consideration.

In Hong Kong SAR, China, from 2014 to 2018, seven external confiscation orders have been registered.

In Cyprus, between 2013 and 2018, five foreign confiscation orders have been registered and enforced, either on the basis of MLA requests or the EU mutual recognition legal framework. Within the same period,

27 foreign freezing orders have been registered and enforced.

In France, the Agency for the Recovery and Management of Seized and Confiscated Assets (AGRASC) provided the following data:

- Direct execution of a foreign freezing and seizure order (execution of a freezing certificate on the basis of EU Framework Decision 2003/577): 80 cases and 131 properties (56 real estate, 55 bank accounts, 12 cash sums, 4 financial instruments, 2 credits, 1 seizure of company shares, and 1 miscellaneous property)
- Execution of MLA requests for freezing and seizure purposes not based on EU Framework Decision 2003/577: 107 files relating to 304 properties (130 real estate, 118 bank accounts, 29 sums seized in cash, 15 financial instruments, 7 claims, 2 boats, 1 seizure of gold or precious metals, and 2 seizures of company shares)

- Direct execution of a confiscation order: 16 cases (13 real estate, 40 bank accounts, 1 financial instrument, 1 cash sum, and 1 claim) on the basis of EU Framework Decision 2006/783 and 18 cases (22 bank accounts, 10 real estate, 4 financial instruments, 4 cash, and 2 claims) on the basis of bilateral or multilateral agreements

The statistics provided by France may be incomplete as AGRASC is only informed of the seizure of moveable property for confiscatory purposes that is entrusted to it for sale before the judgment.

The United Kingdom reports a steadily growing number of foreign restraint and confiscation orders being recognized and executed under the EU legal framework: although there were only 4 in 2014, in 2018 there were 45. (Reported data for the United Kingdom represent requests dealt with by the Crown Prosecution Service and not the United Kingdom, or England and Wales as a whole.) Several jurisdictions were not in a position to provide statistics owing to sheer data unavailability or difficulties in extracting data relating to direct enforcement–related requests from general MLA statistics.

In the United States, requests for restraint have been growing since 2014. However, in recent years, the number of executable requests is about 12 annually because of several reasons: (a) the assets are often no longer in the United States, (b) the orders do not relate to confiscation proceedings, or (c) the foreign jurisdiction does not have the ability to obtain a court order for restraints before charges are filed, which US law requires.

Case Study 4.2: New Zealand's opening of a domestic investigation

Yan committed a significant fraud in China and fled to New Zealand. He was investigated in New Zealand using money-laundering statutes. China supplied New Zealand the evidence to support the fraud. Asset confiscation began and was made final domestically using the Criminal Proceeds (Recovery) Act. A total of $NZ43 million was confiscated, which was shared with China.

The general paucity of requests executed through direct enforcement channels may have different explanations. In some countries, the limited amount of MLA in this area may stem from the narrow size of their economies and thus the limited criminal opportunities offered by small financial centers. Another reason may be that the launch of cross-border financial investigations into criminal assets held abroad is complex and requires specific expertise, time, and resources. In many jurisdictions, such investigations may simply not be carried out or not reach the level of maturity to enable the preparation of sufficiently solid MLA requests. A more specific reason may be jurisdictions' reliance on alternative avenues for asset recovery. As mentioned in this study's section 2.1.2, the use of alternative channels may reflect some countries' propensity to make strategic use of the full range of legal options to recover assets transferred abroad.

For requested jurisdictions, in particular, lack of experience in applying procedures for direct enforcement means that they would not be able to rely on precedents and jurisprudential guidelines, which may offer crucial interpretative tools to clarify ambiguous legal terms or procedures, if a direct enforcement case arises.

4.3 LACK OF SUFFICIENT, OR SUFFICIENTLY PRECISE, INFORMATION

For several requested jurisdictions, a major and frequent concern is that requests do not contain enough information. Reference is often made to so called "fishing expeditions," whereby requested countries are vaguely asked to "please find, freeze and return all properties held by Mr. X." Canada mentions wrong bank account numbers are provided to identify assets in the foreign jurisdiction. Experts from the United States report that, historically, foreign requests often did not provide enough information about the nominees or legal entities that may be used to hide assets in a particular case.[5]

In most countries, MLA requests for confiscation and asset recovery purposes shall, among other things, include as a minimum: (a) a factual summary of the case; (b) a description of the nexus between the underlying criminal activity and the identified asset; (c) text of any applicable statutes, including penalties, on which the investigation or prosecution is based; and (d) an explanation of the assistance sought and its legal and factual relationship to the investigation or proceeding that forms the basis of the request, including identification of any assets thought to be present in the requested jurisdiction.

Failure to include the minimum information, especially according to the terms of the treaties under which the request is being made, can severely slow the process. For example, missing information may include an insufficient depiction of the facts of the case or the precise act of which the person concerned stands accused. Whenever they decide to take a proactive stance, some jurisdictions report contacting their foreign counterparts to solicit additional clarifications, documentation, or explanations. In some cases, according to the same jurisdictions, lack of information prevents the request from being executed altogether.[6]

A recurrent problem appears to be failure by requesting jurisdictions to establish the link between the offenses in question and the assets purportedly held abroad. As criminal proceeds are often held in the names of nominees or shell companies, without sufficient evidence to identify them as criminal proceeds,

Case Study 4.3: Non-execution in France of a request for confiscation regarding immoveable property

On November 6, 2019, the British judicial authority sent a confiscation certificate to the French judicial authority to confiscate a building owned by a person convicted for money laundering in the United Kingdom. The building had not been seized during the investigation and the only information provided by the British was limited to the location of the property and its supposed value. However, after having inquired, the prosecutor of Bobigny discovered that a mortgage had been registered on the building to the benefit of the French treasury.

Thus, the British confiscation request became irrelevant. If the French court had authorized its execution and if the Agency for the Recovery of Seized and Confiscated Assets had been responsible for the sale of the property, the real estate's full price would have been paid to the French tax administration, whose claim over the property had been previously established. Financial investigations carried out upstream, and in particular during the investigation, might have enabled the British to identify this property and the fact that no value could be obtained from the proceeds of its sale.

many countries cannot enforce foreign orders in these cases.[7] However, Egyptian experts mention that requested jurisdictions could support requesting countries more actively by helping the requesting countries prove the link between the asset and the crime committed.

Another highlighted challenge is where the property has not been described correctly or in a way that the requested jurisdiction can readily and easily recognize. For instance, a street address is given instead of the property description. Such challenges are compounded by the fact that, in some countries, different state systems describe property differently.[8]

A specific difficulty reported lies in executing requests for restraint or temporary measures in cases where assets are held by third parties.[9] Frequently, these are complex cases where detailed and tangible evidence needs to be provided on how specific assets flowed from the perpetrator of the offense in question to a third party. As perpetrators try to obscure such asset flows, it is often difficult to supply the necessary evidence. Similar scenarios are particularly prone to problems with the requesting jurisdiction not furnishing sufficient information about the facts of the case.

4.4 DIFFICULTIES STEMMING FROM LACK OF NON-CONVICTION-BASED (NCB) PROCEDURES

Lack of adoption of NCB-related confiscation regimes can hamper action by countries on direct enforcement issues in at least two ways.

First, when the requesting jurisdiction has not obtained a confiscation order and indirect enforcement is the only alternative for having the request executed abroad, some requested jurisdictions may be able to proceed only by NCB confiscation. That is the case of countries such as the United States where the in absentia prosecution of the alleged perpetrator is excluded, and, hence, no possibility exists of obtaining a domestic criminal confiscation judgment.

Second, significant obstacles may be encountered by those jurisdictions seeking to have their NCB orders directly enforced abroad owing to the absence of comparable legislation on NCB proceedings in requested jurisdictions.

Countries such as Australia and the United States indicated that whereas NCB procedures are in many cases essential and increasingly used domestically, especially in internet fraud cases, there are many jurisdictions where this authority still does not exist despite several international instruments encouraging countries to adopt NCB models.

4.5 LACK OF UNDERSTANDING OF FOREIGN PROCEDURES

Differences in legal systems, terminologies, and procedures are at the root of misunderstandings and hindrances in the direct enforcement of foreign confiscation orders. For example, an order that would be described as a "pecuniary penalty order" in some jurisdictions is defined as a "forfeiture order" in others. Also, the Arab Republic of Egypt mentions the refusal by some countries to enforce its "restitution orders" on mere terminological grounds as, under Egyptian law, "restitution" has the same meaning and objectives as "confiscation."

At the same time, this type of difficulty does not appear to be exclusively related to the execution of foreign asset confiscation orders, but rather to the understanding and execution of MLA requests in general. Further, there is broad recognition that these challenges are more pronounced in the relationship between civil and common law countries.

4.6 COMPETING REQUESTS FROM DIFFERENT JURISDICTIONS

When there are competing requests from different jurisdictions, enforcement is not possible unless it is clear who the recipient of the assets in question is.

Singapore experienced a similar scenario. After the registration of a foreign confiscation order through a direct enforcement mechanism, competing claims left matters in a state of limbo; neither of the two competing jurisdictions provided the necessary information or instructions for Singapore to enforce and repatriate the confiscated property. A receiver cannot be appointed to hold onto assets indefinitely.

4.7 RESOURCE CONSTRAINTS IN REQUESTED JURISDICTIONS

Resource constraints in requested jurisdictions may lead to requests for direct enforcement action not being processed with the necessary speed.

Because of limited financial and human resources in the authorities (for example, the central authority or asset recovery offices), and given the number of incoming requests involving both asset recovery and non-asset-recovery matters, priority often has to be given to the most urgent cases. The speed at which a formal request will be enforced may also be delayed by factors such as (a) the seriousness of the offense in question, (b) the net value of the involved assets, (c) the stage of the investigation in the requesting jurisdiction (for example, whether indictments or charges are immediately forthcoming), and (d) the perceived effect of the case on the public interest.[10]

4.8 DIFFERENCES IN LEGAL SYSTEMS AND PROCEDURES

Differences across legal systems represent a significant source of friction. Typically, this occurs in countries that are unable to enforce foreign confiscation orders where the underlying conduct is not an indictable offense in their own legal system.[11]

Sometimes, the discrepancies between requesting and requested jurisdictions touch on the fundamental principles of their respective legal systems. Jurisdictions requiring that the foreign order be issued by a judicial authority face major issues.[12] Accordingly, some jurisdictions[13] report their inability to directly enforce orders issued by senior law enforcement officers in requesting countries. Similarly, due process requirements mean that some jurisdictions are unable to directly enforce provisional measures issued by prosecutors.

Some jurisdictions do not directly enforce foreign confiscation orders handed down in proceedings in absentia.[14] Concerns have also been expressed about the enforcement of foreign orders based on illicit enrichment offenses.

Case Study 4.4: Switzerland's evidentiary challenges with common law countries

Switzerland reports major obstacles in having its provisional measures enforced by common law jurisdictions. Although these jurisdictions apply a lower evidentiary threshold than the one needed to obtain a criminal conviction, they still require a "reasonable suspicion or reasonable ground to believe" threshold, which remains a much higher one than the one used in Switzerland. Accordingly, Swiss prosecutors face insurmountable obstacles in gathering enough information at the beginning of a criminal proceeding to be able to submit an asset-freezing request complying with the threshold set in most common law jurisdictions. Although such jurisdictions may in theory seek to reduce the evidentiary burden by way of legislative action, in practice any such move would have little chances of succeeding because it would require overcoming complex issues of constitutional relevance.

Swiss experts interviewed for this study report that only in a few common law jurisdictions do Swiss provisional orders seem to be enforceable (current cases known include Grand Cayman and Australia). As a rule, these orders need to be confirmed regularly, with the requesting jurisdictions asked to present increasing amounts of evidence to keep the orders in place.

A provisional or confiscation order obtained through such procedures may not be directly enforceable under a number of domestic laws (notably, in the United States) owing to the shift of the burden of proof from the prosecutorial authority to the holder of the property.[15]

The civil law and common law divide represents a major source of "incommunicability" between requested and requesting jurisdictions. In this regard, it appears significantly more challenging for civil law countries to comply with legal thresholds and requirements set by common law countries than the other way around.

4.9 SLOW AND TIME-CONSUMING CONFISCATION PROCEEDINGS IN REQUESTING JURISDICTIONS

Several jurisdictions reported instances where orders providing registration for foreign provisional orders had to be revoked or discontinued because requesting jurisdictions would not secure the final confiscation measure within an acceptable amount of time.[16]

Switzerland and the United States mention a few cases in which restraint orders had to be lifted after waiting several years (in certain cases more than 10) for the corresponding confiscation measure to be issued or not. In the United States, in particular, although there is no statutory time limit, more than 20 foreign provisional orders have been enforced over the past seven or eight years, including in corruption-related cases. Of these, however, only four final confiscation orders have been received for enforcement purposes because of the slow pace of the foreign criminal proceedings. Swiss courts would also lift provisional measures if the requesting state is not seen as advancing swiftly enough with the criminal proceeding.

Case Study 4.5: Singapore's experience with foreign authorities going "cold"

Jurisdiction A made a mutual legal assistance (MLA) request to Singapore for the seizure of funds, alleged to be proceeds of corruption, in an account kept with a fund management company, with a view to subsequent repatriation of the funds. As Singapore law enforcement authorities had simultaneously been alerted by their foreign law enforcement counterparts of the illicit fund flows, the account was seized under domestic investigations shortly before the MLA request was even received.

However, since the domestic seizure of the funds, the authorities of the requesting country became less responsive to Singapore's requests for information needed to maintain the seizure and update on the status of confiscation or criminal proceedings in the requesting country. In April 2019, after more than one and a half years since having secured the assets, Singapore still had no information from the requesting jurisdiction, despite regular follow-ups and even a face-to-face meeting on whether any criminal proceedings or confiscation proceedings had begun.

This situation has been experienced in numerous other cases where authorities go "cold" after assets have been restrained on a temporary and urgent basis.

4.10 BURDENS FOR REQUESTED JURISDICTIONS IN MAINTAINING TEMPORARY MEASURES ON PERISHABLE OR HIGH-COST ITEMS

A significant challenge for requested jurisdictions lies in the costs of maintaining assets (other than cash) frozen or seized for long periods. Such expenses may easily go well beyond the anticipated costs of executing a standard MLA request. Depending on the type of assets to be restrained (for example, real estate, yachts, art requiring temperature-controlled or secure conditions, live animals, and highly speculative investments), their value can significantly diminish over time. Additionally, major expenses may have to be incurred with the management of property (for example, state property taxes; insurance against fire, flooding, or theft; appropriate security to prevent theft and damage; property maintenance that often includes grass cutting, swimming pool maintenance, maintaining electricity and air-conditioning without which mold grows and interiors deteriorate; berthing charges for yachts; and storage and engine maintenance charges for planes, high performance cars and yachts, and so forth).

4.11 LENGTHY PROCESSES IN THE REQUESTED JURISDICTION TO DETERMINE WHETHER THE CONDITIONS FOR DIRECT ENFORCEMENT HAVE BEEN FULFILLED

Whereas direct enforcement procedures ensure that the merits of the case are not relitigated before requested jurisdictions, those jurisdictions may still need to establish that a series of conditions are fulfilled before enforcing the foreign order. Potentially lengthy processes may cause significant delays. Some circumstances may be easier and more straightforward to establish than others, for example, that the court in the requesting country had jurisdiction, or that the confiscation order is not subject to appeal. Other facts may be more difficult to establish as they entail more subjective types of evaluations. For example, it may

Case Study 4.6: The Lucy case in the United States: corruption and the illegal wildlife trade

The Lucy case is an example of the US government directly enforcing a foreign provisional restraint order against proceeds of corruption, namely seven offspring of a rare snake smuggled from Brazil into the United States by US citizens and linked to bribery of an official who had custody of the animals. The United States could assert its jurisdiction over some of the defendants and the assets involved; in addition, the time needed to obtain a foreign final order of forfeiture from Brazil was estimated to be excessively long and the cost of maintaining the offspring in appropriate conditions too high. Therefore, a domestic action was brought that led to the snakes being criminally forfeited from the owners in the United States and returned to Brazil by plane.

Source: Enforcement of a Seizure order by the 2nd Federal Criminal Court of Justice in the State of Roraima, The Federative Republic of Brazil to seize Brazilian Boa Constrictor "Lucy," and its offspring located in Utah or elsewhere in the U.S., no. 1:13-mc-00926 (D.D.C.).

not always be straightforward to determine if the foreign confiscation order is final in relation to an asset where the codefendants are appealing other aspects of the same order. Also, determining whether the foreign court was impartial or independent, as some countries require, could open up debates and lengthy litigation before the courts in requested jurisdictions. In similar scenarios, the risk is that the time advantages gained from implementing direct enforcement models may be lost if authorities in requested jurisdictions spend a long time assessing certain facts. Germany, for example, emphasized the time-consuming nature of examining the admissibility of foreign confiscation orders through its exequatur procedure. Similar remarks are made by Brazilian experts, mentioning the time needed by its Supreme Court to perform the homologation of foreign decisions.

Moreover, according to interviewed practitioners from Spain, major challenges are posed by noncooperative jurisdictions. In their experience, MLA requests sent to those countries are not always formally rejected, but their execution subjected to the receipt of additional unnecessary information. Thus, in practice, making the request is useless as investigative deadlines often expire before the necessary pieces of evidence are obtained.

4.12 CONFISCATION ORDERS CONTAINED IN LONG AND BULKY DOCUMENTS

Some requested jurisdictions face problems in directly enforcing foreign orders that are contained in long and bulky documents. In some cases, those orders are basically lengthy transcripts of the investigation. This leads to significant delays in courts' determination as to whether the foreign order shall be enforced.

The problem appears to be even more acute in foreign orders sent in languages others than the requested jurisdiction's official one. When the request is not immediately rejected, the foreign order requires expensive translation, which in turn extends the time needed by the competent authorities to determine if the request should be processed further. Also, a lengthy foreign order requires more time of the requested country's court to decide whether to enforce it.

4.13 CONDITIONALITY PLACED ON THE DIRECT ENFORCEMENT OF FOREIGN CONFISCATION ORDERS

In some cases, the potential of direct enforcement as a channel for speedy and effective asset recovery may be hampered by conditions posed by some requested jurisdictions that property be returned to a specific fund in the requesting jurisdiction distinct from the general treasury of the state. This form of conditionality is considered by some countries[17] as difficult to implement by requesting jurisdictions and unfairly impacts their sovereign prerogatives as protected by article 4 of UNCAC.

4.14 TAKEAWAYS

- Although use of direct enforcement proceedings hold the potential for delivering fast and effective assistance in international asset recovery operations, this study reveals that their usefulness may be impacted by drawbacks and inefficiencies generally affecting international judicial cooperation in criminal matters.
- To make the most of direct enforcement mechanisms and to limit the effect of differences in legal systems and procedures across jurisdictions (for example, between civil law and common law countries), the following are important to do: (a) engage in enhanced pre-MLA communication through informal consultations among practitioners from requesting and requested jurisdictions; (b) proactively exchange information and best practices through asset recovery informal networks such as Camden Assets Recovery Inter-Agency Network; and (c) leverage existing institutional arrangements, such as liaison magistrates, to help initiate or advance direct enforcement action. See Recommendations 5.2.5 and 5.2.6 in this study.
- Countries would benefit from developing special knowledge and training that covers features and challenges of enforcing foreign orders. For example, such training would benefit MLA central authorities, judicial authorities in charge of the recognition of foreign orders, and asset recovery managers. Countries should also consider assigning one or more authority officials to specifically support the enforcement of foreign requests for asset restraint and confiscation. See Recommendation 5.2.9 of this study.
- Including specific deadlines for handling incoming requests may incentivize requested jurisdictions to take speedy action. This may be further facilitated through ending ad hoc arrangements whereby the requested and the requesting jurisdictions agree on mutually acceptable deadlines for requesting execution. See Recommendation 5.1.6 of this study.
- Countries' ability to directly enforce foreign orders should not be hampered by the narrow definition of key terms. A terminology-neutral approach contributes to avoiding situations where formal differences in how basic concepts are denominated across jurisdictions lead to execution delays or nonexecution altogether. See Recommendation 5.1.4 of this study.
- To further speed and facilitate request examination, courts in requesting jurisdictions could reduce the length of documents containing orders for confiscation or provisional measures to be enforced abroad. See Recommendation 5.2.7 of this study.

- The need for requested jurisdictions to manage frozen or seized property for a long time on behalf of a foreign country—pending the adoption of a final confiscation order by the requesting jurisdiction—may represent a significant financial and logistical burden for requested jurisdictions. To avoid friction as well as the risk that requested jurisdictions cancel the provisional measures ahead of time, countries should seek to enter into adequate cost-sharing arrangements whenever they expect delicate scenarios. See Recommendation 5.2.8 of this study.
- Several countries appear to have not properly regulated situations where frozen assets lose value as time elapses, the assets in question are perishable, or their custody highly expensive. In relation to such assets, countries may consider resorting to interlocutory or anticipated sales. See Recommendation 5.1.12 of this study.

NOTES

1. Canada, for example, mentions the absence of an agreement with requesting countries (as required by its MLA legislation) as the most prevalent reason for rejecting incoming requests for asset freezing, seizure, or confiscation.
2. For example, the Paris region, the French Riviera, and the Alps.
3. Between 2006 and 2017, South Africa received six foreign requests for either asset restraint or confiscation.
4. In the opinion of the Canadian experts, this area of MLA is in a state of infancy, with the jurisprudence still being developed, as evidenced by the fact that only in 2018 was the first appellate-level decision handed down dealing with the provisions of the Mutual Legal Assistance in Criminal Matters Act (see *Georgiou*, Case Study 5 in this study).
5. Whereas searches in the name of the defendant are rarely effective, recent legislative changes in disclosures of beneficial ownership information are improving US investigators' ability to track assets.
6. According to experts from a surveyed country, several foreign authorities do not execute requests for freezing and seizing property, with most queries related to the establishment of the link between the property in question and the proceeds of crime.
7. For example, the United States.
8. Australia and South Africa.
9. Germany.
10. United States.
11. For example, Canada.
12. In UNCAC requirements, however, only the direct enforcement of confiscation orders issued by courts is required (arts. 54.1(a) and 55.1(b)). If States Parties decide to submit, for enforcement purposes, orders issued by a competent authority that is not a court, requested States have the option to enforce them directly or indirectly (arts. 54.1(a) and 55.2).
13. For example, United States and New Zealand. Australia also faces this hurdle with respect to foreign confiscation orders that are not made by a court or equivalent judicial authority. However, owing to a relatively recent amendment, a foreign restraining order needs only to be made under a law of the foreign country (whether or not by a court).
14. According to interviewed US practitioners, the fact that the scope for in absentia criminal proceedings in US law is much more limited than in many other countries explains why NCB proceedings are extensively relied upon, including in grand corruption cases.
15. In some jurisdictions, the enforcement of confiscation orders based on illicit enrichment may be precluded by the lack of dual criminality.
16. For example, Italy.
17. Arab Republic of Egypt, Lebanon, and Nigeria.

5 Recommendations

The recommendations outlined in this chapter are derived from the best available data as well as responses to questionnaires received by surveyed countries. More data may provide grounds for additional or more extensive sets of recommendations.

5.1 ESTABLISHING AND ENHANCING LEGAL FRAMEWORKS

5.1.1 Determine the extent to which the United Nations Convention against Corruption (UNCAC) or other treaty requirements on the direct enforcement of foreign confiscation orders need to be domesticated

In implementing relevant articles of UNCAC and other treaties, each state follows its own procedures. These are often found in constitutional provisions and determine how norms of international law are incorporated into domestic legal systems. In this regard, so-called dualist countries need to invariably adopt implementing legislation. The situation is, at least in principle, different for monist countries, for which norms of duly ratified treaties are normally considered an integral part of domestic legal systems. Thus, in theory, monist countries are in a position to use treaty-based asset confiscation provisions without passing an implementing act. In practice, however, implementing several treaty norms in monist countries also requires enacting legislation, notably when such norms are not self-executing.[1]

A typical example of non-self-executing provisions are UNCAC articles dealing with the enforcement of foreign confiscation orders. Whereas it outlines an obligation for States Parties to introduce a direct enforcement mechanism, UNCAC leaves countries in charge of determining the applicable procedure. As a result, it appears that even monist countries cannot argue that they can comply with the relevant articles of UNCAC only by virtue of their having ratified or adhered to it.

Thus, countries are encouraged to determine the extent to which legislative action may be needed to ensure that requirements of the UNCAC—or another treaty framework—on the direct enforcement of foreign confiscation orders are effectively implemented in domestic mutual legal assistance (MLA) proceedings.

5.1.2 Introduce the possibility to directly enforce foreign confiscation orders

To comply with article 54(1)(a) of UNCAC, jurisdictions shall establish domestic proceedings enabling the direct enforcement of foreign confiscation orders.

From a practical perspective, direct enforcement offers the most significant potential for a swifter and more streamlined handling of asset recovery requests than is possible under indirect enforcement models. Under direct enforcement, requested jurisdictions are able to subject the registration of foreign orders to the fulfilment of a number of conditions (for example, that the foreign order is final, that the rights of the defense were duly respected in the requesting jurisdiction). The main reason for this greater efficiency is that under a direct enforcement model the case is not open to relitigation on its merits before the authorities of the requested jurisdiction. Reducing time between the moment when MLA requests for asset confiscation are received and their execution, whereas still maintaining respect for important due process principles, is a key factor to minimize the chances of tainted assets changing owners and locations and thus hampering the ability to trace them.

When introducing new legal frameworks allowing for the direct enforcement of foreign restraint and confiscation orders, jurisdictions should take into account that the scope of the enforcement action does not necessarily correspond to what is available under domestic proceedings.[2]

5.1.3 Ensure that procedures to directly enforce foreign confiscation orders do not entail the relitigation of the merits of the case

National authorities in requested jurisdictions should be bound by the findings related to the facts of the case as they are stated in the foreign request. This means, in practice, they should avoid making any fresh evaluation of the merits of the case. If the merits have already been tried in the requesting jurisdiction, it would be time consuming and counterproductive to reassess the same facts twice. From this point of view, direct enforcement models are predicated on a degree of trust in foreign authorities' decisions.

In the second cycle of UNCAC's Implementation Review Mechanism, the principle that the merits of the case should not be relitigated before the authorities of the requested jurisdiction is being upheld by government experts while reviewing the implementation of article 54(1)(a).

Additionally, a number of treaties dealing with the same subject matter consider this principle as a key requirement. A good example is article 24(2) of the 2005 Warsaw Convention. Identical wording is found in article 42 of the European Convention on the International Validity of Criminal Judgments.

The explicit inclusion of a similar provision in domestic legal frameworks seems particularly appropriate in that it removes any potential ambiguity or interpretative doubt as to the extent of requested jurisdictions' scrutiny of foreign orders, thus upholding a key advantage of direct enforcement over indirect enforcement models. In this regard, some interviewed practitioners have expressed concerns about the risk that, in the absence of any explicit guidance, the competent authorities in requested jurisdictions may tend to assess the merits of the case before them.

5.1.4 Define key terms broadly and adopt a terminology-neutral approach

Jurisdictions' abilities to directly enforce foreign orders should not be hampered by the narrow definition of key terms. For example, under Singaporean law, "foreign confiscation order" is defined broadly with reference to an order, decree, direction, judgment, or any part thereof, however described. Similarly, Peru's legal framework refers to the enforceability of foreign confiscation orders or similar legal arrangements.

Generally speaking, a terminology-neutral approach helps to avoid situations where formal differences in how basic concepts are denominated across jurisdictions lead to the nonexecution of foreign requests.

5.1.5 Enable direct enforcement action across a broad range of criminal offenses

The implementation of UNCAC requirements on direct enforcement in some States Parties may be facilitated by existing legislation already in place under other bilateral, regional, and multilateral treaties containing similar or identical requirements. In some cases, authorities and procedures that have already been established at the national level to generally enforce foreign confiscation orders will automatically serve the purpose of implementing UNCAC requirements. In other cases, however, relevant procedures and authorities may have been established for specific crime categories (for example, money laundering) or treaty-based offenses. In such cases, it will be necessary to examine the extent to which those procedures and authorities need to be extended to ensure coverage of all UNCAC offenses. For example, if countries decide to use anti-money-laundering legislation, they should ensure that the scope of this legislation allows the direct enforcement of foreign orders beyond proceeds of money-laundering offenses.

Ideally, domestic legal frameworks will allow for direct enforcement to be taken in relation to a broad range of criminal offenses. Countries may thus adopt a single national framework ensuring, for example, that they can directly enforce foreign confiscation orders concerning offenses identified by a minimum level of punishment.

It seems particularly important to avoid a situation where different procedures or authorities come into play depending on whether the foreign request concerns proceeds of corruption or other offenses. A fragmented approach is likely to create confusion, increase the risk of interpretative doubts and inconsistencies, and make it difficult for requesting jurisdictions to determine which channels and procedures to follow in submitting the request.

5.1.6 Include time frames when processing foreign requests via direct enforcement

Including specific time frames (through legislation, MLA guidelines, or other administrative instruments) for handling requests aimed at the direct enforcement of foreign confiscation orders may further speed the process. Also, it provides the requesting jurisdiction with a reliable indication of the time needed for its request to be processed. In Latvia, for example, requests dealing with the recognition of foreign decisions are initially handled by the minister of justice who, after verifying that all the necessary materials have been received, shall within 10 days (or 30 days if the amount of materials is particularly large) send them to a district or city court for decision making.[3]

At the same time, decisions to set specific time frames through normative instruments should be realistic, bearing in mind the requested jurisdiction's available resources and its concrete ability to handle foreign requests within the set deadlines. Ideally, failure to meet such deadlines should trigger an obligation by the requested jurisdiction to automatically revert to the requesting one, explaining the reasons for the delay and setting new time frames.

Even if deadlines are not set by a normative instrument, direct enforcement action may be further facilitated through ad hoc arrangements where requesting and requested jurisdictions negotiate and agree on mutually accepted time frames for request execution purposes. For example, while the requested jurisdiction may indicate that execution would not be easily achieved before a certain date, the requesting jurisdiction may put forward specific time lines linked to the need to comply with a time-barred domestic investigation.

5.1.7 Specify modalities for affected parties' intervention in direct enforcement procedures

Jurisdictions introducing or updating direct enforcement procedures are encouraged to ensure that affected parties shall be notified about an application to register foreign orders and how they can intervene in related proceedings. Although general provisions that can be applied to domestic orders might be applicable once the necessary changes have been made, it might be useful to provide clarity on this matter, especially in countries when direct enforcement procedures are not frequently used or where there are limited opportunities to rely on previous practice and precedents.

Moreover, jurisdictions are invited to consider issuing regulations to ensure that applications for court orders to register foreign freezing and seizing orders can be made ex parte (that is, without notice being given to the affected party). Among surveyed jurisdictions, only a few countries have this requirement explicitly spelled out in their direct enforcement legislation.[4]

5.1.8 Provide for the possibility to confiscate property upon the request of a foreign party (indirect enforcement)

Whereas UNCAC States Parties shall be in a position to recognize and directly enforce foreign confiscation orders stemming from conviction-based proceedings,[5] they also need to be able to execute requests that are not accompanied by a confiscation order or where the foreign order is not deemed recognizable. In such cases, they should be able to resort to indirect enforcement through the institution of new domestic confiscation proceedings. In some cases, the indirect enforcement option (for example, the adoption of a domestic confiscation order to execute the foreign request) may be the only possible course of action. For example, a country may seek the enforcement of a confiscation order against a legal person registered in another country that does not recognize the criminal liability of legal persons. In a similar scenario and to execute the request, the requested jurisdiction may need to establish a new proceeding for identifying the individuals against which to enforce the foreign order (Commonwealth Secretariat 2011, 234).

Also, nothing prevents a jurisdiction from requesting the direct enforcement of a confiscation order in relation to certain property and request that indirect action be taken in relation to other property, even when the underlying offense is the same. This path may be useful when property has been substituted, third-party interests are involved, or where the request concerns indirectly derived proceeds or licitly acquired property intermingled with illicitly acquired property.[6]

5.1.9 Consider introducing the possibility to directly enforce foreign freezing and seizing orders

Jurisdictions that are not in a position to directly enforce freezing and seizing orders are encouraged to consider this possibility. When such orders are no longer subject to appeals in the requesting jurisdiction, their direct enforcement provides the same advantages observed for confiscation. Notably, the requested jurisdiction would not need to institute a domestic proceeding for the purpose of adopting a domestic freezing and seizing order based on the relitigation of the case on its merits.

5.1.10 Ensure that foreign restraint orders can be directly enforced even when they are adopted at very early stages of a proceeding

Countries are encouraged to ensure that they can directly enforce foreign freezing and seizing orders (when this option is available in their domestic legislation) irrespective of the stage of the criminal proceeding in the requesting jurisdiction when the order has been issued (for example, even before the person under investigation has been officially charged with an offense). It is critical that measures be taken at the earliest possible stage to secure the assets that may become subject to a confiscation (Brun and others 2021, 75). If this option is not available domestically, countries may wish to consider introducing it in their domestic legislation.

5.1.11 When domestic restraint orders are issued by non-judicial bodies, consider subjecting them to judicial review for purposes of asset recovery abroad

Some jurisdictions, especially those belonging to the common law legal tradition, face challenges in directly enforcing foreign restraint orders that have not been issued by a court. This is sometimes the case in orders issued by law enforcement officials or prosecutors in civil law jurisdictions.[7] In the United States, for example, the fact that restraint orders have been issued by a neutral fact-finding body in the requesting jurisdiction is central.

To mitigate the risk of having the request rejected on grounds that the foreign order was not issued by a judicial authority, requested jurisdictions may initiate their own cases based on evidence provided by the country seeking asset restraint. However, this route may not always be possible or warranted. Requested jurisdictions may be committing extensive resources by bringing their own case rather than using direct enforcement. In the United States, for example, the types of possible challenges that can be raised in a direct enforcement action are severely limited compared with the issues that can be raised by claimants under other domestic authorities.

Another possibility is for requesting jurisdictions (where restraint orders can be issued by nonjudicial bodies) to provide that, for the purpose of ensuring their enforcement abroad, those orders be specifically subject to judicial review. Such a step was taken by Colombia in 2017, when the national forfeiture law was amended with the addition of a new provision addressing "Precautionary Measures for Property Abroad." The new law now enables "the Office of the Attorney General to request the competent authority of the cooperating country to execute precautionary measures on property overseas subject to asset forfeiture. These measures will be submitted to the corresponding judicial review before the asset forfeiture judges in order that they have full legal effect in the foreign country."[8]

5.1.12 Consider using interlocutory or anticipated sales for seized perishable or high-cost items

Interlocutory or anticipated sales may be usefully employed to address challenges linked to perishable or high-cost items. According to interviewed practitioners, these should be considered key tools to ensure that asset recovery processes, including through MLA, are managed as effectively as possible. And yet, several countries appear to have not properly regulated situations where frozen assets lose value as time elapses, the assets in question are perishable, or their custody highly expensive. In the United States, interlocutory sales are usually granted by courts in unavoidable situations where seized assets are perishable or susceptible to deterioration. However, asset management authorities may not be able to obtain permission to conduct interlocutory sales of assets held under a foreign or domestic provisional order until it can be shown that the property in question is not being maintained adequately, thereby causing its depreciation and leading to costs for the government.

5.2 EFFECTIVELY APPLYING EXISTING LEGAL FRAMEWORKS

5.2.1 Take advantage of the UNCAC implementation review mechanism to obtain guidance and inspiration for the adoption of direct enforcement mechanisms

In drafting or amending legislation dealing with direct enforcement, jurisdictions may consider statutes from countries that already have good experience in this area. Also, jurisdictions that already have experience in direct enforcement action are encouraged to share good practices and challenges with those that are in the process of legislating for the first time. A valuable forum to facilitate such exchanges is the Conference of the States Parties (CoSP) to the UNCAC and its subsidiary bodies, notably the Working Group on Asset Recovery and the Implementation Review Group (IRG). Both settings offer valuable platforms for countries to discuss their actual or potential engagement on matters of directly enforcing foreign freezing or confiscation orders.

Through the IRG and particularly since the start of the second review cycle that focuses on implementing chapter V of the Convention (Asset Recovery), jurisdictions that want to introduce a direct enforcement model in their legislation are encouraged to use avenues created for discussion and exchange of practices, whether in the role of a reviewing or a reviewed country.[9]

5.2.2 To the extent possible, leverage general legal frameworks on the recognition of foreign judgments

Absent a specific legal framework allowing them to directly enforce foreign confiscation orders, jurisdictions may consider the extent they can apply legal framework dealing with recognizing foreign judgments. Reliance on available mechanisms may sometimes ensure that MLA requests for confiscation retain a reasonable chance to be executed swiftly.

For example, Brazil applies a procedure of homologation of final foreign decisions and granting exequatur to letters rogatory. Under this procedure, which has constitutional coverage, the country's Superior Court of Justice carries out a preliminary analysis of the foreign decision and issues an act of authorization.[10]

Also, some jurisdictions are parties to the 1970 European Convention on the International Validity of Criminal Judgments. Whereas this framework was not specifically designed to deal with the recognition of foreign confiscation orders, it offers a procedural framework for jurisdictions lacking a dedicated legal avenue in this area. With currently 23 States Parties, the 1970 Convention's scope of application extends to European criminal judgments, which are defined as "any final decision delivered by a criminal court of a Contracting State as a result of criminal proceeding."[11] According to article 2 of the 1970 European Convention, this includes not only sanctions involving deprivation of liberty, but also "fines or confiscation."

The general approach followed by the 1970 European Convention is to require States Parties to enforce, upon request, foreign judgments issued by other States Parties, unless the case meets one of the grounds for refusal explicitly mentioned. In addition to general provisions, the 1970 European Convention contains "clauses relating specifically to enforcement of fines and confiscations." These clauses deal with technical issues such as the conversion of the amounts into the currency of the requested state in case of foreign confiscation orders for payment of money, the confiscation of specific objects, and so forth.

5.2.3 When direct enforcement is only possible via crime-specific statutes, to the extent possible apply them by analogy to other crime areas

When direct enforcement procedures are exclusively set forth in anti-money-laundering laws, jurisdictions should explore, within the limits of the principles of their legal system, whether these procedures are applicable to cases in which property mentioned in foreign restraint or confiscation orders are not proceeds of money-laundering offenses. If this is not feasible, new legislation should be considered to ensure that foreign confiscation orders can be directly enforced beyond the boundaries of money-laundering legal frameworks.

5.2.4 If foreign orders cannot be directly enforced, to the extent possible assist the requesting jurisdiction through other avenues

A common reason for rejecting an MLA request to enforce a foreign order is that assets are no longer available for restraint or confiscation. In those cases, requested jurisdictions may be able to provide information to requesting ones about the new suspected location of those assets. This could help the formulation of new requests for asset tracing and restraint to be addressed to the jurisdiction where the assets have been presumably moved.

An alternative, though more onerous approach, is for requested parties, if they have jurisdiction, to open their own cases, issue domestic confiscation orders, and request their enforcement by the country where the assets have been presumably transferred. This approach could be a way for well-resourced jurisdictions to help developing jurisdictions recover stolen assets. Establishing parallel proceedings by requested jurisdictions may be useful in cases where executing an MLA request poses insurmountable challenges. To ensure that establishing parallel proceedings is done in the most effective way, the spontaneous transmission of information across jurisdictions may be critical. Consider setting up joint investigative teams as a key enabler.

5.2.5 Work toward enhanced pre-MLA communication

Early consultations between MLA central authorities of the requesting and the requested jurisdictions invariably enhance the effective and timely enforcement of foreign restraint or confiscation orders. Consultations of this nature before the lodging of an official MLA request ensure that any eventual request conforms with what is legally possible in the requested jurisdiction under its domestic laws.

The need to open and sustain effective communications between requesting and requested jurisdictions is especially recognized in asset recovery cases. Such cases often present specific technical and terminological difficulties, in particular in direct enforcement action, with which various countries are still unfamiliar.

Also, by relying on pre-MLA communication networks (for example, through police, financial intelligence units, and asset recovery offices) practitioners from requesting jurisdictions can often obtain key knowledge that will significantly increase the chances of their subsequent MLA request being promptly executed. For example, they can first check whether another jurisdiction has the ability to enforce a certain type of order.[12] This includes whether a criminal or non-conviction-based (NCB) order could be executed in the foreign jurisdiction. Additionally, developing CARIN-styled asset recovery informal networks[13] may help requesting jurisdictions have a better understanding of competent authorities in foreign countries and of how foreign legal systems work. They may also help requesting jurisdictions confirm issues such as the continued ownership of real property or the existence of bank accounts, and so forth.

More generally and holistically, CARIN-style regional bodies may further develop their role beyond platforms for simple information exchange into networks and conduits where countries proactively collaborate and look for enforcement opportunities under the principles of confidence and trust.

Developing informal relationships among practitioners is also key for requesting essential information from jurisdictions, such as on the evidentiary thresholds needed for the enforcement of required measures.[14] Some countries mentioned the importance of forging links among central authorities during workshops or expert groups meetings, which could then lead to the development of personal contacts by email or telephone.[15] Notably, the establishment of personal connections with foreign counterparts can help reduce delays, particularly where differences in legal systems and traditions carry higher risks of misunderstandings. Direct and personal connections contribute to build trust among involved parties.

The newly established Global Operational Network of Anti-Corruption Law Enforcement Authorities supported by UNODC could also become instrumental in improving informal consultations among practitioners in this area.[16]

Overall, MLA requests are best relied upon after a preliminary investigation and informal information gathering has occurred. At the initial stages of an investigation, basic financial information might be provided informally, without the need to invest time and resources in drafting, translating, and submitting a formal MLA request.[17]

5.2.6 Leverage existing institutional arrangements, such as liaison magistrates, to help initiate or advance direct enforcement action

A country exchange of liaison magistrates is typically done to increase the speed and effectiveness of judicial cooperation and to facilitate the mutual understanding of procedures. An exchange's usefulness has been widely recognized in (a) activating direct lines of communication between national central authorities, (b) following up on formal MLA requests, and (c) providing legal and practical advice to authorities of the country of deployment.

In deploying new liaison magistrates, jurisdictions should ensure that posted officials are familiar with asset recovery processes, in particular with (a) facilitating the mutual recognition of foreign restraint and confiscation orders by jurisdictions that adopt a direct enforcement model and (b) actively promoting the adoption or use of direct enforcement models before the competent authorities.

Inspiration may be drawn from the ongoing UNODC's PROMIS project (UNODC 2019) aimed to support the deployment of Nigerian liaison prosecutors to Italy and Spain with a view to establishing direct channels of communications between these countries and more effectively handle MLA requests about smuggling of migrants. Similar multicountry initiatives may be encouraged to ensure that posted magistrates are trained in MLA for asset recovery and that such actions are prioritized.

5.2.7 Reduce the length of documents containing orders for confiscation or provisional measures

For the purpose of swifter and less expensive examinations in requested jurisdictions, courts in requesting jurisdictions could enter more succinct provisional and confiscation orders, thereby limiting the explanatory part to the essential and necessary procedural history, factual findings, and legal conclusions. More detailed information is in the appendixes.

5.2.8 Consider cost-sharing arrangements and other cost-effective solutions for the management of assets subject to provisional measures

A frequently reported problem stems from where foreign assets, once swiftly restrained through direct enforcement action, remain subject to provisional measures for a long time pending the adoption of a final confiscation order in requesting jurisdictions. Such scenarios create high costs (for example, for storage, security, special maintenance) that are associated with preserving the property in the interest of requesting countries.

From the requesting jurisdictions, the time gap between the adoption of provisional orders and final confiscation depends on multiple factors dealing with the specific circumstance of each case and the structure and general effectiveness of their justice systems. Whereas the authorities of requesting jurisdictions that initially requested (and obtained) the provisional measure may not have control of the timing for the issuance of the final confiscation order, they should at least provide regular updates to requested jurisdictions as to the expected or likely evolution of the investigation or judicial proceeding.

Crucially, jurisdictions may explore stopping cost-sharing arrangements envisaging that the cost of maintaining the restrained assets be borne by requesting jurisdictions when obtaining a final confiscation order is expected to take a long time. The financial burden, initially borne by the requested jurisdiction, possibly could be switched to the requesting one if the confiscation order does not intervene before a mutually agreed period.

One way to mitigate the financial burden of requested jurisdictions has been highlighted by the United States. In a number of domestic cases where it has restrained significant property such as freighters or airplanes used for charter, the US government has returned those assets to the custody of the purported owner. This action is done when a bond is posted in cash or by a third-party insurer to shift the costs of maintenance back to the owner pending the proceeding. Such cases allow the authorities to confiscate the proceeds of the bond, if necessary. The same action could be used in direct enforcement cases involving highly valuable assets.

Alternatively, more jurisdictions could explore interlocutory sale authority for restrained assets (See Recommendations, section 5.1.12 of this study).

5.2.9 Develop specialized knowledge about the direct enforcement of foreign confiscation orders within competent authorities (for example, MLA central authorities, courts, and asset recovery managers)

Jurisdictions may consider assigning one or more of their central authority officials to support the enforcement of foreign requests for asset restraint and confiscation (for example, by checking that all legal requirements are complied with and by making the required applications to court). Developing such expertise would benefit from infrequent personnel rotations aimed at fostering a pool of knowledge as well as serving as steady contact with foreign counterparts.

For example, in important corruption cases in France, executing MLA requests can be entrusted to the national financial prosecutor's office, that specializes in cases that are international or that require complex and technical investigations. Also, within the French central authority, MLA requests are drafted by officials with specific knowledge of the countries to which the requests need to be sent. Such action makes those officials the privileged and unique interlocutors with certain states and allows them to establish relationships built on trust.

The US Department of Justice (DOJ), which includes both the MLA central authority and federal prosecutors, has direct enforcement requests considered and enforced by specialists in the DOJ's Money Laundering and Asset Recovery Section (International Unit). This method ensures that focused and timely attention is given to those requests and tries to develop a body of consistent common law in interpreting this authority by filing cases in Washington, D.C.

Developing specialized knowledge about asset recovery actions would also be beneficial within the judicial system, including, notably, the courts that are entrusted with making decisions about recognizing or registering foreign restraint and confiscation orders. Some jurisdictions under survey are heading in this direction. In Italy, most courts of appeal, which are competent for the direct enforcement of confiscation orders, can rely on panels of judges specialized in international legal cooperation.

More generally, all those involved in asset recovery should become familiar with the proceedings aimed at the direct and indirect enforcement of foreign orders. This knowledge may reduce the chance that the competent authorities in the requested jurisdiction fail to enforce a foreign request because they cannot sufficiently master the operational consequences of registering or recognizing a foreign order, for example, in asset management. The easiest option for a country in such a situation might be to invoke a legal barrier to justify the rejection of the foreign request as the alternative might be the need to acknowledge its domestic lack of preparedness, knowledge, or experience.

NOTES

1. A provision is self-executing when it is directly enforceable without the need for the country to adopt implementing legislation.
2. The United States, for example, authorizes the direct enforcement of a foreign confiscation order regarding any property "involved in" the commission of any foreign offense listed as a predicate for the money laundering statute, including foreign public corruption (28 U.S.C. 2467(a)(2)(B)). By contrast, the criminal and civil confiscation statutes that authorize confiscation in connection with domestic public corruption cases are limited to the confiscation of proceeds and do not generally extend to property involved.
3. Criminal Procedure Law, § 754(1) (Latvia).
4. For example, Australia, New Zealand, and United Kingdom.
5. As discussed in section 2.3 of this study, in relation to foreign NCB confiscation orders, under UNCAC the States Parties are technically only required to consider enforcing such orders.
6. As also mentioned in the Explanatory Report to the 2005 Warsaw Convention, ¶ 167, https://rm.coe.int/CoERMPublicCommonSearchServices/DisplayDCTMContent?documentId=09000016800d3813.
7. Experts from India, for example, report problems in having its adjudicating authority recognized as an authority equivalent to a court by some foreign jurisdictions. Under the Prevention of Money Laundering Act (PMLA), 2002, the adjudicating authority is in charge of deciding that any property is involved in money laundering and shall, by an order in writing, confirm the attachment of the property made or retention of property or record seized (as under § 5 of PMLA).
8. Law 1708 of 2014, art. 208-A, as amended by Law 1849 of 2017 (Colombia).
9. Useful guidance may be found in framework documents of the Working Group on Asset Recovery, a subsidiary body of the CoSP to the UNCAC. The Working Group is responsible for assisting and advising the CoSP implement its mandate with the return of proceeds of corruption. Find Working Group documents at www.unodc.org/unodc/en/corruption/WG-AssetRecovery/working-group-on-asset-recovery.html.

   The UNOCD's website explains: "The Implementation Review Group is a subsidiary body of the Conference of the States Parties to the United Nations Convention against Corruption. It is responsible for having an overview of the review process and consider technical assistance requirements for the effective implementation of the Convention." See https://www.unodc.org/unodc/en/corruption/IRG/implementation-review-group.html.

Further useful information can be found on the UNCAC country profile page that contains completed UNCAC Implementation Review executive summaries and many published country reports. See https://www.unodc.org/unodc/en/corruption/country-profile/index.html.

10. Constitution, art. 105.I.i (Brazil).

11. 1970 European Convention on the International Validity of Criminal Judgments, art. 1.

12. US practitioners report that some jurisdictions seek direct enforcement of what are, in fact, civil judgments. These cannot be enforced under the US direct enforcement statute; a completely different process may be required. Under current direct enforcement legislation, the United States cannot enforce foreign restitution orders, foreign civil judgments, or foreign criminal orders that impose fines.

13. CARIN (Camden Assets Recovery Inter-Agency Network) is an informal network of law enforcement and judicial practitioners in the field of asset tracing, freezing, seizure, and confiscation.

14. For example, the United States can enforce orders that do not specify the assets to be seized or confiscated (especially if property is held in names of nominees). But before spending time and resources in directly enforcing foreign orders, US authorities need (a) to receive sufficient information to be sure that the assets intended to be restrained or confiscated can reasonably be located in the United States and (b) to prove that the record owners are not good faith purchasers. Some information may also be needed in the form of an affidavit.

15. For example, France.

16. See the website of Global Operational Network of Anti-Corruption Law Enforcement Authorities, https://globenetwork.unodc.org/.

17. The United States, for instance, might informally advise that an asset (a) cannot be located in its territory, (b) appears to have been sold to a bona fide purchaser, or (c) is not worth pursuing a formal request because certain bank accounts have already been closed.

REFERENCES AND OTHER READINGS

ADB (Asian Development Bank) and OECD (Organisation for Economic Co-operation and Development). 2017. "Mutual Legal Assistance in Asia and the Pacific: Experiences in 31 Jurisdictions." ADB and OECD Anti-Corruption Initiative for Asia and the Pacific, Paris. www.oecd.org/corruption/ADB-OECD-Mutual-Legal-Assistance-Corruption-2017.pdf.

Brun, Jean-Pierre, Anastasia Sotiropoulou, Larissa Gray, Clive Scott, and Kevin M. Stephenson. 2021. *Asset Recovery Handbook: A Guide for Practitioners*. Washington, DC: International Bank for Reconstruction and Development and the World Bank. https://star.worldbank.org/publication/asset-recovery-handbook-guide-practitioners-second-edition.

Commonwealth Secretariat. 2011. *Commonwealth Strategies to Combat Corruption*. London: Commonwealth Secretariat. https://thecommonwealth.org/sites/default/files/key_reform_pdfs/Strategies%20to%20Combat%20Corruption%20141011_0.pdf.

Fazekas, Mihaly, and Eva Nanopoulos. 2016. "The Effectiveness of EU Law: Insights from the EU Legal Framework on Asset Confiscation." *European Journal of Crime, Criminal Law and Criminal Justice* (February): 39–64.

Greenberg, Theodore S., Linda M. Samuel, Wingate Grant, and Larissa Gray. 2009. *Stolen Asset Recovery : A Good Practices Guide for Non-conviction Based Asset Forfeiture*. Washington, DC: World Bank. https://openknowledge.worldbank.org/handle/10986/2615.

Rose, Cecily, Michael Kubiciel, and Oliver Landwehr (eds.). 2019. *The United Nations Convention Against Corruption: A Commentary*. Oxford, UK: Oxford University Press.

Stephenson, Kevin M., Larissa Gray, Ric Power, Jean-Pierre Brun, Gabriele Dunker, and Melissa Panjer. 2011. *Barriers to Asset Recovery: An Analysis of the Key Barriers and Recommendations for Action*. Washington, DC: International Bank for Reconstruction and Development and the World Bank. https://star.worldbank.org/sites/star/files/Barriers%20to%20Asset%20Recovery.pdf.

Tickner, Jonathan, and Sarah Gabriel (eds.). 2015. "Asset Recovery in 26 Jurisdictions Worldwide." Law Business Research Ltd, London.

United Nations. 2010. *Travaux Préparatoires of the Negotiations for the Elaboration of the United Nations Convention Against Corruption.* Vienna: United Nations Office on Drugs and Crime.

UNODC (United Nations Office on Drugs and Crime). 2019. "UNODC Enhances Judicial Cooperation Between Africa and Europe." UNODC in West and Central Africa, PROMIS Judicial Cooperation, September 6. United Nations, New York.

UNCAC Provisions (Excerpts)

ARTICLE 2. USE OF TERMS

For the purposes of this Convention:

> [...]

> (d) "Property" shall mean assets of every kind, whether corporeal or incorporeal, movable or immovable, tangible or intangible, and legal documents or instruments evidencing title to or interest in such assets;

> (e) "Proceeds of crime" shall mean any property derived from or obtained, directly or indirectly, through the commission of an offence;

> (f) "Freezing" or "seizure" shall mean temporarily prohibiting the transfer, conversion, disposition or movement of property or temporarily assuming custody or control of property on the basis of an order issued by a court or other competent authority;

> (g) "Confiscation", which includes forfeiture where applicable, shall mean the permanent deprivation of property by order of a court or other competent authority;

> [...].

ARTICLE 31. FREEZING, SEIZURE AND CONFISCATION

1. Each State Party shall take, to the greatest extent possible within its domestic legal system, such measures as may be necessary to enable confiscation of:

   (a) Proceeds of crime derived from offences established in accordance with this Convention or property the value of which corresponds to that of such proceeds;

   (b) Property, equipment or other instrumentalities used in or destined for use in offences established in accordance with this Convention.

2. Each State Party shall take such measures as may be necessary to enable the identification, tracing, freezing or seizure of any item referred to in paragraph 1 of this article for the purpose of eventual confiscation.

3. Each State Party shall adopt, in accordance with its domestic law, such legislative and other measures as may be necessary to regulate the administration by the competent authorities of frozen, seized or confiscated property covered in paragraphs 1 and 2 of this article.

4. If such proceeds of crime have been transformed or converted, in part or in full, into other property, such property shall be liable to the measures referred to in this article instead of the proceeds.

5. If such proceeds of crime have been intermingled with property acquired from legitimate sources, such property shall, without prejudice to any powers relating to freezing or seizure, be liable to confiscation up to the assessed value of the intermingled proceeds.

6. Income or other benefits derived from such proceeds of crime, from property into which such proceeds of crime have been transformed or converted or from property with which such proceeds of crime have been intermingled shall also be liable to the measures referred to in this article, in the same manner and to the same extent as proceeds of crime.

7. For the purpose of this article and article 55 of this Convention, each State Party shall empower its courts or other competent authorities to order that bank, financial or commercial records be made available or seized. A State Party shall not decline to act under the provisions of this paragraph on the ground of bank secrecy.

8. States Parties may consider the possibility of requiring that an offender demonstrate the lawful origin of such alleged proceeds of crime or other property liable to confiscation, to the extent that such a requirement is consistent with the fundamental principles of their domestic law and with the nature of judicial and other proceedings.

9. The provisions of this article shall not be so construed as to prejudice the rights of bona fide third parties.

10. Nothing contained in this article shall affect the principle that the measures to which it refers shall be defined and implemented in accordance with and subject to the provisions of the domestic law of a State Party.

ARTICLE 46. MUTUAL LEGAL ASSISTANCE

1. States Parties shall afford one another the widest measure of mutual legal assistance in investigations, prosecutions and judicial proceedings in relation to the offences covered by this Convention.

[...]

3. Mutual legal assistance to be afforded in accordance with this article may be requested for any of the following purposes:

[...]

(g) Identifying or tracing proceeds of crime, property, instrumentalities or other things for evidentiary purposes;

[...]

(j) Identifying, freezing and tracing proceeds of crime in accordance with the provisions of chapter V of this Convention;

(k) The recovery of assets, in accordance with the provisions of chapter V of this Convention.

CHAPTER V—ASSET RECOVERY

ARTICLE 51. GENERAL PROVISION

The return of assets pursuant to this chapter is a fundamental principle of this Convention, and States Parties shall afford one another the widest measure of cooperation and assistance in this regard.

ARTICLE 54. MECHANISMS FOR RECOVERY OF PROPERTY THROUGH INTERNATIONAL COOPERATION IN CONFISCATION

1. Each State Party, in order to provide mutual legal assistance pursuant to article 55 of this Convention with respect to property acquired through or involved in the commission of an offence established in accordance with this Convention, shall, in accordance with its domestic law:

   (a) Take such measures as may be necessary to permit its competent authorities to give effect to an order of confiscation issued by a court of another State Party;

   (b) Take such measures as may be necessary to permit its competent authorities, where they have jurisdiction, to order the confiscation of such property of foreign origin by adjudication of an offence of money-laundering or such other offence as may be within its jurisdiction or by other procedures authorized under its domestic law; and

   (c) Consider taking such measures as may be necessary to allow confiscation of such property without a criminal conviction in cases in which the offender cannot be prosecuted by reason of death, flight or absence or in other appropriate cases.

2. Each State Party, in order to provide mutual legal assistance upon a request made pursuant to paragraph 2 of article 55 of this Convention, shall, in accordance with its domestic law:

   (a) Take such measures as may be necessary to permit its competent authorities to freeze or seize property upon a freezing or seizure order issued by a court or competent authority of a requesting State Party that provides a reasonable basis for the requested State Party to believe that there are sufficient grounds for taking such actions and that the property would eventually be subject to an order of confiscation for purposes of paragraph 1 (a) of this article;

(b) Take such measures as may be necessary to permit its competent authorities to freeze or seize property upon a request that provides a reasonable basis for the requested State Party to believe that there are sufficient grounds for taking such actions and that the property would eventually be subject to an order of confiscation for purposes of paragraph 1 (a) of this article; and

(c) Consider taking additional measures to permit its competent authorities to preserve property for confiscation, such as on the basis of a foreign arrest or criminal charge related to the acquisition of such property.

ARTICLE 55. INTERNATIONAL COOPERATION FOR PURPOSES OF CONFISCATION

1. A State Party that has received a request from another State Party having jurisdiction over an offence established in accordance with this Convention for confiscation of proceeds of crime, property, equipment or other instrumentalities referred to in article 31, paragraph 1, of this Convention situated in its territory shall, to the greatest extent possible within its domestic legal system:

   (a) Submit the request to its competent authorities for the purpose of obtaining an order of confiscation and, if such an order is granted, give effect to it; or

   (b) Submit to its competent authorities, with a view to giving effect to it to the extent requested, an order of confiscation issued by a court in the territory of the requesting State Party in accordance with articles 31, paragraph 1, and 54, paragraph 1 (a), of this Convention insofar as it relates to proceeds of crime, property, equipment or other instrumentalities referred to in article 31, paragraph 1, situated in the territory of the requested State Party.

2. Following a request made by another State Party having jurisdiction over an offence established in accordance with this Convention, the requested State Party shall take measures to identify, trace and freeze or seize proceeds of crime, property, equipment or other instrumentalities referred to in article 31, paragraph 1, of this Convention for the purpose of eventual confiscation to be ordered either by the requesting State Party or, pursuant to a request under paragraph 1 of this article, by the requested State Party.

3. The provisions of article 46 of this Convention are applicable, mutatis mutandis, to this article. In addition to the information specified in article 46, paragraph 15, requests made pursuant to this article shall contain:

   (a) In the case of a request pertaining to paragraph 1 (a) of this article, a description of the property to be confiscated, including, to the extent possible, the location and, where relevant, the estimated value of the property and a statement of the facts relied upon by the requesting State Party sufficient to enable the requested State Party to seek the order under its domestic law;

(b) In the case of a request pertaining to paragraph 1 (b) of this article, a legally admissible copy of an order of confiscation upon which the request is based issued by the requesting State Party, a statement of the facts and information as to the extent to which execution of the order is requested, a statement specifying the measures taken by the requesting State Party to provide adequate notification to bona fide third parties and to ensure due process and a statement that the confiscation order is final;

(c) In the case of a request pertaining to paragraph 2 of this article, a statement of the facts relied upon by the requesting State Party and a description of the actions requested and, where available, a legally admissible copy of an order on which the request is based.

4. The decisions or actions provided for in paragraphs 1 and 2 of this article shall be taken by the requested State Party in accordance with and subject to the provisions of its domestic law and its procedural rules or any bilateral or multilateral agreement or arrangement to which it may be bound in relation to the requesting State Party.

5. Each State Party shall furnish copies of its laws and regulations that give effect to this article and of any subsequent changes to such laws and regulations or a description thereof to the Secretary-General of the United Nations.

6. If a State Party elects to make the taking of the measures referred to in paragraphs 1 and 2 of this article conditional on the existence of a relevant treaty, that State Party shall consider this Convention the necessary and sufficient treaty basis.

7. Cooperation under this article may also be refused or provisional measures lifted if the requested State Party does not receive sufficient and timely evidence or if the property is of a de minimis value.

8. Before lifting any provisional measure taken pursuant to this article, the requested State Party shall, wherever possible, give the requesting State Party an opportunity to present its reasons in favour of continuing the measure.

9. The provisions of this article shall not be construed as prejudicing the rights of bona fide third parties.

ARTICLE 59. BILATERAL AND MULTILATERAL AGREEMENTS AND ARRANGEMENTS

States Parties shall consider concluding bilateral or multilateral agreements or arrangements to enhance the effectiveness of international cooperation undertaken pursuant to this chapter of the Convention.

Questionnaire for National Experts

QUESTIONS FOR ALL COUNTRIES

1. Before receiving this questionnaire, were you aware of articles 54(1)(a) and 55(1)(b) of UNCAC dealing with the direct enforcement of confiscation orders?

   [ ]

2. Regardless of UNCAC, were you aware that some countries are in a position to directly enforce foreign confiscation orders?

   [ ]

3. Is your country in a position to directly enforce foreign confiscation orders? (If your answer is positive, go straight to question 6)

   [ ]

4. Have the authorities of your country ever debated the possibility to introduce normative changes to enable the direct enforcement of foreign confiscation orders?

   [ ]

5. Would the possibility to directly enforce foreign confiscation orders be something that should be considered introducing in your legal system? If so, why? If not, why?

   [ ]

6. Has any foreign country (to which you have requested the freezing/seizure/confiscation of assets) handled your requests via a direct enforcement mechanism?

```

```

7. If your answer to question 6 is positive, what challenges, if any, have you/ the authorities of your jurisdiction encountered in having your request executed via a direct enforcement mechanism? (It would be very useful if you could provide one or more case studies highlighting successes and/or failures. In case of challenges encountered, what could have been done better?)

```

```

If your country is not in a position to directly enforce foreign confiscation orders, there are no more questions for you. Thank you for participating in this questionnaire.

QUESTIONS ONLY FOR COUNTRIES THAT ARE IN A POSITION TO DIRECTLY ENFORCE FOREIGN CONFISCATION ORDERS

8. Please describe the procedure, requirements and authorities involved in the process of directly enforcing foreign confiscation orders. Mention articles of relevant legal texts. To the extent possible, provide web links to legal texts, explanatory notes, jurisprudence, relevant scholarly articles, etc.

```

```

9. Does your jurisdiction have authority to directly enforce foreign provisional orders for asset freezing/seizure? If so, please describe procedure, requirements and authorities involved. Mention articles of relevant legal texts. To the extent possible, provide web links to legal texts, explanatory notes, jurisprudence, relevant scholarly articles, etc.

```

```

10. Does your jurisdiction have authority to directly enforce foreign non-conviction-based confiscation orders? Please provide details.

```

```

11. Does your jurisdiction require the existence of a treaty in order to directly enforce foreign orders for asset freezing/seizure or confiscation? If so, are you aware of the requirement set forth in article 55.6 of UNCAC?

```

```

12. Has your jurisdiction ever triggered in practice its authority to directly enforce foreign orders for asset freezing/seizure or confiscation? To the extent possible, provide numbers and statistics. If exact data are unknown or unavailable, provide best estimates based on your experience.

```
```

13. If the authorities of your jurisdiction have a choice between executing a foreign request via "direct enforcement" and other legal means (e.g. taking a domestic order on behalf of the requesting country), what avenue is more likely to be chosen, and why?

```
```

14. It would be very useful if you could provide case studies highlighting successes and/or failures in the process of directly enforcing foreign orders for asset freezing/seizure/confiscation. If challenges were encountered, what could have been done better?

```
```

15. Has a foreign request for asset freezing/seizure/confiscation via direct enforcement ever been rejected? If yes, what were the most prevalent reasons for the rejection?

```
```

16. In your opinion, are the authorities of your jurisdiction well-acquainted with the procedure leading to the direct enforcement of foreign freezing/seizure and confiscation orders? Is this procedure followed as a routine practice or only on rare occasions?

```
```

17. What legal, institutional and practical challenges, if any, do the authorities of your country experience in applying the procedure for the direct enforcement of foreign orders for asset freezing/seizure/confiscation (e.g. legislative gaps, inconsistencies, inadequate information provided by requesting countries, etc.)?

```
```

18. Are the challenges you mentioned under question 17 specific to the execution of requests for asset confiscation via enforcement of foreign orders, or are they common to the execution of asset recovery and MLA requests in general? Please elaborate.

```
```

19. In your opinion, what could be improved to make the procedure leading to the enforcement of foreign freezing/seizure/confiscation orders more effective and faster?

```
┌─────────────────────────────────────────────────────┐
│                                                       │
│                                                       │
└─────────────────────────────────────────────────────┘
```

20. Do you experience any specific challenges in directly enforcing the confiscation orders of certain countries (e.g. countries from certain regions or sharing a certain legal system) as opposed to others? Please elaborate.

```
┌─────────────────────────────────────────────────────┐
│                                                       │
│                                                       │
└─────────────────────────────────────────────────────┘
```

21. Provide any additional feedback, comment or suggestion you may have on the broad subject of executing foreign requests for asset freezing/seizure/confiscation via direct enforcement mechanisms.

```
┌─────────────────────────────────────────────────────┐
│                                                       │
│                                                       │
└─────────────────────────────────────────────────────┘
```

Surveyed Countries' Legal Frameworks (Excerpts)

AUSTRALIA

Mutual Assistance in Criminal Matters Act 1987

PART VI–PROCEEDS OF CRIME
DIVISION 2–REQUESTS BY FOREIGN COUNTRIES
Subdivision A–Enforcement of foreign orders

Object of Subdivision–SECT 33A

(1) The object of this Subdivision is to facilitate international cooperation in the recovery of property through the registration and enforcement of foreign orders in Australia.

(2) For the purpose of achieving this object, it is the intention of the Parliament that the validity of foreign orders not be examined.

Requests for enforcement of foreign orders–SECT 34

(1) If:

(a) a foreign country requests the Attorney-General to make arrangements for the enforcement of:

(i) a foreign forfeiture order, made in respect of a foreign serious offence, against property that is reasonably suspected of being located in Australia; or

(ii) a foreign pecuniary penalty order, made in respect of a foreign serious offence, where some or all of the property available to satisfy the order is reasonably suspected of being located in Australia; and

(b) the Attorney-General is satisfied that:

(i) a person has been convicted of the offence; and

(ii) the conviction and the order are not subject to further appeal in the foreign country;

the Attorney-General may authorise a proceeds of crime authority, in writing, to apply for the registration of the order.

(2) If a foreign country requests the Attorney-General to make arrangements for the enforcement of:

(a) a foreign forfeiture order that:

(i) has the effect of forfeiting a person's property on the basis that the property is, or is alleged to be, the proceeds or an instrument of a foreign serious offence (whether or not a person has been convicted of that offence); and

(ii) is made against property that is reasonably suspected of being located in Australia; or

(b) a foreign pecuniary penalty order in respect of which both of the following apply:

(i) the order has the effect of requiring a person to pay an amount of money on the basis that the money is, or is alleged to be, the benefit derived from a foreign serious offence (whether or not the person has been convicted of that offence);

(ii) some or all of the property available to satisfy the order is reasonably suspected of being located in Australia;

the Attorney-General may authorise a proceeds of crime authority, in writing, to apply for the registration of the order.

(3) If a foreign country requests the Attorney-General to make arrangements for the enforcement of a foreign restraining order, against property that is reasonably suspected of being located in Australia, that is:

(a) made in respect of a foreign serious offence for which a person has been convicted or charged; or

(b) made in respect of the alleged commission of a foreign serious offence (whether or not the identity of the person who committed the offence is known);

the Attorney-General may authorise a proceeds of crime authority, in writing, to apply for the registration of the order.

Registration of foreign orders–SECT 34A

(1A) An application to a court for registration of a foreign order in accordance with an authorisation under this Subdivision must be to a court with proceeds jurisdiction.

(1) If a proceeds of crime authority applies to a court with proceeds jurisdiction for registration of a foreign order in accordance with an authorisation under this Subdivision, the court must register the order accordingly, unless the court is satisfied that it would be contrary to the interests of justice to do so.

(2) The proceeds of crime authority must give notice of the application:

(a) to specified persons the authority has reason to suspect may have an interest in the property; and

(b) to such other persons as the court directs.

(3) However, the court may consider the application without notice having been given if the proceeds of crime authority requests the court to do so.

(4) If a foreign pecuniary penalty order or a foreign restraining order is registered in a court under this Subdivision:

    (a) a copy of any amendments made to the order (whether before or after registration) may be registered in the same way as the order; and

    (b) the amendments do not, for the purposes of this Act and the Proceeds of Crime Act, have effect until they are registered.

(5) An order or an amendment of an order is to be registered in a court by the registration, in accordance with the rules of the court, of:

    (a) a copy of the appropriate order or amendment sealed by the court or other authority making that order or amendment; or

    (b) a copy of that order or amendment duly authenticated in accordance with subsection 43(2).

Enforcement of foreign forfeiture orders–SECT 34B

(1) A foreign forfeiture order registered in a court under this Subdivision has effect, and may be enforced, as if it were a forfeiture order made by the court under the Proceeds of Crime Act at the time of registration.

(2) In particular, section 68 of the Proceeds of Crime Act applies in relation to the forfeiture order as if:

    (a) the reference in subparagraph 68(1)(b)(i) of that Act to a proceeds of crime authority having applied for the order were a reference to the foreign forfeiture order having been made; and

    (b) subparagraph 68(1)(b)(ii) of that Act did not apply if the person in question died after the authority applied for registration of the order under section 34A of this Act.

(3) Subject to section 34C, property that is subject to a foreign forfeiture order registered under this Subdivision may be disposed of, or otherwise dealt with, in accordance with any direction of the Attorney-General or of a person authorised by the Attorney-General in writing for the purposes of this subsection.

(4) Sections 69 and 70 and Divisions 5 to 7 of Part 2-2 of the Proceeds of Crime Act do not apply in relation to a foreign forfeiture order registered under this Subdivision.

Effect on third parties of registration of foreign forfeiture orders—SECT 34C

Applications by third parties

(1) If a court registers under section 34A a foreign forfeiture order against property, a person who:

    (a) claims an interest in the property; and

    (b) either:

        (i) if the registration relates to an authorisation given under subsection 34(1)—was not convicted of a foreign serious offence in respect of which the order was made; or

        (ii) if the registration relates to an authorisation given under subsection 34(2)—is not a person whom the court has reason to believe committed a foreign serious offence in respect of which the order was made;

may apply to the court for an order under subsection (2).

Orders by the court

(2) If, on an application for an order under this subsection, the court is satisfied that:

(a) the applicant was not, in any way, involved in the commission of a foreign serious offence in respect of which the foreign forfeiture order was made; and

(b) if the applicant acquired the interest in the property at the time of or after the commission of such an offence—the property was neither proceeds nor an instrument of such an offence;

the court must make an order:

(c) declaring the nature, extent and value (as at the time when the order is made) of the applicant's interest in the property; and

(d) either:

(i) directing the Commonwealth to transfer the interest to the applicant; or

(ii) declaring that there is payable by the Commonwealth to the applicant an amount equal to the value declared under paragraph (c).

Certain people need leave to apply

(3) A person who was given notice of, or appeared at, the hearing held in connection with the making of the foreign forfeiture order is not entitled to apply under subsection (1) unless the court gives leave.

(4) The court may give leave if satisfied that there are special grounds for doing so.

(5) Without limiting subsection (4), the court may grant a person leave if the court is satisfied that:

(a) the person, for a good reason, did not attend the hearing referred to in subsection (3) although the person had notice of the hearing; or

(b) particular evidence that the person proposes to adduce in connection with the proposed application under subsection (1) was not available to the person at the time of the hearing referred to in subsection (3).

Period for applying

(6) Unless the court gives leave, an application under subsection (1) is to be made before the end of 6 weeks beginning on the day when the foreign forfeiture order is registered in the court.

(7) The court may give leave to apply outside that period if the court is satisfied that the person's failure to apply within that period was not due to any neglect on the person's part.

Procedural matters

(8) A person who applies under subsection (1) must give to the proceeds of crime authority authorised under section 34 notice, as prescribed, of the application.

(9) That proceeds of crime authority is to be a party to proceedings on an application under subsection (1). The Attorney-General may intervene in the proceedings.

Enforcement of foreign restraining orders—SECT 34E

(1) A foreign restraining order registered in a court under this Subdivision has effect, and may be enforced, as if it were a restraining order that:

   (a) was made by the court under the Proceeds of Crime Act at the time of the registration; and

   (b) directed that the property specified in the order is not to be disposed of or otherwise dealt with by any person.

(2) In particular:

   (a) section 288 of that Act applies as if:

      (i) the reference in that section to the Official Trustee's exercise of powers under that Act included a reference to the Official Trustee's exercise of those powers in relation to a foreign restraining order so registered; and

      (ii) the reference in that section to the Official Trustee's performance of functions or duties under that Act included a reference to the Official Trustee's performance of those functions or duties in relation to such a foreign restraining order; and

   (b) section 289 of that Act applies as if the reference in that section to controlled property included a reference to property that is subject to an order under section 35; and

   (c) section 290 of that Act applies as if the reference in that section to the controlled property were a reference to the property that is subject to an order under section 35.

(3) Divisions 1, 2 and 3 of Part 2-1, section 33, Divisions 5 and 6 of Part 2-1 and sections 142, 143, 169, 170 and 282 to 287 of the Proceeds of Crime Act do not apply in relation to a foreign restraining order registered under this Subdivision.

Copies of foreign orders sent by fax, email or other electronic means—SECT 34F

(1) If a copy of a sealed or authenticated copy of:

   (a) a foreign order; or

   (b) an amendment of a foreign order;

is sent by fax, email or other electronic means, the copy is to be regarded, for the purposes of this Act, as the same as the sealed or authenticated copy.

(2) However, if registration of the order under this Subdivision is effected by means of the copy, the registration ceases to have effect at the end of 45 days unless the sealed or authenticated copy has been filed by then in the court that registered the order.

Cancelling registration—SECT 34G

(1) The Attorney-General may direct the proceeds of crime authority authorised under section 34 to apply to a court in which:

(a) a foreign pecuniary penalty order; or

(b) a foreign restraining order;

has been registered under this Subdivision for cancellation of the registration.

(2) Without limiting subsection (1), the Attorney-General may give a direction under that subsection in relation to an order if the Attorney-General is satisfied that:

(a) the order has ceased to have effect in the foreign country in which the order was made; or

(b) cancellation of the order is appropriate having regard to the arrangements entered into between Australia and the foreign country in relation to the enforcement of orders of that kind.

(3) The court to which a proceeds of crime authority applies in accordance with a direction under subsection (1) must cancel the registration accordingly.

BRAZIL

Brazilian Code of Civil Procedure (Law n° 13.105, March 16, 2015) Chapter VI—Ratification of a Foreign Decision and Granting of *Exequatur* of a Letter (Arts. 960 to 965)

Art. 960. The ratification of a foreign decision shall be requested by an action for the ratification of a foreign decision, unless otherwise provided by a treaty.

§ 1 A foreign interlocutory decision may be executed in Brazil by means of a letter rogatory.

§ 2 The ratification shall comply with the provisions of the treaties in effect in Brazil and the Internal Regulations of the Superior Court of Justice.

§ 3 The ratification of a foreign arbitral decision shall observe the provisions of treaties and statutory law, applying, subordinately, the provisions of this Chapter.

Art. 961. A foreign decision shall only be enforceable in Brazil after the homologation or the granting of the exequatur of the letters rogatory, unless otherwise provided by law or treaty.

§ 1 A final judicial decision, as well as a non-judicial one that would be of a judicial nature under Brazilian law, may be ratified.

§ 2 A foreign decision may be partially homologated.

§ 3 The Brazilian judicial authority may grant applications for urgency and perform acts of provisional execution in an action for the homologation of a foreign decision.

§ 4 A foreign decision for the purpose of tax foreclosure shall be homologated when provided for by treaty or by a promise of reciprocity made to the Brazilian authority.

§ 5 A foreign sentence of a consensual divorce is enforceable in Brazil, independently of its ratification by the Superior Court of Justice.

§ 6 In the case of § 5, it shall be up to any judge to examine the validity of the decision, as the main issue or incidentally, when this matter is raised in a case under its jurisdiction.

Art. 962. A foreign judgment granting interlocutory relief may be executed.

§ 1 A foreign decision granting interlocutory relief shall be executed by means of a letter rogatory.

§ 2 Interlocutory relief granted without having heard the defendant may be executed provided that the right to be heard, *audi alteram partem*, shall be assured at a later stage.

§ 3 The judgment regarding the urgency of the relief falls exclusively to the judicial authority that rendered the foreign decision.

§ 4 When ratification is waived for the foreign judgment to be enforced in Brazil, the decision that grants the interlocutory relief shall depend, in order to be enforced, on the express recognition of its validity by the judge with jurisdiction to order its satisfaction, waiving ratification by the Superior Court of Justice.

Art. 963. The following are indispensable requirements for the ratification of the decision:
   I–that it be rendered by an authority with jurisdiction;
   II–that it be preceded by suitable service of process, even if there is default;
   III–that it be effective in the country where it was rendered;
   IV–that it does not violate a Brazilian *res judicata* [final] decision;
   V–that it be accompanied by an official translation, unless its waiver is provided for in a treaty;
   VI–that it does not contain an express violation of public policy.

Sole paragraph. In order to grant the exequatur of the letters rogatory, the conditions laid down in the head provision of this article and in art. 962, § 2 shall be observed.

Art. 964. The foreign decision shall not be ratified when the Brazilian courts have exclusive jurisdiction.

Sole paragraph. The provision is also applicable to the grant of exequatur of the letter rogatory.

Art. 965. The satisfaction of the foreign judgment shall occur before the federal court jurisdiction, at the request of the party, in accordance with the rules established for the satisfaction of Brazilian decisions.

Sole paragraph. The request for execution shall be accompanied by a certified copy of the ratification decision or exequatur, as the case may be.

Brazilian Penal Code (Decree-Law nº 2.848, December 7, 1940)

Effectiveness of the foreign judgement

Art. 9–The foreign sentence, when the application of the Brazilian law produces the same consequences in the species, may be homologated in Brazil to:

> I–compel the condemned to repair the damage, to make restitutions and to other civil effects; (Included by Law nº 7.209 of July 11, 1984)
>
> II–subject him/her to a security measure. (Included by Law nº 7.209 of July 11, 1984)

Sole paragraph–The homologation depends on: (Included by Law nº 7.209 of July 11, 1984)

> a. for the purposes provided for in item I, the request of the interested party;
> b. for the other purposes, the existence of an extradition treaty with the country from which the judicial authority pronounced the sentence, or, in the absence of a treaty, a request of the Minister of Justice. (Included by Law nº 7.209 of July 11, 1984).

Brazilian Penal Procedure Code (Decree-Law nº 3.689, October 3, 1941)

Book I

Procedure in General

Title IV

Civil Action

Art. 63. Once the judicial decision has become final, the offended party, his legal representative or his heirs may enforce it in the civil court for the purpose of reparation of the damage.

Book V

Jurisdictional Relations with Foreign Authorities

Single Title

Chapter I

General Provisions

Art. 780. Without prejudice to conventions or treaties, the provisions of this Title shall apply to the homologation of foreign criminal sentences and to the dispatch and fulfillment of letters rogatory for summons, inquiries and other measures necessary for the instruction of criminal proceedings.

Art. 781. Foreign sentences will not be homologated, nor letters rogatory fulfilled, if they are contrary to public order and good customs.

Art. 782. The transit, through diplomatic channels, of the documents presented will constitute enough proof of their authenticity.

Chapter III

The Homologation of Foreign Judgments

Art. 787. Foreign sentences must be previously homologated by the Supreme Court to produce the effects of Article 7 of the Penal Code.

Art. 788. The foreign criminal judgment will be homologated when the application of Brazilian law to similar crimes produces the same consequences and the following requirements concur:

I–is covered by the necessary external formalities, according to the legislation of the country of origin;

II–was handed down by a competent judge, through regular summons, according to the same legislation;

III–is a final judicial decision;

IV–is duly authenticated by a Brazilian consul;

V–is accompanied by a translation, made by a public translator.

Art. 789. The Prosecutor General of the Republic, whenever he becomes aware of the existence of a foreign criminal sentence issued by a State that has an extradition treaty with Brazil and that has imposed a personal security measure or an accessory penalty that must be served in Brazil, shall request to the Minister of Justice to make arrangements to obtain elements that will enable him to request the homologation of the sentence.

§ 1 The homologation of a sentence issued by a judicial authority of a State, which does not have an extradition treaty with Brazil will depend on the request of the Minister of Justice.

§ 2 Once the request for homologation has been distributed, the rapporteur will order the summons of the interested party to submit his objections, within ten days, if he resides in the Federal District, or thirty days, if he resides elsewhere.

§ 3 If the interested party does not deduce its objections within that period, the rapporteur shall appoint him a defender, who shall produce the defense within ten days.

§ 4 The objections may only be based on doubt over the authenticity of the document, over the understanding of the sentence, or over the lack of any of the requirements listed in articles 781 and 788.

§ 5 Once the objections have been challenged within ten days by the general prosecutor, the process will go to the rapporteur and to the reviser, observing in its judgment the Internal Rules of the Federal Supreme Court.

§ 6 Once the sentence has been homologated, the respective letter will be sent to the president of the Court of Appeals of the Federal District, the State, or the Territory.

§ 7 Upon receipt of the letter of sentence, the president of the Court of Appeals shall send it to the judge of the place of residence of the convict, for the application of the security measure or accessory penalty, in compliance with the provisions of Title II, Chapter III, and Title V of Book IV of this Code.

Art. 790. The interested party in the execution of a foreign criminal sentence, for the reparation of the damage, restitution and other civil effects, may request the Federal Supreme Court for its homologation, observing what the Code of Civil Procedure prescribes in this regard.

BRITISH VIRGIN ISLANDS

Criminal Justice (International Co-Operation) (Enforcement of Overseas Forfeiture Orders) Order, 1996

10. Registration of external forfeiture orders.

(1) On an application made by or on behalf of the government of a designated country, the High Court may register an external forfeiture order made there if,

(a) it is satisfied that at the time of registration the order is in force and not subject to appeal;

(b) it is satisfied, where the person against whom the order is made did not appear in the proceedings, that he received notice of the proceedings in sufficient time to enable him to defend them; and

(c) it is of the opinion that enforcing the order in the Territory would not be contrary to the interests of justice.

(2) In subsection (1) "appeal" includes,

(a) any proceedings by way of discharging or setting aside a judgment, and

(b) an application for a new trial or stay of execution.

(3) The High Court shall cancel the registration of an external forfeiture order if it appears to the court that the order has been satisfied by the forfeiture of the property liable to be recovered under the external forfeiture order or by any other means.

11. Proof of orders and judgment of court in a designated country.

(1) For the purposes of this Order,

(a) any order made or judgment given by a court in a designated country purporting to bear the seal of that court, or to be signed by any person in his capacity as a judge, magistrate or officer of the court, shall be deemed without further proof to have been duly sealed or, as the case may be, to have been signed by that person, and

(b) a document, duly authenticated, which purports to be a copy of any order made or judgment given by a court in a designated country shall be deemed without further proof to be a true copy.

(2) A document purporting to be a copy of any order made or judgment given by a court in a designated country is duly authenticated for the purposes of subsection (1) (b) if it purports to be certified by any person in his capacity as a judge, magistrate or officer of the court in question or by or on behalf of the appropriate authority of the designated country.

12. Evidence in relation to proceedings and orders in a designated country.

(1) For the purposes of this Order, a certificate purporting to be issued by or on behalf of the appropriate authority of a designated country stating:

    (a) that proceedings have been instituted and have not been concluded, or that proceedings are to be instituted, there,

    (b) in a case to which section 2 (5) (b) applies, that the defendant has been notified as specified in that subsection,

    (c) that an external forfeiture order is in force and is not subject to appeal,

    (d) that property recoverable in the designated country under an external forfeiture order remains unrecoverable there,

    (e) that any person has been notified of any proceedings in accordance with the law of the designated country, or

    (f) that an order (however described) made by a court of the designated country is for the forfeiture and destruction or the forfeiture and other disposal of anything in respect of which an offence to which this order applies has been committed or which was used or intended for use in connection with the commission of such an offence, shall, in any proceedings in the High Court, be admissible as evidence of the facts so stated.

(2) In those proceedings a statement contained in a document, duly authenticated, which purports to have been received in evidence or to be a copy of a document so received, or to set out or summarise evidence given in proceedings in a court in a designated country, shall be admissible as evidence of any fact stated therein.

(3) A document is duly authenticated for the purposes of subsection (2) if it purports to be certified by any person in his capacity as judge, magistrate or officer of the court in the designated country, or by or on behalf of the appropriate authority of the designated country, to have been received in evidence or to be a copy of a document so received, or, as the case may be, to be the original document containing or summarising the evidence or a true copy of that document.

(4) Nothing in this section shall prejudice the admission of any evidence, whether contained in any document or otherwise, which is admissible apart from this section.

13—Certificate of appropriate authority.

Where in relation to any designated country no authority is specified in Schedule 2, a certificate made by the Governor to the effect that the authority specified therein is the appropriate authority for the purposes of this Order shall be sufficient evidence of that fact.

14—Representation of government of a designated country.

A request for assistance sent to the Governor by the appropriate authority of a designated country shall, unless the contrary is shown, be deemed to constitute the authority of the government of that country for the crown prosecution service or the Comptroller of Customs to act on its behalf in any proceedings in the High Court under section 10 or any other provision of this Order.

CANADA

Mutual Legal Assistance in Criminal Matters Act
Foreign Orders for Restraint, Seizure and Forfeiture of Property in Canada

Orders for restraint or seizure

9.3 (1) When a written request is presented to the Minister by a state or entity, other than the International Criminal Court referred to in section 9.1, for the enforcement of an order for the restraint or seizure of property situated in Canada issued by a court of criminal jurisdiction of the state or entity, the Minister may authorize the Attorney General of Canada or an attorney general of a province to make arrangements for the enforcement of the order.

Filing of order

(2) On receipt of an authorization, the Attorney General of Canada or an attorney general of a province may file a copy of the order with the superior court of criminal jurisdiction of the province in which the property that is the subject of the order is believed to be located. On being filed, the order shall be entered as a judgment of that court and may be executed anywhere in Canada.

Conditions

(3) Before filing an order, the Attorney General of Canada or an attorney general of a province must be satisfied that

  (a) the person has been charged with an offence within the jurisdiction of the state or entity; and

  (b) the offence would be an indictable offence if it were committed in Canada.

Effect of registered order

(4) On being filed,

  (a) an order for the seizure of proceeds of crime may be enforced as if it were a warrant issued under subsection 462.32(1) of the Criminal Code;

  (b) an order for the restraint of proceeds of crime may be enforced as if it were an order made under subsection 462.33(3) of the Criminal Code;

  (c) an order for the seizure of offence-related property may be enforced as if it were a warrant issued under subsection 487(1) of the Criminal Code, subsection 11(1) of the Controlled Drugs and Substances Act or subsection 87(1) of the Cannabis Act, as the case may be; and

  (d) an order for the restraint of offence-related property may be enforced as if it were an order made under subsection 490.8(3) of the Criminal Code, subsection 14(3) of the Controlled Drugs and Substances Act or subsection 91(3) of the Cannabis Act, as the case may be.

Filing of amendments

(5) When an order is filed under subsection (2), a copy of any amendments made to the order may be filed in the same way as the order, and the amendments do not, for the purpose of this Act, have effect until they are registered.

Orders of forfeiture

9.4 (1) When a written request is presented to the Minister by a state or entity, other than the International Criminal Court referred to in section 9.1, for the enforcement of an order of forfeiture of property situated in Canada issued by a court of criminal jurisdiction of the state or entity, the Minister may authorize the Attorney General of Canada or an attorney general of a province to make arrangements for the enforcement of the order.

Grounds for refusal of request

(2) The Minister shall refuse the request if he or she

(a) has reasonable grounds to believe that the request has been made for the purpose of punishing a person by reason of their race, sex, sexual orientation, religion, nationality, ethnic origin, language, colour, age, mental or physical disability or political opinion;

(b) is of the opinion that enforcement of the order would prejudice an ongoing proceeding or investigation;

(c) is of the opinion that enforcement of the order would impose an excessive burden on the resources of federal, provincial or territorial authorities;

(d) is of the opinion that enforcement of the order might prejudice Canada's security, national interest or sovereignty; or

(e) is of the opinion that refusal of the request is in the public interest.

Filing of order

(3) On receipt of an authorization, the Attorney General of Canada or an attorney general of a province may file a copy of the order with the superior court of criminal jurisdiction of the province in which all or part of the property that is the subject of the order is believed to be located. On being filed, the order shall be entered as a judgment of that court and may be executed anywhere in Canada.

Deemed filing

(4) An order that is filed under subsection (3) by an attorney general of a province is deemed to be filed by the Attorney General of Canada.

Conditions

(5) Before filing an order, the Attorney General of Canada or an attorney general of a province must be satisfied that

(a) the person has been convicted of an offence within the jurisdiction of the state or entity;

(b) the offence would be an indictable offence if it were committed in Canada; and

(c) the conviction and the order are not subject to further appeal.

Effect of registered order

(6) From the date it is filed under subsection (3), subject to subsection (4),

(a) an order of forfeiture of proceeds of crime has the same effect as if it were an order under subsection 462.37(1) or 462.38(2) of the Criminal Code; and

(b) an order for the forfeiture of offence-related property has the same effect as if it were an order under subsection 490.1(1) or 490.2(2) of the Criminal Code, subsection 16(1) or 17(2) of the Controlled Drugs and Substances Act or subsection 94(1) or 95(2) of the Cannabis Act, as the case may be.

Filing of amendments

(7) When an order is filed under subsection (3), a copy of any amendments made to the order may be filed in the same way as the order, and the amendments do not, for the purpose of this Act, have effect until they are registered.

Notice

(8) When an order has been filed under subsection (3),

(a) an order of forfeiture of proceeds of crime shall not be executed before notice in accordance with subsection 462.41(2) of the Criminal Code has been given to any person who, in the opinion of the court, appears to have a valid interest in the property; and

(b) an order of forfeiture of offence-related property shall not be executed before

(i) notice in accordance with subsection 490.41(2) of the Criminal Code, subsection 19.1(2) of the Controlled Drugs and Substances Act or subsection 98(2) of the Cannabis Act has been given to any person who resides in a dwelling-house that is offence-related property and who is a member of the immediate family of the person charged with or convicted of the offence in relation to which property would be forfeited, and

(ii) notice in accordance with subsection 490.4(2) of the Criminal Code, subsection 19(2) of the Controlled Drugs and Substances Act or subsection 97(2) of the Cannabis Act has been given to any person who, in the opinion of the court, appears to have a valid interest in the property.

CYPRUS

The Prevention and Suppression of Money Laundering and Terrorist Financing Laws of 2007–Updated 2018

PART IV–INTERNATIONAL CO-OPERATION

Interpretation of principal terms.

37. For the purposes of this Part:

"appeal" for the purposes of subsection 3(a) of section 38 (Procedure for the enforcement of foreign orders) shall include any proceedings the object of which is the setting aside of a judgement of the court or the retrial of the case or the stay of its execution;

"Convention" means

(a) The United Nations Convention against Illicit Traffic in Narcotic Drugs and Psychotropic Substances which was ratified with the United Nations Convention against Illicit Traffic in Narcotic Drugs and Psychotropic Substances (Ratification) Law;

(aa) The European Convention on Laundering, Search, Seizure and Confiscation of the Proceeds from Crime of 1990, which was ratified with the European Convention on Laundering, Search, Seizure and Confiscation of the Proceeds from Crime (Ratification) Law of 1995;

(b) the Convention of the Council of Europe on Laundering, Search, Seizure and Confiscation of the Proceeds from Crime and Financing of Terrorism which was ratified with the European Convention on Laundering, Search, Seizure and Confiscation of the Proceeds from Crime and Financing of Terrorism (Ratification) Law.

(c) The United Nations Convention Against Transnational Crime; and

(d) The Treaty on Mutual Legal Assistance in Penal Matters between Cyprus and USA, which has been ratified by the Treaty between the Government of the Republic of Cyprus and the Government of the U.S.A. on Mutual Legal Assistance in Criminal Matters (Ratification) Law and the Instrument which is provided for under subsection (2) of Section 3 of the Agreement on Mutual Legal Assistance between the European Union and the USA signed on 25 June 2003, relating to the application of the Convention between the Republic of Cyprus and the USA for Mutual Legal Assistance in Penal Matters, signed on 20 December 1999 (Ratification) Law of 2008.

(e) The United Nations Convention against Corruption which was ratified with the United Nations Convention against Corruption (Ratification) Law.

"court" means the President or a Senior District Judge of the District Court of Nicosia;

"foreign country" means a country which at the time of submitting an application for the execution of a foreign order is a Contracting Party to the Convention;

"foreign order" means an order made by a court of a foreign country, which is made for the purposes of the Conventions or legislation enacted for the purpose of implementing the Conventions and shall include—

(a) Orders for the confiscation of proceeds and instrumentalities as these are defined in the Convention and includes—

(i) An order for the confiscation of proceeds, which is in the possession of the accused or a third person or other assets equal to the value of the proceeds.

(ii) A confiscation order without conviction, issued by a court within the framework of the procedure relating to a criminal offence, and

(iii) A restitution order to the legitimate owners or victims which was issued, either before or after the coming into force of the provisions of the Prevention and Suppression of Money Laundering Activities (Amendment) Law of 2018:

Provided that, for the purpose of the present paragraph, 'confiscation order without conviction' includes an order without conviction issued either before or after the coming into force of the provisions of the Prevention and Suppression of Money Laundering Activities (Amendment) Law of 2018, from a court of a foreign country which leads to the deprivation of property and does not constitute a criminal sanction, to the extent that it is ordered by the court of a foreign country in relation to a criminal offence, provided it has been proven that the property relating to the order constitutes proceeds.

(b) restraint orders and orders for the seizure of property made temporarily for the purposes of future confiscation of proceeds and instrumentalities;

(c) any order which the Council of Ministers may, by notification published in the Official Gazette of the Republic, wish to include in the term "foreign order."

Procedure for the enforcement of external orders.

38. —(1) The request for enforcement shall be submitted by or on behalf of a foreign country to the Ministry of Justice and Public Order which, if satisfied that the request comes from a foreign country and concerns a foreign order within the meaning of this Part, shall thereafter transmit the request to the Unit which submits it to the court, if the Unit considers that the requirements of this law are met.

(2) Subject to the provisions of subsection (3), the court, after a request of a foreign country is transmitted to it, shall register the foreign order for the purpose of its enforcement.

(3) The court shall register an external order, if satisfied that—

(a) At the time of registration the external order was in force and enforceable and no appeal is pending against the said order;

(b) in the event where the foreign order relating to the confiscation of property was issued upon conviction of the accused in his absence, he was notified of the relevant proceedings in the country of issuance of the foreign order to be able to appear and present his position and opinions;

(b1) in the event where the foreign order relating to the freezing of property was issued in the absence of the accused or the suspect, he was notified of the relevant proceedings in the country of issuance of the foreign order to be able to appear and present his position and opinions;

(c) the enforcement of the order would not be contrary to the interests of justice of the Republic;

(d) the grounds for refusal of co-operation mentioned in the International Conventions or Bilateral do not concur.

(4) The Court, after the registration of the foreign order, issues directions that notification be given to all persons affected by the order.

(5) The provisions of paragraphs (a), (b), (c) and (d) of subsection (7) of section 43C apply by analogy in the case of a Court order for registration and execution of a restraint and seizure order issued pursuant to the provisions of the present section.

(6) Subject to the provisions of the present section, the rights of bona fide third parties are safeguarded.

Transmission to a foreign country of an order issued on the basis of the provisions of this law.

38. A. Any restraint, charging or confiscation order issued, on the basis of the provisions of this law by a Court of the Republic of Cyprus following an application of the Attorney-General, which relates to property situated aboard, it is transmitted by the Unit for execution and/or service to the competent authorities of the foreign country, through the Ministry of Justice and Public Order.

Effect of registration.

39. –(1) Subject to the provisions of subsection (2) of this section, a foreign order registered by virtue of section 38 (Procedure for the enforcement of foreign orders) shall become enforceable as if the order had been made by a competent court of the Republic under this Law.

(2) The enforcement of the order may be subject to a condition of the foreign country that the penalty of imprisonment or other deprivation of liberty, in case there is compliance with the order, shall not be imposed.

(3) Where the foreign order concerns the confiscation of proceeds or property, the proceeds or property may, after the enforcement of the said order, be distributed among the competent authorities of the foreign country and the Republic of Cyprus.

(4) In the event of registration of a confiscation order, this is executed by the Unit, if within six (6) weeks from the date the persons affected by the order received notification in accordance with section 38(4), the said persons took no action for the cancellation or the setting aside of the registration order:

Provided that, in the event it is not possible to provide the notification mentioned in section 38 (4) or the accused or the third person in the possession of whom the proceeds are held cannot be located, despite making reasonable efforts, the confiscation order is executed immediately by the Unit.

Cancellation of registration.

40. —(1) The court shall cancel the registration of a foreign order if it appears to the court that the order has been complied with.

    (a) by the payment of the amount due under the order; or

    (b) in any other way that may be provided for under the legislation of a foreign country.

(2) The court may cancel the registration of a restraint order if, within a reasonable period of time, the criminal proceedings have not been initiated or there was no progress in the investigation of the criminal case which could lead to criminal proceedings during which a confiscation order may be issued.

(3) In the event that an application for cancellation of the registration of a restraint order pursuant to the provisions of subsection (2) is submitted the foreign country which issued the order is notified in advance, and is permitted to submit its comments.

External order shall be binding.

41. —(1) A foreign order may be amended or revised only by a court or any other competent authority of the foreign country which made the order.

(2) The court, when exercising the powers conferred upon it by section 39 (Effect of registration) as well as other powers in respect of the execution of a foreign order, shall be bound by the findings as to the facts in so far as they are stated in the conviction or decision of a court of the foreign country or in so far as such conviction or judicial decision is implicitly based on them.

External order shall be binding.

Amount of the order.

42. —(1) Where in the foreign order there is a reference to a sum of money to be received in the currency of another country, this amount shall be converted into the currency of the Republic at the rate of exchange ruling at the time the request for registration was made.

(2) Under no circumstances shall the total value of the confiscated property exceed the sum of money to be paid which is referred to in the foreign order.

Implementation of the provisions of this law in foreign orders.

43. —(1) Subsections (7), (8), (10), (11) of section 14, subsections (9) and (10) of section 15 and sections 17, 18, 19, 20, 22 and 23 shall also apply in cases of foreign orders subject to any amendments or limitations that the Council

of Ministers may wish to prescribe by regulations made under this Implementation of the provisions of this law in foreign orders.

(2) The Council of Ministers may include in the Regulations any other provision it considers necessary for the better implementation of this Part and in particular anything relating-

  (a) to the proof of any matter or thing;

  (b) to the circumstances which in any foreign country may be considered as constituting the commencement or conclusion of procedures for the making of an external order.

(3) Where on the request of or on behalf of a foreign country the court is satisfied that proceedings have been instituted but not concluded in this country during which a foreign order may be made, the court shall make a restraint or charging order by applying sections 14 and 15 of this Law.

(3A) Subject to the provisions of section 72 A, in the event that the Court cancels a restraint or charging order issued pursuant to the provisions of section 14 or section 15, the property which is the subject matter of the order is released completely, to the extent possible without reducing or affecting its value or amount in any way, for the benefit of the person in whose name it is held.

(4) The application of this section does not depend on the issue of Regulations and until such Regulations are issued, the sections referred in paragraph (1) will apply without any amendments or limitations.

FRANCE

Code of criminal procedure

Book V: Enforcement Procedures
Title I: Enforcement of Criminal Sentences
Chapter III: International cooperation in the enforcement of confiscation orders

Section 2: Enforcement of confiscation orders issued by foreign judicial authorities

713-36

In the absence of an international convention providing otherwise, Articles 713-37 to 713-40 are applicable to the enforcement of confiscation orders issued by foreign judicial authorities, aimed at the confiscation of movable or immovable property of any kind that was used or intended to be used to commit the offence or that appears to be the direct or indirect proceeds thereof, as well as any property the value of which corresponds to the proceeds of the offence.

713-37

Without prejudice to the application of Article 694-4, the execution of the confiscation shall be refused;

1. If the facts at the origin of the request do not constitute an offence under French law;

2. If the property to which it relates is not subject to confiscation under French law;

3. If the foreign decision was pronounced under conditions that do not offer sufficient guarantees with regard to the protection of individual liberties and the rights of the defense;

4. If it is established that the foreign decision was issued for the purpose of prosecuting or convicting a person because of his or her sex, race, religion, ethnic origin, nationality, language, political opinions or sexual orientation or gender identity;

5. If the French Public Prosecutor's Office had decided not to prosecute the acts for which the confiscation was ordered by the foreign court, or if these acts have already been the object of a final judgement by the French judicial authorities or by those of a State other than the requesting State, provided, in the event of a conviction, that the sentence has been served, is being served or can no longer be reduced to execution under the laws of the sentencing State;

6. If it relates to a political offence.

713-38

The execution of the confiscation ordered by a foreign judicial authority in application of article 713-36 is authorized by the criminal court, at the request of the public prosecutor.

Enforcement is authorized on condition that the foreign decision is final and enforceable under the law of the requesting State.

The authorization of enforcement may not have the effect of infringing rights lawfully established in favor of third parties, in application of French law, over property whose confiscation was ordered by the foreign decision. However, if this decision contains provisions relating to the rights of third parties, it is binding on the French courts unless the third parties have not been able to assert their rights before the foreign court under conditions analogous to those provided for by French law.

Refusal to authorize enforcement of the confiscation order issued by the foreign court automatically results in the release of the seizure. The same applies when proceedings initiated abroad have ended or have not led to the confiscation of the seized property.

713-39

If it deems it useful, the criminal court hears, if necessary by rogatory commission, the owner of the seized property, the convicted person and any person having rights over the property that was the subject of the foreign confiscation order.

The persons mentioned in the preceding paragraph may be represented by an attorney.

The criminal court is bound by the findings of fact of the foreign decision. If these findings are insufficient, it may request, by letter rogatory, the foreign authority that issued the decision to provide, within a period of time that it determines, the necessary additional information.

713-40

The enforcement on the territory of the Republic of a confiscation order issued by a foreign court entails the transfer to the French State of ownership of the confiscated property, unless otherwise agreed with the requesting State.

The property thus confiscated may be sold in accordance with the provisions of the Code of State Property.

The costs of enforcing the confiscation order are deducted from the total amount recovered.

The sums of money recovered and the proceeds from the sale of the confiscated property, after deduction of the costs of enforcement, are vested in the French State when this amount is less than €10,000 and vested half in the French State and half in the requesting State in other cases.

If the foreign order provides for value confiscation, the order authorizing its enforcement renders the French State a creditor of the obligation to pay the corresponding sum of money. In the event of non-payment, the State has its claim recovered from any property available for this purpose. The amount recovered, after deduction of all costs, shall be shared in accordance with the rules provided for in this Article.

713-41

For the application of the present section, the competent criminal court is that of the location of one of the assets that are the object of the request or, failing that, the criminal court of Paris.

GERMANY

Act on International Cooperation in Criminal Matters

Part IV.
Assistance through Enforcement of Foreign Judgments

Section 48

Principle

For criminal proceedings assistance may be provided through enforcement of a penalty or any other sanction imposed with final and binding force in a foreign country. Part IV of this Law shall also apply to requests for the enforcement of an order for confiscation or deprivation, made by a court exercising other than criminal jurisdiction in the requesting State if the order is based on a punishable offence.

Section 49
Additional Prerequisites for Admissibility of Assistance

(1) The enforcement shall not be admissible unless

1. a competent authority of the foreign State submitting the complete, legally binding and enforceable decision has requested it;

2. in the proceedings on which the foreign decision is based the convicted person had an opportunity to be heard and to present an adequate defense, and the sanction has been imposed by an independent court or, in the case of a fine, was imposed by an authority whose decision may be appealed to an independent court;

3. under German law notwithstanding possible procedural obstacles and, if necessary mutatis mutandis, a criminal penalty, measure of rehabilitation and incapacitation or a regulatory fine could have been imposed in respect of the offence on which the foreign judgment is based or, where enforcement of an order for confiscation or deprivation is requested, such an order could have been made, notwithstanding section 73(1) 2nd sentence of the German penal code;

4. a decision of the kind mentioned in section 9 no. 1 has been made, unless the enforcement of an order for confiscation or deprivation is requested and such an order could be made independently under section 76a of the German penal code;

5. the statute of limitations for the enforcement under German law has not lapsed or would not have lapsed mutatis mutandis; the above notwithstanding the enforcement of an order for confiscation or deprivation shall be admissible if

   a) German criminal law does not apply to the offence on which the order is based or

   b) such an order could be made mutatis mutandis by analogous application of section 76a(2) no. 1 of the German penal code.

(2) If a custodial sanction has been imposed in a foreign State and the convicted person is located there, enforcement shall not be admitted unless the convicted person, after having been advised, consented and his consent was entered into the record of a court in the requesting State or the consent was declared before a German consular career official empowered to certify legally relevant declarations. The consent cannot be revoked.

(3) If German law does not recognize any type of sanction corresponding to the sanction imposed in the foreign State, enforcement shall not be admissible.

(4) If in the foreign order for confiscation or deprivation a decision has been made concerning the rights of third parties, it shall be binding unless

   a) the third party had not been given sufficient opportunity to defend their rights, or

   b) the decision is incompatible with a German civil court decision issued in the same matter or

c) the decision relates to third party rights to real estate located on German territory or to real estate rights; third party rights shall also include priority notices.

(5) Orders depriving of or suspending a right, or ordering prohibitions or the loss of a capacity, shall extend to German territory if so provided for in an international agreement approved by law in accordance with Article 59(2) of the Basic Law.

Section 50

Subject-Matter Jurisdiction

Jurisdiction regarding the enforceability of a foreign decision shall lie with the regional court. The public prosecution service at the regional court shall prepare the decision.

Section 51

Local Jurisdiction

(1) Jurisdiction for the decision regarding the enforceability of a foreign decision shall be determined by the place of residence of the convicted person.

(2) If the convicted person does not have a permanent place of residence on German territory, jurisdiction shall be determined by the place where that person normally lives or, if such a place is not known, by the last place of residence, otherwise by the place where that person was apprehended, or, if that person has not been apprehended, where that person was first located. If the request relates solely to enforcement of an order for confiscation or deprivation or a fine or a regulatory fine, jurisdiction shall lie with the court in whose district the object described in the order for confiscation or deprivation is located, or, if no particular object is specified in the order for confiscation or deprivation or if a fine or regulatory fine is to be enforced, jurisdiction shall lie with the court in whose district the convicted person's assets are located. If the convicted person has assets in the districts of several regional courts jurisdiction shall be determined by which regional court was first seized of the matter or, if no regional court has been seized of the matter yet, with that public prosecution office at the regional court which was first seized of the case.

(3) If jurisdiction cannot be otherwise established, it shall be determined by the seat of the Federal Government.

Section 52

Preparation of Decision

(1) If the documents submitted are insufficient to permit a determination as to enforcement, the court shall issue its decision only after the requesting State has been given an opportunity to submit additional documents.

(2) Section 30(1) 2nd sentence, (2) 2nd and 4th sentences, (3) and section 31(1) and (4) shall apply mutatis mutandis. If the convicted person is on German territory, section 30(2) 1st sentence and section 31(2) and (3) shall also apply mutatis mutandis.

(3) In respect of requests for enforcement of foreign orders for confiscation or deprivation, the convicted person as well as third parties who could, depending on the circumstances of the case, claim rights to the object, must be given an opportunity to be heard prior to the decision.

Section 53

Assistance of Counsel

(1) In respect of requests for enforcement of foreign orders for confiscation or deprivation, the convicted person as well as third parties who could, depending on the circumstances of the case, claim rights to the object, may avail themselves of the assistance of counsel at any stage of the proceedings.

(2) If the convicted person did not privately appoint counsel, he shall be assigned counsel if

    1.   because of the complexity of the factual and legal situation, the assistance of counsel appears necessary,

    2.   it is apparent that the convicted person cannot himself adequately protect his rights or

    3.   the convicted person is in detention outside German territory and there are doubts whether he himself can adequately protect his rights.

[...]

(6) The provisions of Chapter 11 of Book 1 of the Code of Criminal Procedure with the exception of sections 140, 141(1) to (3) and section 142(2) shall apply mutatis mutandis.

Section 54

Conversion of Foreign Sentence

(1) To the extent that enforcement of the foreign judgment is admissible, it shall be declared enforceable. The penalty imposed shall at the same time be converted into a penalty which under German law corresponds most closely to it. The extent of the penalty to be imposed shall be determined by the foreign decision; it must, however, not exceed the maximum of the penalty which could be imposed for the offence under German law. This maximum shall be substituted with a maximum term of two years' imprisonment if under German law the offence is punishable

    1.   by a term of imprisonment not exceeding two years or

    2.   sanctionable as a regulatory offence by a regulatory fine yet the foreign penalty must be converted into a term of imprisonment pursuant to the 2nd sentence above.

(2) In the case of a fine the foreign currency amount shall be converted into Euros at the exchange rate applicable on the day of the foreign decision.

(2a) Where an order for confiscation or deprivation concerns a specific object the declaration of enforceability shall refer to that object. Instead of a specific object the declaration can also refer to the monetary amount equal to the value of the object if

    1.   the foreign State has made a request to that effect and

2. the conditions of section 76 of the German penal code are fulfilled mutatis mutandis.

If the order is defined in terms of monetary value, subsection (2) above shall apply mutatis mutandis.

(3) When converting a sentence imposed against a juvenile or a young adult the provisions of the Juvenile Court Act shall apply mutatis mutandis.

(4) Any part of the sentence previously served in the requesting State or a third State, and any detention served pursuant to section 58, shall be credited towards the sentence to be determined. If this credit was not taken into account at the time of the decision about enforcement of the judgment or if the conditions for a credit arise at a later date, the decision shall be amended.

Section 55

Decision Concerning Enforceability

(1) The regional court shall decide on the enforceability by order. To the extent that the foreign decision is declared enforceable, that finding and the type and extent of the penalty to be enforced shall be stated in the order.

(2) The public prosecution service at the regional court, the convicted person and third parties who when a request for enforcement of an order for confiscation or deprivation was made have claimed rights to the object, may appeal the order within one week. For the subsequent procedure, section 42 shall apply mutatis mutandis.

(3) Copies of the final orders entered by the court shall be passed on to the Federal Central Criminal Register. This shall not apply if the penalty imposed in the foreign judgment has been converted into a fine or if the final order related solely to an order for confiscation or deprivation. If the foreign decision is to be entered in the Federal Central Criminal Register the decision regarding the enforce ability is to be noted in the entry. Ss. 12 to 16 of the Federal Central Criminal Register Act shall apply mutatis mutandis.

Section 56

Granting Assistance

(1) Legal assistance shall not be granted unless the foreign decision has been declared enforceable.

(2) The decision regarding legal assistance shall be notified to the Federal Central Criminal Register. Section 55(3) 2nd to 4th sentences shall apply mutatis mutandis.

(3) If upon request the enforcement of a fine or a sentence of imprisonment is granted, the offence may no longer be prosecuted under German law.

(4) The granting of a request for legal assistance seeking the enforcement of an order for confiscation or deprivation shall be equivalent to a final order and decision within the meaning of sections 73, 74 of the German penal code. Section 493 of the Code of Criminal Procedure shall apply mutatis mutandis.

Section 56a

Compensation of the Injured Party

(1) If upon the request of another State a foreign decision ordering confiscation was executed into the assets of the convicted person within German territory, the party injured by the offence on which the foreign decision is based shall receive compensation from public funds if

1. a German or foreign court has issued an enforceable decision awarding damages against the convicted person or if the latter has declared his obligation to pay to the injured person in an enforceable document (title),

2. the title is enforceable within German territory,

3. the injured person shows that the title covers the damages arising from the offence on which the decision for confiscation is based and

4. the injured person shows that he could not obtain full satisfaction of his claim from the enforcement of the title.

Compensation shall be awarded in exchange for cession of the claim for damages to an equal amount.

(2) Compensation shall not be granted if the rights of the injured person under section 73e(1) 2nd sentence continue to exist.

(3) The amount of compensation shall be limited by the remaining revenue accruing to German public funds from the enforcement of the confiscation order into the domestic assets. If several injured parties have filed an application under subsection (1) above, their compensation shall be determined by the sequence of their applications. If several applications are filed on the same day and the revenue is insufficient to satisfy these persons they shall receive compensation pro rata according to the amount of the claims for damages.

(4) The application shall be filed with the competent enforcement authority. It may be denied if six months have passed since the end of the enforcement proceedings related to the asset from which compensation could be paid. The enforcement authority may set appropriate time limits in which the injured person must adduce the necessary documentation.

(5) The decision of the enforcement authority may be reviewed in the civil courts.

Section 56b

Agreement on Disposal, Return and Distribution of Seized Assets

(1) The authority in charge of granting assistance may enter into an ad hoc agreement with the competent authority of the requesting State about the disposal, return or distribution of the assets resulting from the enforcement of an order for confiscation or deprivation if reciprocity is assured.

(2) Agreements relating to objects within the meaning of sections 1 and 10 of the Act on the Protection of Cultural Property require the consent of the Representative of the Federal Government for Cultural and Media Affairs. If the consent is refused, section 16(3) 2nd sentence of the Act on the Protection of Cultural Property* shall apply mutatis mutandis.

Section 57

Enforcement

(1) Upon legal assistance having been granted, the prosecution service having jurisdiction under s. 50(2) shall execute the enforcement as enforcement authority. The jurisdiction for the enforcement of a sanction which was converted into a sanction admissible under the Juvenile Court Act shall be determined by the provisions of the Juvenile Court Act.

(2) The enforcement of the remainder of a custodial sanction may be suspended. The provisions of the German penal code shall apply mutatis mutandis.

(3) The decision under subsection (2) above and any subsequent decision relating to suspension shall lie with the court having jurisdiction under section 462a(1) 1st and 2nd sentences of the Code of Criminal Procedure, or, if its jurisdiction is not established under this provision, with the court having jurisdiction under section 50.

(4) The enforcement of a converted sanction shall follow, mutatis mutandis, the provisions applicable to a similar sanction if issued in the Federal Republic of Germany.

(5) The enforcement related to a monetary value shall cease or be restricted if the convicted person adduces a document which shows that the amount was enforced in another State or if the enforcing authority obtains knowledge thereof in another manner.

(6) Enforcement shall not be executed if a competent authority of the requesting State provides notice that the conditions for enforcement no longer exist.

(7) If a foreign order for confiscation was enforced and there is reason to believe from that order that a person identifiable by name might have a claim for damages against the convicted person arising from the offence on which the order was based, that person must without undue delay be informed by the enforcing authority by simple letter to the last known address, about his rights under section 56a. The authority may decide not to send such information if the period under section 56a(4) 2nd sentence has lapsed.

Section 57a

Costs of enforcement

The convicted person shall bear the costs of the enforcement.

Section 58

Measures Safeguarding Enforcement

(1) If a request for enforcement in the meaning of section 49(1) no. 1 has been received, or if prior to its receipt it has been so requested by a competent authority of the requesting State with details of the offence on which the sentence is based, the time and place when it was committed and as exact a description of the convicted person as possible, the detention of the convicted person for the purpose of ensuring enforcement of a sentence of imprisonment may be ordered provided that on the basis of ascertainable facts

1. there is reason to believe that he would abscond from the enforcement proceedings or from enforcement, or

2. if there is a strong reason to believe that in the enforcement proceedings he would dishonestly obstruct the ascertainment of the truth.

(2) The court having jurisdiction pursuant to s. 50 shall issue the decision regarding detention. Ss. 17, 18, 20, 23 to 27 shall apply mutatis mutandis. The higher regional court shall be substituted by the regional court, the public prosecution service at the higher regional court shall be substituted by the public prosecution service at the regional court. Decisions of the regional court shall be subject to appeal.

(3) If the request for enforcement relates to a fine, a regulatory fine or an order for confiscation or deprivation, or if a competent authority of the requesting State has, with identification of the person sought, the offence on which the criminal proceedings are based and the time and place of its commission prior to receipt of such request, requested preliminary measures for the purpose of ensuring enforcement under ss. 111b to 111d of the Code of Criminal Procedure, section 67(1) shall apply mutatis mutandis. For the purpose of the preparation of an order for confiscation or deprivation in the requesting State, which may also relate to the monetary value, decisions under sections 111b to 111d of the Code of Criminal Procedure may be issued if the conditions of section 66(2) nos. 1 and 2 are fulfilled.

(4) Subsections (1) and (3) above shall not apply if it appears ab initio that enforcement will not be admissible.

HONG KONG SAR, CHINA

Mutual Legal Assistance in Criminal Matters Ordinance

PART VI
ASSISTANCE IN RELATION TO CONFISCATION, ETC. OF PROCEEDS OF CRIME

Section 25 Requests by Hong Kong for enforcement of Hong Kong confiscation order

The Secretary for Justice may request an appropriate authority of a place outside Hong Kong to make arrangements—(Amended L.N. 362 of 1997)

(a) for the enforcement of a Hong Kong confiscation order; or

(b) where a Hong Kong confiscation order may be made in a proceeding which has been or is to be instituted in Hong Kong, to restrain dealing in any property against which the order may be enforced or which may be available to satisfy the order.

Section 26 Satisfaction of Hong Kong confiscation order

(1) Where, in execution of a Hong Kong confiscation order pursuant to a request under section 25, property is recovered in a place outside Hong Kong but the order requires an amount specified therein to be payable, then that amount shall be treated as reduced by the value of property so recovered.

(2) For the purposes of this section and without prejudice to the admissibility of any evidence which may be admissible apart from this subsection, a certificate purporting to be issued by or on behalf of an appropriate authority of a place outside Hong Kong stating that property has been recovered there in execution of a request under section 25, stating the value of the property so recovered and the date on which it was recovered shall, in any proceedings in a court in Hong Kong, be admissible as evidence of the facts so stated.

(3) Where the value of property recovered as described in subsection (1) is expressed in a currency other than that of Hong Kong, the extent to which the amount payable under the Hong Kong confiscation order is to be reduced under that subsection shall be calculated on the basis of the exchange rate prevailing on the date on which the property was recovered in the place outside Hong Kong concerned.

(4) For the purposes of subsection (3), a certificate purporting to be signed by the Monetary Authority and stating the exchange rate prevailing on a specified date shall be admissible in any proceedings as evidence of the facts so stated.

Section 27 Requests to Hong Kong for enforcement of external confiscation order

(1) Where a place outside Hong Kong requests the Secretary for Justice to make arrangements—

(a) for the enforcement of an external confiscation order; or

(b) where an external confiscation order may be made in a proceeding which has been or is to be instituted in that place, to restrain dealing in any property against which the order may be enforced or which may be available to satisfy the order,

then the Secretary for Justice may, in relation to that request, act for that place under the provisions of Schedule 2.

(2) A request under subsection (1) shall, unless the contrary is shown, be deemed to constitute the authority of the place outside Hong Kong concerned for the Secretary for Justice to act on its behalf in any proceedings in the Court of First Instance under section 28 or under any provision of Schedule 2.

Section 28 Registration of external confiscation orders

(1) On an application made by the Secretary for Justice, the Court of First Instance may register an external confiscation order if—(Amended L.N. 362 of 1997; 25 of 1998 s. 2)

(a) it is satisfied that at the time of registration the order is in force and not subject to appeal;

(b) it is satisfied, where any person against whom, or in relation to whose property, the order is made does not appear in the proceedings, that he received notice of the proceedings, in accordance with the law of the place outside Hong Kong concerned, in sufficient time to enable him to defend them; and

(c) it is of the opinion that enforcing the order in Hong Kong would not be contrary to the interests of justice.

(2) In subsection (1), "appeal" (上訴) includes—

    (a) any proceedings by way of discharging or setting aside a judgment; and

    (b) an application for a new trial or a stay of execution.

(3) For the purposes of this section, an external confiscation order is subject to appeal so long as an appeal, further appeal or review is pending against the order; and for this purpose an appeal, further appeal or review shall be treated as pending (where one is competent but has not been instituted) until the expiration of the time prescribed for instituting the appeal, further appeal or review under the law of the place outside Hong Kong concerned.

(4) The Court of First Instance shall cancel the registration of an external confiscation order if it appears to the Court of First Instance that the order has been satisfied by—

    (a) payment of the amount due under it or by the person against whom it was made serving imprisonment in default of such payment;

    (b) recovery of property specified in it (or the value of such property) or by the person against whom it was made serving imprisonment in default of such recovery; or

    (c) any other means.

(5) Where an amount of money, if any, payable or remaining to be paid under an external confiscation order registered in the Court of First Instance under this section is expressed in a currency other than that of Hong Kong, for the purpose of any action taken in relation to that order under Schedule 2 the amount shall be converted into the currency of Hong Kong on the basis of the exchange rate prevailing on the date of registration of the order.

(6) For the purposes of subsection (5), a certificate purporting to be signed by or on behalf of the Monetary Authority and stating the exchange rate prevailing on a specified date shall be admissible in any proceedings as evidence of the facts so stated.

Section 29 Proof of orders and judgments of court in place outside Hong Kong

(1) For the purposes of sections 27 and 28 and Schedule 2—

    (a) any order made or judgment given by a court in a place outside Hong Kong purporting to bear the seal of that court or to be signed by any person in his capacity as a judge, magistrate or officer of the court, shall be deemed without further proof to have been duly sealed or, as the case may be, to have been signed by that person; and

    (b) a document, duly certified, which purports to be a copy of any order made or judgment given by a court in a place outside Hong Kong shall be deemed without further proof to be a true copy.

(2) A document purporting to be a copy of any order made or judgment given by a court in a place outside Hong Kong is duly certified for the purpose of subsection (1)(b) if it purports to be certified by any person in his capacity as a judge, magistrate or officer of the court in question or by or on behalf of the appropriate authority of the place outside Hong Kong concerned.

Section 30 Evidence in relation to proceedings and orders in place outside Hong Kong

(1) For the purposes of sections 27 and 28 and Schedule 2, a certificate purporting to be issued by or on behalf of the appropriate authority of a place outside Hong Kong stating—

    (a) that a proceeding has been instituted and has not been concluded, or that a proceeding is to be instituted, in the place;

    (b) that an external confiscation order is in force and is not subject to appeal;

    (c) that all or a certain amount of the sum payable under an external confiscation order remains unpaid in the place, or that other property recoverable under an external confiscation order remains unrecovered in the place;

    (d) that any person has been notified of any proceeding in accordance with the law of the place; or

    (e) that an order (however described) made by a court in the place has the purpose of—

        (i) recovering (including forfeiting and confiscating)—

            (A) payments or other rewards received in connection with an external serious offence or their value;

            (B) property derived or realised, directly or indirectly, from payments or other rewards received in connection with an external serious offence or the value of such property; or

            (C) property used or intended to be used in connection with an external serious offence or the value of such property; or

        (ii) depriving a person of a pecuniary advantage obtained in connection with an external serious offence, shall, in any proceeding in the Court of First Instance, be admissible as evidence of the facts so stated.

(2) In any such proceeding a statement contained in a document, duly certified, which purports to have been received in evidence or to be a copy of a document so received, or to set out or summarise evidence given in proceedings in a court in a place outside Hong Kong, shall be admissible as evidence of any fact stated therein.

(3) A document is duly certified for the purposes of subsection (2) if it purports to be certified by any person in his capacity as a judge, magistrate or officer of the court in the place outside Hong Kong concerned, or by or on behalf of an appropriate authority of the place, to have been received in evidence or to be a copy of a document so received or, as the case may be, to be the original document containing or summarising the evidence or a true copy of that document.

(4) Nothing in this section shall prejudice the admission of any evidence, whether contained in any document or otherwise, which is admissible apart from this section.

INDIA

The Prevention of Money Laundering Act, 2002

60. Attachment, seizure and confiscation, etc., of property in a contracting State or India.

(1) Where the Director has made an order for attachment of any [property under section 5 or for freezing under sub-section (1A) of section 17 or where an Adjudicating Authority has made an order relating to a property under section 8 or where a Special Court has made an order of confiscation relating to a property under sub-section (5) or sub-section (6) of section 8], and such property is suspected to be in a contracting State, the Special Court, on an application by the Director or the Administrator appointed under sub-section (1) of section 10, as the case may be, may issue a letter of request to a court or an authority in the contracting State for execution of such order.

(2) Where a letter of request is received by the Central Government from a court or an authority in a contracting State requesting [attachment, seizure, freezing or confiscation] of the property in India, derived or obtained, directly or indirectly, by any person from the commission of an offence under a corresponding law committed in that contracting State, the Central Government may forward such letter of request to the Director, as it thinks fit, for execution in accordance with the provisions of this Act.

[(2A) Where on closure of the criminal case or conclusion of trial in a criminal court outside India under the corresponding law of any other country, such court finds that the offence of money-laundering under the corresponding law of that country has been committed, the [Special Court] shall, on receipt of an application from the Director for execution of confiscation under sub-section (2), order, after giving notice to the affected persons, that such property involved in money-laundering or which has been used for commission of the offence of money-laundering stand confiscated to the Central Government.]

(3) The Director shall, on receipt of a letter of request under section 58 or section 59, direct any authority under this Act to take all steps necessary for tracing and identifying such property.

(4) The steps referred to in sub-section (3) may include any inquiry, investigation or survey in respect of any person, place, property, assets, documents, books of account in any bank or public financial institutions or any other relevant matters.

(5) Any inquiry, investigation or survey referred to in sub-section (4) shall be carried out by an authority mentioned in sub-section (3) in accordance with such directions issued in accordance with the provisions of this Act.

(6) The provisions of this Act relating to attachment, adjudication, confiscation and vesting of property in Central Government contained in Chapter III and survey, searches and seizures contained in Chapter V shall apply to the property in respect of which letter of request is received from a court or contracting State for attachment or confiscation of property.

[(7) When any property in India is confiscated as a result of execution of a request from a contracting State in accordance with the provisions of this Act, the Central Government may either return such property to the requesting State or compensate that State by disposal of such property on mutually agreed terms that would take into account deduction for reasonable expenses incurred in investigation, prosecution or judicial proceedings leading to the return or disposal of confiscated property.]

ITALY

Code of Criminal Procedure

Title IV
Effects of foreign criminal judgments. Enforcement of Italian criminal judgments abroad.

Chapter I
Effects of foreign criminal judgments

Article 731

Recognition of foreign criminal judgments pursuant to international agreements

1.   The Minister of Justice, if he/she considers that—pursuant to an international agreement—a criminal judgment delivered abroad must be enforced in the State, or however, that other effects must be attributed to it in the state, shall request its recognition. To that end, he/she shall forward to the Prosecutor General at the Court of Appeal in the district where the competent office of the judicial records is located, a copy of judgment, together with a translation into the Italian language, along with the acts attached to it, and with the available documentation and information. He/she shall also forward a possible request—for enforcement in the [Italian] State—from the foreign state, or the document by which this state agrees to enforcement.

     1-bis. The provisions of paragraph 1 shall also apply in cases of execution of confiscation and when the relevant measure has been adopted by the foreign judicial authority by means of a decision other than a judgment of conviction.

2.   The Prosecutor General shall request the recognition to the Court of Appeal. Where the necessary conditions are met, he/she shall request that recognition be also approved for the purposes provided for in Article 12, paragraph 1, numbers 1), 2) and 3) of the Criminal Code.

Article 733

Requirements for recognition

1.   The foreign judgment cannot be recognized if:
     a)   the judgment has not become final according to the laws of the state in which it was delivered;
     b)   the judgment contains provisions contrary to the fundamental principles of the legal system of the State;

c) the judgment was not rendered by an independent and impartial judge or the defendant was not summoned to appear in court before a foreign authority or he/she was not given the right to be questioned in a language which he/she can understand and be assisted by a lawyer;

d) there are reasonable grounds to believe that considerations concerning race, religion, gender, nationality, language, political opinions or personal or social conditions have affected the development or outcome of the trial;

e) the fact for which the judgment was delivered is not considered to be an offence under the Italian law;

f) a final judgment was delivered in the State for the same fact and against the same person;

g) criminal proceedings are taking place in the State for the same fact and against the same person.

1-bis. Without prejudice to Article 735-bis, a foreign judgment may not be recognized for the purposes of confiscation if this involves property whose confiscation would not be possible under the Italian law, should the same fact be prosecuted in the State.

Article 734

Decision of the Court of Appeal

1. The Court of Appeal shall decide upon the recognition, complying with the procedure set out in Article 127, by means of a judgment in which the effects resulting from it are expressly stated.

2. An appeal against the judgment may be lodged with the Supreme Court (606) by the Prosecutor General at the Court of Appeal and by the person concerned.

Article 735

Determination of the penalty and confiscation order

1. When it pronounces the recognition of a foreign judgment for enforcement purposes, the Court of Appeal shall determine the sentence that must be executed in the State.

2. To that end, it converts the penalty established in the foreign judgment into one of the penalties provided for the same act by the Italian law. Such penalty must correspond in nature, as far as possible, to the penalty imposed by the foreign judgment. The amount of the penalty is determined, taking possibly into account the criteria provided by the Italian law, on the basis of the amount fixed in the foreign judgment; however, the amount cannot exceed the maximum amount provided for the same fact by the Italian law. When the amount of the penalty is not established in the foreign judgment, the Court shall determine it on the basis of the criteria set out in Articles 133, 133-bis and 133-ter of the Criminal Code.

3. In no case may the penalty thus determined be more severe than the one established in the foreign judgment.

4. If in the foreign State where the judgment was delivered, the sentence was conditionally suspended, the Court shall also order, along with the judgment of recognition, the suspended sentence under the Criminal Code (Article 163 of the Criminal Code); if in that State the sentenced person was conditionally released, the Court shall replace the foreign measure with parole (Article 176 of the Criminal Code) and, in determining the requirements for probation [libertà vigilata], the supervising judge cannot make the overall treatment—in terms of penalties established in foreign provisions, more severe.

5. To determine the pecuniary penalty, the amount established in the foreign judgment shall be converted into the equivalent value in Italian liras at the exchange rate of the day when the recognition is deliberated.

6. When the Court pronounces recognition for the purpose of execution of a confiscation (Article 240 of the Criminal Code), the latter shall be ordered with the same judgment of recognition.

Article 736

Coercive measures

1. At the request of the Prosecutor General, the Court of Appeal—competent for the recognition of a foreign judgment for the enforcement of a penalty restricting personal liberty—may order a coercive measure (281-286) against the sentenced person who is in the State.

2. Where applicable, the provisions of Title I of Book IV on coercive measures shall be complied with, except for those referred in Article 273.

3. The Presiding Judge of the Court of Appeal shall, as soon as possible and in any event within five days of execution of the coercive measures, see to the identification of the person. The provision under Article 717, paragraph 2, shall apply.

4. The coercive measure, ordered pursuant to this Article, shall be revoked if since the beginning of its execution six months have elapsed without the Court of Appeal having pronounced judgment of recognition, or, in the case of an appeal lodged with the Court of Cassation against that judgment, ten months have passed without a final judgment of recognition having been handed down.

5. The revocation and substitution of the coercive measure shall be ordered in chambers (Article 127) by the Court of Appeal.

6. A copy of the measures issued by the Court shall be communicated and transmitted, after their execution, to the Prosecutor General, the person concerned and his/her defense counsel, who may lodge an appeal with the Court of Cassation for violation of law.

Article 738

Execution following recognition

1. In cases of recognition for the purpose of execution of a foreign judgment, the penalties and confiscation following recognition shall be executed

according to the Italian law. The sentence served in the sentencing State shall be counted for the purpose of execution.

2. The Prosecutor General at the Court of Appeal which deliberated the recognition shall see to the execution ex officio. This Court shall be—to all intents and purposes—treated as equivalent to the judge who pronounced the conviction in an ordinary criminal proceeding.

Article 739

Ban on extradition and new proceedings

1. In cases of recognition for the purpose of execution of the foreign judgment, except in the case of execution of a confiscation (240 Criminal Code), the sentenced person cannot be extradited; neither can he/she be subjected once again to criminal proceedings in the State for the same offense, even if the latter is considered differently in terms of nomen iuris, degree or circumstances (649).

JAPAN

Act on Punishment of Organized Crimes, Control of Crime Proceeds and Other Matters

Chapter VI
Procedures for International Mutual Assistance in the Execution of Adjudication of Confiscation and Collection of Equivalent Value and in the Securance thereof and other Matters

Article 59 Implementation of assistance

When there is a request, with respect to a criminal case in a foreign country (except for a case involving any act constituting a drug offence or the like provided for in Paragraph 2 of Article 16 of the Anti-Drug Special Law) from such foreign country for assistance in the execution of a finally-binding adjudication of confiscation or collection of equivalent value or in the securance of property for the purpose of confiscation or collection of equivalent value, such assistance may be provided except in any of the following cases:

(1) when the act involving the offence for which assistance is requested (Such term means an offence which is alleged to have been committed in the request for the assistance. The same shall apply hereinafter in this paragraph.) does not constitute an offence provided for in the Schedule, (A) through (D) of Item 2 of Paragraph 2 of Article 2, Item 3 or 4 of that paragraph, Paragraphs 1 through 3 of Article 9, Article 10 or Article 11, if committed in Japan

(2) when it is found that, under the laws and regulations of Japan, any penalty may not be imposed for the act involving the offence for which assistance is requested, if committed in Japan

(3) when any criminal case involving the offence, for which assistance is requested, is pending before a Japanese court or there is a finally-binding judgment by a Japanese court for such case

(4) as for assistance in the execution of a finally-binding adjudication of confiscation or in the securance for the purpose of confiscation, when, if the act involving the offence for which assistance is requested is committed in Japan, the property concerned is not the kind of property in respect of which confiscation or securance of confiscation may be ordered under the laws and regulations of Japan for the offence for which assistance is requested

(5) as for assistance in the execution of a finally-binding adjudication of collection of equivalent value or in the securance for the purpose of collection of equivalent value, when, if the act involving the offence for which assistance is requested is committed in Japan, such request does not fall under a case for which adjudication of the requested collection of equivalent value or securance of collection of equivalent value may be made under the laws and regulations of Japan for the offence for which assistance is requested

(6) when it is found that as for assistance in the execution of a finally-binding adjudication of confiscation any person who is reasonably deemed to hold the property concerned or the superficies hypothec or other right existing on such property, or as for assistance in the execution of a finally-binding adjudication of collection of equivalent value any person against whom the adjudication of collection of equivalent value has been made, was not able to claim such person's right in the proceeding in respect of such adjudication for any reason which may not be attributable to such person

(7) as for assistance in the securance for the purpose of confiscation or collection of equivalent value, when there is no reasonable ground to suspect that the act involving the offence for which assistance is requested has been committed or when it is found that, if the act is committed in Japan, there is no ground provided for in Paragraph 1 of Article 22 or Paragraph 1 of Article 42, except when such request is based on an adjudication of securance of confiscation or collection of equivalent value made by a judge or a court of the requesting country or when such request is made after the adjudication of confiscation or collection of equivalent value has become finally binding, or

2. When there is a request referred to in the preceding paragraph with respect to a criminal case in a foreign country involving an act constituting a drug offence or the like provided for in Paragraph 2 of Article 16 of the Anti-Drug Special Law, not pursuant to any treaty, such assistance may be provided except in cases referred to in Item 8 of the preceding paragraph or in items of Article 21 of the Anti-Drug Special Law.

3. In assisting the execution of a finally-binding adjudication of confiscation of any property on which the superficies hypothec or other right exists, such right shall be left as it stands, if such right is to be left as it stands should such property be confiscated under the laws and regulations of Japan.

Article 60 Confiscation deemed to be collection of equivalent value

When there is a request for assistance in the execution of a finally-binding adjudication of confiscation of any property, in lieu of illicit property or property referred to in items of Paragraph 1 or Paragraph 3 of Article 11 of the Anti-Drug Special Law (hereinafter referred to as "illicit property or the like" in this article) the value of which is equivalent to that of the illicit property or the like and which is held by the person to whom such adjudication is addressed, such finally-binding adjudication shall be deemed to be the finally-binding adjudication to collect equivalent value to such property from such person for the purpose of the implementation of assistance under this Law. The same shall apply to a request for assistance in the execution of a finally-binding adjudication of confiscation of property referred to in items of Paragraph 1 of Article 13 other than immovable property, movable property or money claim, which is held by the person to whom such adjudication is addressed.

2. The provisions of the preceding paragraph shall apply mutatis mutandis to a request for assistance in the securance for the purpose of confiscation of any property, in lieu of illicit property or the like, the value of which is equivalent to that of the illicit property or the like or in the securance for the purpose of confiscation of property referred to in items of Paragraph 1 of Article 13 other than immovable property, movable property or money claim.

Article 61 Receipt of Request

A request for assistance shall be received by the Minister of Foreign Affairs; except that the Minister of Justice shall carry out these tasks when a treaty confers the authority to receive requests for assistance on the Minister of Justice or when the Minister of Foreign Affairs gives consent in an emergency or under other special circumstances.

2. When the Minister of Justice receives a request for assistance pursuant to the proviso of the preceding paragraph, the Minister of Justice may ask the Minister of Foreign Affairs for cooperation necessary for the execution of matters relating to the assistance.

Article 62 Examination by the Court

When a request for assistance is for the execution of a finally-binding adjudication of confiscation or collection of equivalent value, a public prosecutor shall apply to a court for an examination whether such request falls under a case for which assistance may be provided.

2. If an application for the examination proves to be unlawful as the result of such examination, the court shall make a decision to dismiss the application, and if the request falls under a case for which the assistance may be provided with respect to the whole or a part of the finally-binding adjudication concerned or assistance may not be provided with respect to any part of such finally-binding adjudication, the court shall make a decision to such effect respectively.

3. When the court makes a decision that the request falls under a case for which the assistance may be provided in the execution of the finally-binding adjudication of confiscation, the court shall concurrently make a decision that such right shall be left as it stands if there is any right which shall be left as it stands in accordance with the provisions of Paragraph 2 of Article 59.

4. When the court makes a decision that the request falls under a case for which the assistance may be provided in the execution of the finally-binding adjudication of collection of equivalent value the court shall concurrently specify the sum to be collected in Japanese yen.

5. In making the examination provided for in Paragraph 1 of this article, the court may not review whether the finally-binding adjudication concerned is justifiable or not.

6. The court may not make a decision with respect to the examination provided for in Paragraph 1 of this article that the request falls under a case for which the assistance may be provided, unless any person enumerated in the following hereinafter the "interested person" is permitted to intervene in the proceeding of such examination.

    (1) as for assistance in the execution of a finally-binding adjudication of confiscation, any person reasonably deemed to hold the property concerned or the superficies hypothec or other right existing on such property, or the execution creditor or provisional execution creditor if a decision to commence compulsory auction, attachment pursuant to the provisions of compulsory execution or provisional attachment has been made in respect of such property or right before the securance of confiscation is made, or

    (2) as for assistance in the execution of a finally-binding adjudication of collection of equivalent value, any person against whom such adjudication has been made.

7. In making a decision with respect to an application for the examination the court shall hear opinions of the public prosecutor and any person permitted to intervene in the proceeding of the review hereinafter referred to as the ("intervenor").

8. The court shall hold a hearing at a public courtroom and give the intervenor an opportunity to be present at such session, if the intervenor expresses the wish to make an oral presentation of such intervenor's opinion or if the court examines any witness or expert. In such case, the intervenor who is unable to be present shall be deemed to be given an opportunity to be present if such intervenor is given an opportunity to be represented by an attorney at the hearing session or to present such intervenor's opinion in writing.

9. The public prosecutor may be present at the hearing provided for in the preceding paragraph.

Article 63 Kokoku Appeal

The public prosecutor and the intervenor may lodge a kokoku appeal against a decision with respect to the application for the review.

2. A special kokoku appeal may be lodged with the Supreme Court against a decision by a kokoku appeal court if there is a cause provided for in each item of Article 405 of the Code of Criminal Procedure.

3. The period for a kokoku appeal provided for in the preceding two paragraphs shall be fourteen days.

Article 64 Effect of Decision

When a decision that the request falls under a case for which the assistance may be provided in the execution of a finally-binding adjudication of confiscation or collection of equivalent value becomes finally binding, such finally-binding adjudication shall be deemed to be a finally-binding adjudication of confiscation or collection of equivalent value pronounced by a Japanese court for the purpose of the implementation of assistance.

Article 64-2 (Grant of Property, etc., for Execution to the Requesting Country, etc.)

When a foreign country that requests assistance in the execution of a final and unappealable adjudication of confiscation or collection of equivalent value (referred to as the "requesting country for assistance in execution" in paragraph 3) requests for grant of the property or money equivalent to the value thereof pertaining to execution of such assistance (hereinafter in this Article referred to as executed property, etc.), the whole or part of the executed property, etc., may be granted.

2. When the Minister of Justice finds it appropriate to grant the whole or part of executed property, etc., the Minister shall order the Chief Prosecutor of the district public prosecutors office whom the Minister ordered to take necessary measures for assistance in the execution of the final and unappealable adjudication of confiscation or collection of equivalent value to retain such executed property, etc., for the purpose of making the grant.

3. When any executed property, etc., falls under either of the following items, the Minister of Justice may order the Chief Prosecutor prescribed in the preceding paragraph to temporarily retain the whole or part of such executed property, etc.:

    (1) In the event that the requesting country for assistance in execution requests grant of executed property, etc., when the Minister finds it necessary in order to determine whether to accept or decline the request; or

    (2) In the event that the Minister anticipates that the requesting country for assistance in execution will request grant of executed property, etc., when the Minister finds necessary.

Article 65 Revocation of Decision

Upon application by a public prosecutor or an interested person, the court shall, by a decision, revoke its prior decision that the request falls under a case for which the assistance may be provided in the execution of a finally-binding adjudication of confiscation or collection of equivalent value, if such finally-binding adjudication concerned is revoked or otherwise becomes invalid after such prior decision was made.

2. When a decision of revocation provided for in the preceding paragraph becomes finally binding, compensation shall be made pursuant to the provisions for compensation for the execution of confiscation or collection of equivalent value provided for in the Criminal Compensation Law.

3. The provisions of Article 63 shall apply mutatis mutandis to a decision with respect to an application provided for in Paragraph 1 of this article.

Article 66 Request for securance of confiscation

When a request for assistance is for the securance for the purpose of confiscation, a public prosecutor shall apply to a judge for the proscription of disposition of the property concerned with a securance order for confiscation. In such case, the public prosecutor may, if such prosecutor finds it necessary, apply for the proscription of disposition of the superficies hypothec or other right existing on such property with a collateral securance order.

2.   After an application for the examination provided for in Paragraph 1 of Article 62 has been made, disposition concerning securance of confiscation shall be made by the court to which such application for the examination has been made.

Article 67 Request for securance of collection of equivalent value

When a request for assistance is for the securance for the purpose of collection of equivalent value, a public prosecutor shall apply to a judge to proscribe a person, against whom an adjudication for collection of equivalent value is to be made, to dispose of such person's property with a securance order for collection of equivalent value.

2.   The provisions of Paragraph 2 of the preceding article shall apply mutatis mutandis to disposition concerning securance of collection of equivalent value.

Article 68 Duration of securance before the institution of prosecution

When a request for assistance in the execution of securance for the purpose of confiscation or collection of equivalent value is made with respect to a case for which a prosecution has not been instituted, a securance order for confiscation or collection of equivalent value shall become invalid unless it shall be notified from the requesting country within 45 days from the date of issuance of such order that a prosecution has been instituted for such case.

2.   When the requesting country makes a notification containing an explanation that the prosecution may not be instituted within the period provided for in the preceding paragraph for a compelling reason the court may upon application by a public prosecutor renew the duration of the securance not more than thirty days. The same shall apply when a notification is made with an explanation that the prosecution may not be instituted within the renewed period for a certain cause beyond the control of the requesting country.

Article 69 Revocation of procedures

When there is a notification to withdraw the request for assistance, a public prosecutor shall promptly revoke the application for the examination or for securance of confiscation or collection of equivalent value, or apply for the revocation of the securance order for confiscation or collection of equivalent value.

2.   When the application provided for in the preceding paragraph is made, the court or the judge shall promptly revoke the securance order for confiscation or collection of equivalent value.

Article 70 Examination of facts

When it is necessary for the examination or disposition concerning securance of confiscation or collection of equivalent value under the provisions of this chapter, a court or a judge may examine the facts. In such case, the court or the judge may examine a witness, carry out inspection, or order an expert examination, interpreting or translation.

Article 71 Disposition by public prosecutor

When a public prosecutor deems it necessary for an application for the securance of confiscation or collection of equivalent value or for the execution of a securance order for confiscation or collection of equivalent value under the provisions of the chapter, the public prosecutor may request the appearance of any person concerned and interrogate such person, request an expert to make an examination, carry out voluntary inspection, request the owner, possessor or custodian of any document or other thing to submit it, request a public office or a public or private organization to make reports on necessary matters, or carry out seizure, search or inspection upon a warrant issued by a judge.

2. The public prosecutor may have a public prosecutor's assistant officer make any disposition provided for in the preceding paragraph.

Article 72 Jurisdiction of court

Any application for the examination, for the securance of confiscation or collection of equivalent value or for the issuance of a warrant under the provisions of this chapter shall be made to a court or a judge having jurisdiction over the place where a public prosecutors office to which the public prosecutor making such application belongs is located.

KAZAKHSTAN

Criminal Procedure Code
Chapter 62. Recognition and enforcement of judgments and decisions of foreign courts

Article 601. Judgments and decisions of foreign courts, recognized in the Republic of Kazakhstan

1. In accordance with the procedure provided by this Code and the international treaties of the Republic of Kazakhstan, the judgments and decisions of foreign courts may be recognized and enforced in the Republic of Kazakhstan in the following cases:

   1) upon receipt of a citizen of the Republic of Kazakhstan, who was convicted to imprisonment in a foreign state for serving the sentence;

   2) upon receipt of a citizen of the Republic of Kazakhstan, who committed in a foreign state a socially dangerous act in a state of insanity, for which there is a court decision of a foreign state on the application to him (her) of compulsory medical measures, for compulsory treatment;

3) in respect of a person, extradited to the Republic of Kazakhstan, who was convicted by a foreign court and did not serve the sentence;

4) in respect of a person, convicted by a foreign court, and the Republic of Kazakhstan refused the extradition (extradition) of which to a foreign state;

5) when deciding on the confiscation of property located on the territory of the Republic of Kazakhstan, or its monetary equivalent;

6) other cases stipulated by the international treaties of the Republic of Kazakhstan.

2. The decision on the recognition and enforcement of the judgment of the foreign courts in a part of the civil claim shall be resolved in accordance with the Civil Procedure Code of the Republic of Kazakhstan.

Article 607. Consideration of an application for admission of a citizen of the Republic of Kazakhstan to serve the sentence or carrying out compulsory treatment, as well as the recognition and enforcement of the sentence or decision of the foreign court

1. The citizens of the Republic of Kazakhstan, referred to in Article 602 of this Code, their legal representatives or close relatives, as well as the competent authorities of a foreign state with the consent of the convicted person or the person, applied to the compulsory medical measures, and in case of his (her) inability to free will—with the consent of his (her) legal representative may apply to the Procurator General of the Republic of Kazakhstan with the request of serving by the convicted person of a sentence or compulsory treatment in the Republic of Kazakhstan.

2. The competent institution of a foreign state may apply to the Procurator General of the Republic of Kazakhstan with the request for the recognition and enforcement of the sentence or decision of a foreign court in relation to the persons, referred to in paragraphs 3) and 4) of the first part of Article 601 of this Code, as well as the judicial acts providing for the confiscation of property, located on the territory of the Republic of Kazakhstan or its cash equivalent.

3. After the request to the Procurator General of the Republic of Kazakhstan for admission of the citizens of the Republic of Kazakhstan referred to in Article 602 of this Code, for further punishment or compulsory treatment in the Republic of Kazakhstan and confirmation of the citizenship of the Republic of Kazakhstan of that person, the General Procurator's Office of the Republic of Kazakhstan requests from the appropriate authority of a foreign state the documents required for resolving the issue on its merits.

4. In the case of approval of the requests, provided for in the first, second parts of this Article, the Procurator General of the Republic of Kazakhstan shall submit a representation on the recognition and enforcement of the sentence or decision of a foreign court to the district or equivalent court in the place of residence of persons against whom the sentence or decision of a foreign court is made. In the absence of these persons permanent residence, the representation shall be made to the district court at the location of the General Procurator's Office of the Republic of Kazakhstan.

Article 608. The order for resolving by the court the issues, related to the execution of the sentence or decision of a foreign court

1. The representation of the Procurator General of the Republic of Kazakhstan is considered by the judge at the hearing in the absence of the convicted person or the person, applied to the compulsory medical measures, in the manner and within the timeframe established by this Code for resolving the issues related to the execution of the sentence.

2. The decision of the judge on the execution of the sentence or decision of a foreign court shall indicate:

    1) the name of the court of a foreign state, the time and place of sentencing or ruling on the application of compulsory medical measures;

    2) the information about the last place of residence in the Republic of Kazakhstan of the convicted person or the person, applied to the compulsory medical measures, the place of work and occupation before the conviction or the application of compulsory medical measures;

    3) the qualification of the criminal offence, in the commission of which the person is found guilty, and on the basis of which criminal law he (she) is convicted or the compulsory medical measures are applied;

    4) the Criminal law of the Republic of Kazakhstan providing for the liability for a criminal offence, committed by the convicted person or the person, applied to the compulsory medical measures;

    5) the type and term of the punishment (primary and secondary), the start date and the end of the punishment, which the convicted person shall serve in the Republic of Kazakhstan; the type of penal institution, the order of compensation for the claim; the kind of compulsory medical measures, which shall apply in relation to a person in compulsory treatment.

3. If under the law of the Republic of Kazakhstan the time limit of imprisonment for this crime is less than fixed by the sentence of the foreign court, the judge shall determine the maximum term of imprisonment for the commission of the offence under the Criminal Code of the Republic of Kazakhstan. If the imprisonment is not provided as a punishment, the judge shall determine another punishment within the proportion established by the Criminal Code of the Republic of Kazakhstan for this criminal offence and most relevant to the fixed by the sentence of the foreign court.

4. If the sentence relates to two or more acts, not all of which are recognized as crimes in the Republic of Kazakhstan, the judge shall determine what part of the punishment imposed by the sentence of the foreign court, applies to the act that constitutes a crime.

5. When considering the issue of execution of the punishment, the court may at the same time decide on the execution of the sentence of the foreign court in part of the civil claim and procedural costs if there is a corresponding request.

6. In case of cancellation or changes in the sentence or decision of the foreign court or the use of amnesty or pardon, issued in a foreign state or in the Republic of Kazakhstan, to the person serving the punishment or undergoing compulsory treatment in the Republic of Kazakhstan, the issues of

execution of the revised sentence or decision of the court, as well as the use of amnesty or pardon shall be resolved by the rules of this Article.

7. If when considering the representation of the Procurator General of the Republic of Kazakhstan, the court concludes that the act for which the person is convicted or applied to the compulsory medical measures, is not a crime under the legislation of the Republic of Kazakhstan, or the sentence or the decision of the foreign court may not be executed due to the expiration of the statute of limitations, as well as on other grounds stipulated by the legislation of the Republic of Kazakhstan or international treaties of the Republic of Kazakhstan, he (she) shall make a decision to refuse to recognize the sentence or decision of the foreign court.

8. The decision of the court may be appealed or protested in the manner and terms, established by this Code for the revision of the court decision, which entered into force.

Article 610. Notification of change or cancellation of the sentence or decision of the foreign court

1. Any issues, relating to the revision of the sentence or decision of the foreign court shall be settled by the court of the state, where the sentence or decision is made.

2. In case of change or cancellation of the sentence or decision of the foreign court, the issue of execution of this decision is considered in the manner provided by this Code.

3. If the sentence or decision of the foreign court is canceled, and a new pre-trial investigation or a new trial is assigned, the issue of the subsequent criminal proceedings shall be decided by the General Procurator's Office of the Republic of Kazakhstan in accordance with this Code.

LATVIA

[The following excerpts reflect the status of Latvian legislation in October 2020.]

Criminal Procedure Law

Division Sixteen
Recognition of Judgments of a Foreign State and Execution of Punishments

Chapter 69
General Provisions for the Execution in Latvia of a Punishment Imposed in a Foreign State

Section 749. Content of the Execution of a Punishment Imposed in a Foreign State

(1) Execution of a punishment imposed in a foreign state shall be the recognition of the validity and lawfulness of such punishment on an uncontested basis and execution according to the same procedures as in case where the punishment would have been specified in criminal proceedings taking place in Latvia.

(2) Recognition of the validity and lawfulness of a punishment imposed in a foreign state shall not preclude the co-ordination thereof with the sanction provided for in The Criminal Law for the same offence.

Section 750. Conditions for the Execution of a Punishment Imposed in a Foreign State

(1) Execution of a punishment imposed in a foreign state shall be possible if:

1) the foreign state has submitted a request regarding the execution of the punishment imposed therein;

2) the punishment in the foreign state has been specified by an adjudication that has entered into effect in terminated criminal proceedings;

3) the limitation period has not set it for the execution of the punishment in the foreign state or Latvia;

4) the person convicted in the foreign state is a Latvian citizen or his or her permanent place of residence is in Latvia, or he or she is serving a punishment related to deprivation of liberty in Latvia and has been convicted with deprivation of liberty or arrest in a foreign state, which could be executed right after serving of the punishment imposed in Latvia;

5) the foreign state would not be able to execute the punishment, even by requesting extradition of the person;

6) execution of the punishment of Latvia would promote resocialization of the person convicted in the foreign state.

(2) Execution of a fine or confiscation of property imposed in a foreign state shall be possible also if the person convicted in the foreign state owns a property or has other income in Latvia.

Section 751. Reasons for Refusal of the Execution in Latvia of a Punishment Imposed in a Foreign State

A request regarding the execution of a punishment imposed in a foreign state may be refused if:

1) there is a reason to believe that the punishment has been imposed because of race, religious affiliation, nationality, gender or political views of the person, or if the offence may be deemed political or military;

2) execution of the punishment would be in contradiction with international commitments of Latvia to another state;

3) execution of the punishment may harm the sovereignty, security, public order or other essential interests of the State of Latvia;

4) a person convicted in a foreign state for the same offence could not be punished in accordance with The Criminal Law;

5) execution of the punishment would be in contradiction with the basic principles of the legal system of Latvia;

6) criminal proceedings regarding the same offence, for which a punishment has been imposed in a foreign state, are taking place in Latvia;

7) execution of the punishment in Latvia is not possible;

8) the offence has not been committed in the foreign state, which imposed the punishment to be executed;

9) expenditure for execution of the punishment are not commensurate with the seriousness of and harm caused by the criminal offence;

10) the foreign state itself is able to execute the judgment;

11) Latvia does not have a contract with the foreign state regarding the execution of punishments imposed in another state.

Section 752. Time Limitations for Execution of a Punishment

(1) Execution of a punishment imposed in a foreign state shall be limited by both the time limitations for the execution of a punishment provided for in The Criminal Law and the time limitations for the execution of a punishment provided for in laws of the relevant foreign state.

(2) Circumstances affecting the running of limitation periods in a foreign state shall also affect it to the same extent in Latvia.

Section 753. Inadmissibility of Double Trial

A punishment imposed in a foreign state shall not be executed in Latvia, if a person convicted in the foreign state has served a punishment imposed in Latvia or a third country for the same offence, has been convicted without determination of a punishment, has been released by amnesty or clemency or has been acquitted for the same offence.

Section 754. Procedures for Examination of a Request Regarding Execution of a Punishment Imposed in a Foreign State

(1) Having received a request of a foreign state regarding the execution of a punishment imposed therein, the Ministry of Justice shall, within 10 days, but if the amount of materials is particularly large within 30 days, verify whether all the necessary materials have been received.

(2) If translation of documents is necessary, verification of a request of a foreign state shall take place within the time periods referred to in Paragraph one of this Section after receipt of translation.

(3) If several requests of foreign states regarding the execution of a punishment imposed in such foreign states in relation to the same person or property have been received concurrently, the Ministry of Justice shall combine the verification of such requests in one process.

(4) Upon a request verification materials shall be sent to a district (city) court for taking of a decision on recognition of the judgment of a foreign state and execution of a punishment in Latvia. The request shall be examined by a judge according to the place of residence of a convicted person in a foreign state. If the place of residence of the person is unknown, the request of the foreign state shall be examined by a judge of a district (city) court according to the location of the Ministry of Justice.

(5) If information provided by the foreign state is insufficient, the Ministry of Justice or a court with the intermediation of the Ministry of Justice may request additional information or documents, specifying a deadline for the submission thereof.

Section 755. Examination of a Request Regarding Execution of a Punishment Imposed in a Foreign State in the Absence of a Person (in absentia)

(1) If a judgment has been rendered in a foreign state, except a European Union Member State, in the absence of a person (in absentia) and Latvia has a contract with the foreign state regarding the execution of a punishment imposed in the absence of a person (in absentia), prior to taking a decision on recognition of a judgment of a foreign state and execution of a punishment in Latvia a court shall issue a notification to the person convicted in the relevant foreign state, indicating that:

   1) the request regarding the execution of a punishment has been submitted by a foreign state, with which Latvia has a contract regarding the execution of a punishment imposed in the absence of a person (in absentia);

   2) the person convicted in the foreign state has the right, within 30 days from the day of receipt of the notification, to submit an application regarding examination in his or her presence in the relevant foreign state or Latvia of the case adjudicated in his or her absence (in absentia);

   3) the punishment will be conformed and executed in accordance with general procedures, if examination of the case in the presence of the person convicted in the foreign state or Latvia is not requested within 30 days or if the application is rejected due to nonarrival of the person.

(2) The person shall submit the application provided for in Paragraph one of this Section to a court. If the state of examination has not been indicated in the application, it shall be examined in Latvia.

(3) The Ministry of Justice shall send a copy of the notification to the relevant state with a note regarding issuance of the notification to the person convicted in the foreign state.

Section 756. Submission of an Application of a Person Convicted in a Foreign State in his or her Absence (in absentia) to the Relevant Foreign State

(1) If a person convicted in a foreign state in his or her absence (in absentia) submits an application within the specified deadline, requesting re-examination of the case in his or her presence in the foreign state, which imposed the punishment, a court shall postpone examination of the request of such state regarding the execution of a punishment.

(2) If the application referred to in Paragraph one of this Section has been cancelled, recognised invalid or unacceptable, a court shall, after receipt of information, examine a request regarding the execution of a punishment imposed in the relevant foreign state according to the same procedures as if the case was examined in the presence of the person.

(3) If as a result of examining the application a judgment of conviction is repealed, a court with the intermediation of the Ministry of Justice shall send the request of the foreign state regarding the execution of a punishment undecided to the requesting state.

(4) If the person convicted in a foreign state in his or her absence (in absentia) is under temporary arrest upon the request of the foreign state, such person shall be transferred to the relevant foreign state for examination of an application in his or her presence. In such case the state which imposed the

punishment shall decide on the matter of further holding under arrest of such person.

(5) If the person convicted in a foreign state in his or her absence (in absentia) who has submitted an application to the state which imposed the punishment has been placed under arrest due to other criminal proceedings or is serving a punishment for another offence, a court with the intermediation of the Ministry of Justice shall inform the foreign state thereof and assign the State Police to co-ordinate the time when the person may be transferred to the relevant foreign state for participation in examination of the application.

(6) If the law of the foreign state allows it, the person convicted in such foreign state in his or her absence (in absentia) may participate in examination of the application, using technical means. Participation, using technical means, shall not affect the procedural rights of the person convicted in the foreign state in the process taking place in such foreign state. If the person has invited an advocate of the foreign state for receipt of legal assistance, the advocate has the right to meet with the person in confidential conditions in Latvia and to participate in examination of the application, using technical means, together with the client.

(7) Invitation of an advocate of the foreign state shall not affect the right of the person convicted in such foreign state in his or her absence (in absentia) to legal assistance in Latvia.

Section 757. Submission of an Application of a Person Convicted in a Foreign State in his or her Absence (in absentia) to Latvia and Procedures for Examination Thereof

(1) If a person convicted in a foreign state in his or her absence (in absentia) requests examination of an application in a court of Latvia, the Ministry of Justice shall, without delay after receipt of information from the court, inform the relevant foreign state thereof.

(2) A summons to a court in a foreign state shall be issued to the person convicted in the foreign state in his or her absence (in absentia) not more than 21 days prior to the day of examination of the application, unless such person has expressed an explicit consent for the application of a shorter period of time.

(3) As a result of examination a court shall take one of the following decisions:
   1) on rejection of the application due to non-arrival of the person and recognition of the judgment of the foreign state and execution of the punishment in Latvia;
   2) on allowing the application of the person convicted in the foreign state in his or her absence (in absentia).

(4) Having taken the decision referred to in Paragraph three, Clause 2 of this Section, a court shall send it to the Ministry of Justice, which shall request the foreign state to send the necessary materials related to adjudication of the offence at the disposal of the foreign state, specifying the deadline by which materials should be sent. Having received the materials of the foreign state, the Ministry of Justice shall ensure their translation and assess

them in accordance with the conditions and procedures referred to in Chapter 67 of this Law. If the person is placed under temporary arrest, the procedural time periods referred to in Section 732 of this Law shall be applied.

(5) The evidence obtained in accordance with the procedures specified in the foreign state shall be assessed in the same way as the evidence obtained in Latvia.

Section 759. Recognition and Execution of a Punishment Imposed in a Foreign State

(1) A judge of a district (city) court shall, within 30 days, examine a request of a foreign state regarding the execution of a punishment imposed in the foreign state in a written procedure and, after evaluating the conditions and reasons for refusal, take one of the following decisions:

1) on consent to recognise the judgment and execute the punishment imposed in the foreign state;

2) on refusal to recognise the judgment and execute the punishment imposed in the foreign state.

(2) If an adjudication of a foreign state applies to two or more offences, not all of which are offences, for which execution of the punishment is possible in Latvia, a judge shall request to specify more precisely, which part of the punishment applies to offences conforming to such requirements.

(3) The decision referred to in Paragraph one of this Section shall not be subject to appeal, and a judge shall notify the decision taken to the person convicted in the foreign state and with the intermediation of the Ministry of Justice—to the foreign state and the person convicted therein, if he or she is in the foreign state.

Section 760. Determination of a Punishment to be Executed in Latvia

(1) After taking of the decision referred to in Section 759, Paragraph one, Clause 1 of this Law a judge shall determine a punishment to be executed in Latvia in a written procedure, if a person convicted in a foreign state and a public prosecutor does not object thereto.

(2) The factual circumstances established in a court adjudication of a foreign state and the guilt of a person shall be binding to a court of Latvia.

(3) The punishment determined in Latvia shall not deteriorate the condition of a person convicted in a foreign state, however, it shall conform to the punishment determined in the relevant foreign state as much as possible.

(4) Concurrently with a notification regarding the decision referred to in Section 759, Paragraph one, Clause 1 of this Law a judge shall inform a person convicted in a foreign state and a public prosecutor regarding the right, within 10 days from the day of receipt of the notification, to submit objections against the determination of the punishment to be executed in Latvia in a written procedure, to submit recusation for a judge, to submit an opinion on the punishment to be executed in Latvia, as well as on the day of availability of the decision.

(5) If a person convicted in a foreign state is serving a punishment of deprivation of liberty in the state that submitted the request, the relevant person shall be informed regarding the right referred to in Paragraph four of this Section immediately after transfer thereof to Latvia.

(6) If a person convicted in a foreign state or a public prosecutor has submitted objections against the determination of the punishment to be executed in Latvia in a written procedure, a judge shall take a decision in accordance with the procedures of Section 651 of this Law. If a person convicted in a foreign state is under arrest in the foreign state or is serving a punishment of deprivation of liberty in the relevant foreign state, and an issue on determination of the punishment to be executed in Latvia, which is not related to deprivation of liberty, is being decided, technical means shall be used for ensuring of the participation or temporary transfer of the person to Latvia shall be requested.

(7) A person convicted in a foreign state or a public prosecutor may appeal a decision of a judge on determination of the punishment to be executed in Latvia to the Senate of the Supreme Court within 10 days from the day of availability of the decision in accordance with cassation procedures.

(8) A complaint shall be examined according to the same procedures as a cassation complaint or protest submitted in criminal proceedings taking place in Latvia, and in such extent as allowed by the international agreements binding to Latvia and this Chapter.

(9) If a decision of a judge on determination of the punishment to be executed in Latvia has not been appealed within the time period specified in Law or a decision has been appealed and the Senate of the Supreme Court has left it in effect, the decision shall be executed in accordance with the procedures referred to in Section 634 of this Law. The request of a foreign state shall be appended to the decision.

Section 761. Compliance with a Foreign State Judgment in Criminal Proceedings Taking Place in Latvia

(1) In determining a punishment in criminal proceedings taking place in Latvia to a person, in relation to whom a foreign state has requested to execute the punishment in Latvia, the punishment to be executed in Latvia shall be added to the punishment imposed in the foreign state according to the norms of The Criminal Law regarding determination of a punishment after several adjudications.

(2) When classifying offences according to The Criminal Law, an offence, for which the punishment imposed in the foreign state is being executed, shall have the same significance as an offence examined in criminal proceedings taking place in Latvia.

Section 762. Legal Consequences Caused by the Execution in Latvia of a Punishment Imposed in a Foreign State

(1) Execution of a punishment, which has been imposed in a foreign state, determined for execution in Latvia shall take place according to the same procedures as execution of the punishment imposed in criminal proceedings that have taken place in Latvia.

(2) Clemency and amnesty acts adopted in Latvia and conditions of early conditional release, as well as decisions of the relevant foreign state on reduction of the punishment, amnesty or clemency shall apply to a person.

(3) Only the state in which the judgment was rendered has the right to re-examine the judgment.

(4) Execution of a punishment shall be discontinued and a request of a foreign state regarding the execution of a punishment shall be cancelled by a decision taken in the relevant foreign state on revocation of a judgment of conviction.

(5) A notification of a foreign state on the legal facts provided for in Paragraphs two and four of this Section shall be received and its execution shall be organised by the Ministry of Justice. If a decision of a foreign state contains an unequivocal information regarding immediate termination of the execution of a punishment or the final date, it shall be transferred to the institution executing the punishment and in other cases—for examination in a court, which shall take a decision on matters related to execution of the judgment.

(6) A person who is serving a punishment related to deprivation of liberty shall be released without delay as soon as information regarding revocation of the judgment of conviction is received, if concurrently a request of a foreign state for application of temporary arrest has not been received in the cases provided for in this Section.

Section 763. Notifications of the Ministry of Justice to a Foreign State

(1) The Ministry of Justice shall notify a foreign state that a request thereof regarding the execution of a punishment applied in the foreign state has been forwarded to a district (city) court.

(2) After receipt of a notification of a court the Ministry of Justice shall notify the relevant foreign state regarding:
    1) a decision to recognise the judgment and to execute the punishment imposed in the foreign state;
    2) a refusal to recognise the judgment and to execute the punishment imposed in the foreign state;
    3) a decision on determination of the punishment to be executed in Latvia;
    4) an amnesty and clemency decision;
    5) completion of execution of the punishment;
    6) if the foreign state has requested a special report.

(3) In relation to an adjudication rendered in the foreign state, by which the punishment of deprivation of liberty has been imposed, the Ministry of Justice shall, in addition to the notifications referred to in Paragraphs one and two of this Section, also inform the relevant foreign state regarding:
    1) the beginning and the end of the early conditional release term, if the state that rendered the judgment has requested it;
    2) regarding the escape of the convicted person from prison.

(4) In relation to an adjudication rendered in the foreign state, by which a fine has been imposed, the Ministry of Justice shall, in addition to the notifications referred to in Paragraphs one and two of this Section, also inform the relevant foreign state regarding:

1) substitution of the fine;

2) inability to execute the adjudication.

(5) In relation to an adjudication rendered in the foreign state, by which confiscation of property has been applied, the Ministry of Justice shall, in addition to the notifications referred to in Paragraphs one and two of this Section, also inform the relevant foreign state regarding:

1) a decision on impossibility of execution of the confiscation of property.

2) a decision on complete or partial non-execution of the confiscation of property.

(6) In relation to an adjudication rendered in the foreign state, by which an alternative sanction has been applied, the Ministry of Justice shall, in addition to the notifications referred to in Paragraphs one and two of this Section, also inform the relevant European Union Member State regarding determination of an alternative sanction, if it does not conform to the alternative sanction specified in the relevant European Union Member State.

Chapter 74
Execution in Latvia of a Confiscation of Property Applied in a Foreign State

Section 790. Principles for the Assessment of a Confiscation of Property Applied in a Foreign State

The procedures referred to in Chapter 69 of this Law shall be applied to the assessment of a request of a foreign state regarding the execution of a confiscation of property, if it has not been specified otherwise in this Chapter.

Section 791. Determination of a Confiscation of Property to be Executed in Latvia

(1) A confiscation of property to be executed in Latvia shall be determined, if such confiscation has been imposed in a foreign state and if The Criminal Law provides for such confiscation as a basic punishment or additional punishment regarding the same offence, or if property would be confiscated in criminal proceedings taking place in Latvia on grounds provided for in another law.

(2) If a judgment of a foreign state provides for the confiscation of property, but The Criminal Law does not provide for the confiscation of property as a basic punishment or additional punishment, confiscation shall be applied only in the amount established in the judgment of the foreign state, that the object to be confiscated is an instrumentality of the committing of the offence or has been obtained by criminal means.

(3) The amount of a confiscation of property imposed in a foreign state, if an adjudication has been rendered regarding a certain amount of money, shall be calculated according to the currency exchange rate specified by the Bank

of Latvia which was in force on the day of proclamation of the judgment of conviction.

(4) If several adjudications have been received concurrently regarding the confiscation of property in respect of an amount of money and these adjudications have been issued in respect of one person who does not have sufficient resources in Latvia to execute all the adjudications, or several adjudications have been received concurrently regarding the confiscation of property in respect of a certain part of property, a court shall take a decision on which of the adjudications will be executed, taking into account:

1) the severity of a criminal offence;

2) attachment imposed on the property;

3) succession in which adjudications regarding the confiscation of property have been received in Latvia.

Section 792. Conditions in Respect of the Division of Money or Property Acquired as a Result of a Confiscation of Property with Foreign States

(1) A request regarding the division of money or property acquired as a result of a confiscation of property shall be decided by the Ministry of Justice in each particular case.

(2) In examining a request regarding division of money acquired as a result of a confiscation of property, the amount of money acquired, the harm caused by a criminal offence and location of victims shall be taken into account.

(3) If the money obtained as a result of confiscation of property does not exceed the equivalent of EUR 10000 in lats (recalculating in accordance with the currency exchange rate specified by the Bank of Latvia which was in effect on the day of the announcement of the adjudication regarding the confiscation of property), the Ministry of Justice shall take a decision on refusal to transfer the money to a foreign state. If the money obtained as a result of confiscation of property exceeds the equivalent of EUR 10 000 in lats (recalculating in accordance with the currency exchange rate specified by the Bank of Latvia which was in effect on the day of the announcement of the adjudication regarding the confiscation of property), the Ministry of Justice, upon consulting with a foreign state, shall take a decision to transfer to the foreign state not more than half of the money or the amounts specified in a request of the foreign state.

(4) The Ministry of Justice, upon consulting with a foreign state, may take a decision on different division of the money, which has not been referred to in Paragraph three of this Section and which does not harm the financial interests of Latvia. The conditions of Paragraph two of this Section shall be taken into account in consultations.

(5) Upon the request of a foreign state the Ministry of Justice may take a decision on return of the property acquired as a result of a confiscation of property to the foreign state.

(6) The Ministry of Justice shall refuse a request regarding the division of money or property acquired as a result of a confiscation of property, if the request is received after one year from the day of sending of a notification

regarding the execution of the adjudication regarding a confiscation of property.

(7) The Cabinet shall determine the procedures by which money or property acquired as a result of a confiscation of property shall be divided with foreign states and the procedures by which money shall be transferred, as well as the criteria for the division of money or property.

LEBANON

Penal code

Article 29

Sentences imposed by foreign criminal courts in respect of acts characterized as felonies or misdemeanours by Lebanese law may be invoked:

1. With a view to the enforcement of preventive measures and the measures of incapacity and extinguishment of rights resulting therefrom, provided that they are in conformity with Lebanese law, and the enforcement of awards of restitution, damages and other civil awards;

2. With a view to imposing sentences pursuant to Lebanese law in respect of preventive measures and measures of incapacity and extinguishment of rights, comprising awards of restitution, damages and other civil awards;

3. With a view to applying the provisions of Lebanese law concerning recidivism, habitual criminal conduct, plurality of offences, stay of execution and rehabilitation.

The Lebanese judge shall assess the validity of the foreign sentence in procedural and substantive terms in the light of the documents in the case file.

NEW ZEALAND

Mutual Assistance in Criminal Matters Act 1992
Requests to enforce foreign restraining orders and foreign forfeiture orders

54 Request to enforce foreign restraining order

(1) A foreign country may request the Attorney-General to assist in enforcing a foreign restraining order that relates to property that is believed to be located in New Zealand.

(2) The Attorney-General may authorise the Commissioner to apply to the High Court to register a foreign restraining order in New Zealand if satisfied—

   (a) that the request from the foreign country relates to—

      (i) tainted property (as defined in relation to Part 3); or

      (ii) property of a person who has unlawfully benefited from significant foreign criminal activity; or

(iii) an instrument of crime (as defined in relation to Part 3); or

(iv) property that will satisfy some or all of a foreign pecuniary penalty order; and

(b) that there are reasonable grounds to believe some or all of the property that is able to be restrained under the foreign restraining order is located in New Zealand.

(3) An authority issued under subsection (2) must be in writing.

55 Request to enforce foreign forfeiture order

(1) A foreign country may request the Attorney-General to assist in enforcing a foreign forfeiture order that relates to property that is reasonably believed to be located in New Zealand.

(2) The Attorney-General may authorise the Commissioner to apply to the High Court to register the foreign forfeiture order in New Zealand if satisfied—

(a) that the request from the foreign country relates to property that may be forfeited under the foreign forfeiture order and is specific property that—

(i) is tainted property (as defined in relation to Part 3); or

(ii) belongs to a person who has unlawfully benefited from significant foreign criminal activity; or

(iii) is an instrument of crime (as defined in relation to Part 3); or

(iv) will satisfy some or all of a foreign pecuniary penalty order; and

(b) that there are reasonable grounds to believe that some or all of the property to which the order relates is located in New Zealand.

(3) An authority issued under subsection (2) must be in writing.

56 Method for registering foreign orders in New Zealand

(1) If the High Court is satisfied that a foreign order that the Commissioner has applied to register under section 54 or 55 is in force in a foreign country, the High Court must make an order that it be registered in New Zealand.

(3) A foreign order, or an amendment to a foreign order (an amendment), may be registered in the High Court in New Zealand by registering either of the following under the prescribed procedure:

(a) a copy of the foreign order or amendment sealed by the court or other judicial authority who made it; or

(b) a copy of the foreign order or amendment authenticated in accordance with section 63.

(4) A copy of an amendment (whether made before or after registration) may be registered in the same way as a foreign order.

(5) A foreign order or an amendment to a foreign order does not have effect under this Act or the Criminal Proceeds (Recovery) Act 2009 until it is registered.

(6) An exact copy of a sealed or authenticated copy of a foreign order or an amendment must for the purposes of this Act be treated as if it is the sealed or authenticated copy.

(7) However, registration of an exact copy ceases to have effect on the expiry of the period of 21 days commencing on the date of registration unless, before the expiry of that period, the sealed or authenticated copy is registered.

57 Effect of registering foreign orders in New Zealand

(1) A foreign restraining order registered in New Zealand under section 56 has effect, and may be enforced, as if it is a restraining order—

    (a) made by the High Court under the Criminal Proceeds (Recovery) Act 2009; and

    (b) entered on the date it is registered.

(2) Subsection (1) is subject to sections 136 to 139 of the Criminal Proceeds (Recovery) Act 2009.

(3) A foreign forfeiture order registered in New Zealand under section 56 has effect, and may be enforced, as if it is a forfeiture order—

    (a) made by the High Court under the Criminal Proceeds (Recovery) Act 2009; and

    (b) entered on the date it is registered.

(4) Subsection (3) is subject to sections 140 to 149 of the Criminal Proceeds (Recovery) Act 2009.

Section 57: substituted, on 1 December 2009, by section 10 of the Mutual Assistance in Criminal Matters Amendment Act 2009 (2009 No 9).

58 Cancelling registration of foreign orders in New Zealand

(1) The Attorney-General may at any time direct the Commissioner to apply to the High Court to cancel the registration in New Zealand of—

    (a) a foreign restraining order; or

    (b) a foreign forfeiture order.

(2) Without limiting subsection (1), the Attorney-General may give a direction of that kind if the Attorney-General is satisfied—

    (a) that the order has, since being registered in New Zealand, ceased to have effect in the foreign country in which it was made; or

    (b) that cancelling the order is appropriate having regard to arrangements entered into between New Zealand and the foreign country in relation to the enforcing of orders of that kind; or

    (c) that the registration of the order in New Zealand contravened section 56; or

    (d) [Repealed]

    (e) that, after consultation with the foreign country where the order was made, it is desirable that the registration of the foreign order be cancelled; or

    (f) that the foreign order has been discharged, wholly or in part.

(3) The High Court must cancel the registration of a foreign order in New Zealand if the Commissioner applies, under a direction under subsection (1), to the High Court to cancel the registration.

60 Interim foreign restraining order

(1) A foreign country may request the Attorney-General to obtain the issue of an interim foreign restraining order in respect of property that is believed to be located in New Zealand.

(2) After a request is made, the Attorney-General may authorise the Commissioner to make an application under section 128 of the Criminal Proceeds (Recovery) Act 2009 for an interim foreign restraining order if the Attorney-General is satisfied that—

(a) there is a criminal investigation in relation to—

(i) tainted property (as defined in relation to Part 3); or

(ii) property that belongs to a person who has unlawfully benefited from significant foreign criminal activity; or

(iii) an instrument of crime (as defined in relation to Part 3); or

(iv) property that will satisfy some or all of a foreign pecuniary penalty order; and

(b) there are reasonable grounds to believe all or part of the property to which the criminal investigation relates is located in New Zealand.

Criminal Proceeds (Recovery) Act 2009

Subpart 8—Foreign restraining orders and foreign forfeiture orders

Interim foreign restraining orders

128 Interim foreign restraining order

(1) The Commissioner may apply for an interim foreign restraining order if authorised by the Attorney-General under section 60 of the Mutual Assistance in Criminal Matters Act 1992.

(2) An application under subsection (1) is an application made without notice.

(3) Subpart 2 of Part 2 (except sections 21, 22(1), and 37 to 42) applies to an application made under subsection (1)—

(a) with any necessary modifications:

(b) without limiting paragraph (a), with the following specific modifications:

(i) a reference to significant criminal activity must be read as a reference to significant foreign criminal activity:

(ii) the reference in section 28(2) to a respondent's legal expenses must be read as including a reference to a person's expenses in defending allegations of the commission of significant foreign criminal activity in a foreign country.

(4) An interim foreign restraining order is to be treated in all respects (other than under sections 37 to 42) as if it were a restraining order.

(5) This section applies, with any necessary modifications, to an application for a restraining order made under section 112 of the International Crimes and International Criminal Court Act 2000.

129 Expiry of interim foreign restraining orders

(1) An interim foreign restraining order expires when the earlier of the following occurs:

    (a) the date is reached that is the end of 28 days (commencing on the day on which the order is made):

    (b) a foreign restraining order relating to some or all of the property to which the interim foreign restraining order relates is registered in New Zealand.

(2) Despite subsection (1), if the duration of an interim foreign restraining order is extended by a court, the interim foreign restraining order expires on the date specified by the court under section 130.

130 Extending duration of interim foreign restraining order

(1) If a court has made an interim foreign restraining order, the applicant for that order may, before the interim foreign restraining order expires, apply to that court to extend its duration.

(2) If an application is made under subsection (1), the court may order that the interim foreign restraining order be extended for a period not exceeding 3 months.

(3) The duration of an interim foreign restraining order may be extended more than once under this section.

(4) If, before an interim foreign restraining order would otherwise expire under section 129(1), an application is made to a court under this section and the application is granted, the interim foreign restraining order ceases to be in force on the date specified in the court's order, unless it is further extended on an application under this section.

131 Additional matters relating to extending duration of interim foreign restraining order

(1) On making an order under section 130, the court may vary the interim foreign restraining order in any way it considers fit, including, without limitation, by specifying whether all or part of the property is to remain subject to the interim foreign restraining order during the extended period of operation.

(2) An applicant for an order under section 130 must serve, so far as is practicable, a copy of the application on any person who, to the knowledge of the applicant, has an interest in the property that is the subject of the application.

Registering foreign restraining orders

132 Who may apply to register foreign restraining order

The Commissioner may apply to register a foreign restraining order in New Zealand if authorised by the Attorney-General under section 54 of the Mutual Assistance in Criminal Matters Act 1992.

133 Application to register foreign restraining order made to High Court

If authorised to register a foreign restraining order in New Zealand under section 54 of the Mutual Assistance in Criminal Matters Act 1992, the Commissioner may apply to the High Court.

134 Provisions of subpart 2 of Part 2 applying to registering foreign restraining orders

(1) The following sections of subpart 2 of Part 2 apply, with all necessary modifications, if an application is made to register a foreign restraining order in New Zealand under section 54 of the Mutual Assistance in Criminal Matters Act 1992 or an application is made to register a restraining order under section 112(2) of the International Crimes and International Criminal Court Act 2000:

  (a) section 19 (application to identify proposed restrained property, respondent (if any), and interest holders):

  (b) section 21 (application for restraining order on notice):

  (ba) section 22 (application for restraining order without notice):

  (c) section 27 (registration of restraining orders on registers):

  (d) section 28(1), (3), and (4) (conditions on restraining order):

  (e) section 29 (undertakings as to damage or costs in relation to restraining orders):

  (f) section 32 (certain dispositions or dealings set aside):

  (g) section 33(1) and (2) (applying for further order):

  (h) section 34 (making further orders):

  (i) section 35 (types of further order):

  (j) section 36 (impact of certain further orders):

  (k) any other provisions of subpart 2 of Part 2 specified as applicable for the purposes of this subsection by regulations made under section 173(d).

(2) Without limiting subsection (1), a reference in any of the provisions listed in subsection (1) to a restraining order must be read as a reference to a foreign restraining order.

(3) Sections 30 and 31 (relating to relief) apply in relation to a foreign restraining order registered in New Zealand only if the person applying for relief,—

  (a) in a case where the foreign restraining order was made without a hearing in a court in the foreign country where it was made, was given no opportunity to make representations to the person or body that made the foreign restraining order:

  (b) in a case where the foreign restraining order was made at a hearing of a court in the foreign country where it was made, was not served with any notice of, and did not appear at, the hearing held in the court:

  (c) in any other case, obtains the leave of the court to make the application.

(4) Sections 23 and 33(3) apply, in relation to an application to register a foreign restraining order or in relation to an application for a further order in relation to that order or in relation to an application for relief in respect of a foreign restraining order, but confer a right of appearance on the person who is subject to the order or the applicant for relief only if that person,—

(a) in a case where the foreign restraining order was made without a hearing in a court in the foreign country where it was made, was given no opportunity to make representations to the person or body that made the foreign restraining order:

(b) in a case where the foreign restraining order was made at a hearing of a court in the foreign country where it was made, was not served with any notice of, and did not appear at, the hearing held in the court:

(c) in any other case, obtains the leave of the court to appear at the hearing of the application.

(5) The court may grant special leave under subsection (3)(c) or (4)(c) if—

(a) the applicant for relief or the person who is the subject of the foreign restraining order had good reasons—

(i) for failing to make representations to the decision-making person or body who made the order in the foreign country; or

(ii) in a case where the order was made by a court in the foreign country, for failing to attend the hearing at which the foreign restraining order was made; or

(b) the evidence proposed to be adduced by the applicant for relief or other person who is subject to the foreign restraining order was not reasonably available to the applicant for relief or other person at the time when the applicant or other person—

(i) was required to make submissions to the person or body that made the foreign restraining order in a foreign country; or

(ii) at the time of the hearing at which the foreign restraining order was made by the court in a foreign country.

135 Effect of registering foreign restraining order in New Zealand

(1) If a foreign restraining order is registered in New Zealand under section 56 of the Mutual Assistance in Criminal Matters Act 1992, the property specified in the foreign restraining order that is located in New Zealand—

(a) is not to be disposed of, or dealt with, other than is provided for in the order; and

(b) is to be under the Official Assignee's custody and control.

(2) If a foreign restraining order is registered in New Zealand, the Commissioner must give written notice of the order to any persons whose property is the subject of the order.

Duration of foreign restraining order and further orders

136 Duration of foreign restraining order registered in New Zealand and associated further orders

(1) The registration of a foreign restraining order in New Zealand expires on the earliest of the following dates:

(a) the date when the foreign restraining order to which it relates expires or is revoked:

(b) the date that is the end of 2 years after the date on which the foreign restraining order is registered in New Zealand:

(c) the date when the Commissioner registers a foreign forfeiture order in New Zealand in respect of some or all of the property specified in the foreign restraining order:

(d) the date on which the registration of the foreign restraining order in New Zealand has been cancelled under section 58 of the Mutual Assistance in Criminal Matters Act 1992.

(2) Despite subsection (1), if the registration of a foreign restraining order in New Zealand is extended as a result of an application to the High Court, it expires on the date specified by the High Court under section 137.

(3) On the expiry of the registration of a foreign restraining order in New Zealand, any further order made in relation to the foreign restraining order also expires.

137 Extension of duration of registration of foreign restraining order

(1) If the High Court has registered a foreign restraining order in New Zealand, the applicant for that order may, before the registration of the restraining order expires, apply to the High Court for an extension of the duration of the registration of the foreign restraining order in New Zealand.

(2) If an application is made under subsection (1), the High Court may order that the registration of a foreign restraining order be extended for a further period not exceeding 1 year.

(2A) The duration of the registration of a foreign restraining order may be extended more than once under this section.

(3) If an application is granted under this section, the registration of the foreign restraining order in New Zealand ceases at the time specified in the Court's order.

138 Additional matters relating to extension of registration of foreign restraining order

(1) On making any order of the kind referred to in section 137, the High Court may vary the foreign restraining order in any way it considers fit, including, without limitation, by specifying whether all or part of the property is to remain subject to the foreign restraining order during the extended period of registration in New Zealand.

(2) An applicant for an order under subsection (1) must serve a copy of the application on any person who, to the knowledge of the applicant, has an interest in the property that is the subject of the application.

139 Exclusion of interest from foreign restraining order registered in New Zealand

(1) A person (other than the respondent) who has a severable interest in property restrained under a foreign restraining order that is registered in New Zealand may apply to the High Court for the exclusion of that interest if the person—

(a) has not already been a party to proceedings associated with the making of the foreign restraining order in the foreign country where it was made; and

(b) has good reason for failing to have attended the hearing connected with the making of the foreign restraining order in the foreign country where it was made; and

(c) has not unlawfully benefited from the significant foreign criminal activity to which the foreign restraining order relates; and

(d) has already made an application (whether granted or not) under section 30 (as made applicable by section 134(3)).

(2) The High Court may, if it is satisfied of the matters in subsection (1), make an order—

(a) directing the Crown to transfer the interest to the applicant; or

(b) that the Crown pay to the applicant an amount equal to the value of the interest declared by the Court.

(3) An order under subsection (1) does not affect a restraining order, insofar as it applies to property that is not the subject of the order.

Registering foreign forfeiture orders

140 Who may apply to register foreign forfeiture order

The Commissioner may apply to register a foreign forfeiture order in New Zealand if authorised by the Attorney-General under section 55 of the Mutual Assistance in Criminal Matters Act 1992.

141 Application to register foreign forfeiture order made to High Court

If authorised to apply to register a foreign forfeiture order in New Zealand under section 55 of the Mutual Assistance in Criminal Matters Act 1992, the Commissioner may apply to the High Court.

142 Notice of registration of foreign forfeiture order

(1) The Commissioner must serve notice of having applied to register a foreign forfeiture order in New Zealand, so far as it is practicable to do so, on every person who, to the knowledge of the Commissioner, has an interest in the property to which the order relates.

(2) The Commissioner must also serve notice of the intention to register the foreign forfeiture order in New Zealand on the Official Assignee.

143 Provisions of subpart 3 of Part 2 applying to registering foreign forfeiture orders

(1) The following sections of subpart 3 of Part 2 apply, with all necessary modifications, if an application is made to register a foreign forfeiture order in New Zealand under section 55 of the Mutual Assistance in Criminal Matters Act 1992:

(a) section 47 (amending application for civil forfeiture order):

(b) any other provision of subpart 3 of Part 2 specified as applicable for the purposes of this subsection by regulations made under section 173.

(2) Section 148 (which relates to relief) applies in relation to a foreign forfeiture order registered in New Zealand only if the person applying for relief,—

(a) in a case where the foreign forfeiture order was made without a hearing in a court in the foreign country where it was made, was given no opportunity to make representations to the person or body that made the foreign forfeiture order:

(b) in a case where the foreign forfeiture order was made at a hearing of a court in the foreign country where it was made, was not served with any notice of, and did not appear at, the hearing held in the court:

(c) in any other case, obtains the leave of the court to make the application.

(3) Sections 46 and 64 apply, in relation to an application to register a foreign forfeiture order or in relation to an application for relief in respect of a foreign forfeiture order, but confer a right of appearance on the person who is subject to the order or the applicant for relief only if that person,—

(a) in a case where the foreign forfeiture order was made without a hearing in a court in the foreign country where it was made, was given no opportunity to make representations to the person or body that made the foreign forfeiture order:

(b) in a case where the foreign forfeiture order was made at a hearing of a court in the foreign country where it was made, was not served with any notice of, and did not appear at, the hearing held in the court:

(c) in any other case, obtains the leave of the court to appear at the hearing of the application.

(4) The court may grant special leave under subsection (2)(c) or (3)(c) if—

(a) the applicant for relief or the person who is the subject of the foreign forfeiture order had good reasons—

(i) for failing to make representations to the decision-making person or body who made the order in the foreign country; or

(ii) in a case where the order was made by a court in the foreign country, for failing to attend the hearing at which the foreign forfeiture order was made; or

(b) the evidence proposed to be adduced by the applicant for relief or other person who is subject to the foreign forfeiture order was not reasonably available to the applicant for relief or other person at the time when the applicant or other person—

(i) was required to make submissions to the person or body that made the foreign forfeiture order in a foreign country; or

(ii) at the time of the hearing at which the foreign forfeiture order was made by the court in a foreign country.

144 Registering foreign forfeiture order

The effect of registering a foreign forfeiture order in New Zealand under section 56 of the Mutual Assistance in Criminal Matters Act 1992 is that the property specified in the foreign forfeiture order—

(a) vests in the Crown absolutely; and

(b) is in the custody and control of the Official Assignee.

145 Notice of registration of foreign forfeiture order may be recorded on registers

(1) Subsection (2) applies if an application is made for a foreign forfeiture order to be registered in New Zealand against property of a kind covered by a New Zealand enactment that enables the registration of—

  (a) title to that property; or

  (b) charges over that property.

(2) If this subsection applies, the High Court may, at any time before finally determining the application, order any authority responsible for administering an enactment of the kind referred to in subsection (1) (an Authority) to enter on a register a note of the fact that an application has been made to register a foreign forfeiture order against the property in New Zealand.

(3) The Court must order an Authority to cancel an entry made on a register under subsection (2) if—

  (a) the foreign forfeiture order to which registration relates is cancelled or expired; or

  (b) the specified period (as described in section 86(2)) has expired; or

  (c) the foreign forfeiture order in relation to which registration is sought is amended to exclude that property.

146 Additional matters in respect of registering foreign forfeiture order

(1) On registering a foreign forfeiture order in New Zealand, the High Court may do either or both of the following:

  (a) declare the nature, extent, and value of any person's interest in property specified in the order:

  (b) give any directions that may be necessary and convenient for giving effect to the foreign forfeiture order.

(2) Without limiting the generality of subsection (1)(b), if a Court registers a foreign forfeiture order in New Zealand against any property the title to which is passed by registration on a register maintained under any New Zealand enactment, the Court may direct an officer of the Court to do anything reasonably necessary to obtain possession of any document required to effect the transfer of the property and for that purpose may, by warrant, authorise an officer to enter and search any place or thing and seize any document.

(3) Part 4 of the Search and Surveillance Act 2012 (except subpart 6), so far as applicable and with all necessary modifications, applies in relation to a warrant issued under subsection (2) as if it were a warrant issued under section 101 to a member of the police.

147 Registering foreign forfeiture order relating to land

(1) Nothing in section 144 affects the operation of section 89 of the Land Transfer Act 2017 in respect of an estate or interest in land under that Act.

(2) If the High Court registers a foreign forfeiture order in New Zealand in respect of an estate or interest in land, the order must be transmitted by the Registrar of the Court to the Registrar-General of Land or the Registrar of Deeds, as the case may be, for the purposes of registration under the Land Transfer Act 2017 or the Deeds Registration Act 1908, as the case may require.

Section 147(1): amended, on 12 November 2018, by section 250 of the Land Transfer Act 2017 (2017 No 30).

Relief from foreign forfeiture order registered in New Zealand

148 Relief from foreign forfeiture order registered in New Zealand

A person who claims an interest in property sought to be forfeited under a foreign forfeiture order registered in New Zealand may, before the date that is 6 months from the date on which the foreign forfeiture order is registered, apply to the High Court for an order if the person is a person to whom section 143(2)(a), (b), or (c) applies.

149 High Court may grant relief from foreign forfeiture order registered in New Zealand

(1) The High Court may make an order of the kind described in subsection (2) if it is satisfied—

    (a) of the matters in section 148; and

    (b) that the applicant has an interest in the property to which the order relates.

(2) The High Court may make an order—

    (a) directing the Crown to transfer the interest to the applicant; or

    (b) that the Crown pay to the applicant an amount equal to the value of the interest declared by the Court.

(3) The Court may refuse to make an order of the kind described in subsection (2) if it is satisfied that—

    (a) the applicant was involved in the significant foreign criminal activity to which the foreign forfeiture order relates; or

    (b) the applicant did not acquire the interest in the property in good faith or for value (without knowing or having reason to believe that the property was tainted property) in circumstances where the applicant acquired the interest at the time of, or after, the commission of the offence or serious criminal activity; or

    (c) the applicant has unlawfully benefited from the significant foreign criminal activity to which the foreign forfeiture order relates.

(4) Nothing in subsection (3) requires the Court to refuse making an order.

NIGERIA

Mutual Assistance in Criminal Matters within the Commonwealth (Enactment and Enforcement) Act

Part II
Provisions as to the proceeds of criminal activities

22. Confirmation and enforcement of orders for forfeiture of the proceeds of criminal activity

(1) A request under this Part of the Act may seek assistance in invoking procedures in the requested country leading to the recognition or review and confirmation and the enforcement of an order for the forfeiture of the proceeds of criminal activities made by a court or other authority in the requesting country.

(2) A request under this section shall be accompanied by a certified copy of the order and shall contain, so far as is reasonably practicable, all such information available to the Central Authority of the requesting country as may be required in connection with the procedures to be followed in the requested country.

(3) The law of the requested country shall apply to determine the circumstances and manner in which an order may be recognised, confirmed or enforced.

PERU

Regulation of Legislative Decree N.1373 on the Extinction of Ownership

Title XII
International Legal Cooperation

Article 75. Effect in Peru of judgments issued by foreign courts

Judgments of confiscation, extinction of ownership or similar legal institutes issued by foreign courts on assets that are in the national territory and that are sought through international judicial cooperation are enforceable in Peru.

Their enforcement is subject to the provisions of international treaties, conventions or agreements signed, approved and ratified by Peru, or in the absence thereof, to an offer of reciprocity. For this purpose, it is provided that, in the case of movable property other than cash, the requesting State may choose to receive the asset in question or its cash value obtained as a result of the auction carried out by the authority in charge of its administration. In the case of real estates, they are subject to auction and their proceeds will be delivered to the requesting State in cash.

REPUBLIC OF KOREA

Act on Regulation and Punishment of Criminal Proceeds Concealment

Article 11 (Implementation of Mutual Cooperation)

When a foreign country has requested cooperation in relation to a foreign criminal case against an act that falls under specific crimes and the crimes referred to in Articles 3 and 4 of this Act in the execution of a finally-binding adjudication of confiscation or collection of equivalent value or in the preservation of property for the purpose of confiscation or collection of equivalent value, mutual assistance may be provided except in any of the following cases:

1. Where activities related to the crimes that require mutual cooperation take place in the Republic of Korea and such activities are not regarded as specific crimes or the crimes referred to in Articles 3 and 4 of the Acts and subordinate statutes of the Republic of Korea;

2. Where there is no assurance of the requesting country providing assistance for similar requests made by the Republic of Korea;

3. Where it falls under any of the subparagraphs of Article 64 (1) of the Act on Special Cases concerning the Prevention of Illegal Trafficking in Narcotics, etc.

[This Article Wholly Amended by Act No. 10201, Mar. 31, 2010]

Article 12 (Act on Special Cases Concerning the Prevention of Illegal Trafficking in Narcotics, etc. to Be Applied mutatis mutandis)

The provisions of Articles 19 through 63, 64 (2) and 65 through 78 of the Act on Special Cases concerning the Prevention of Illegal Trafficking in Narcotics, etc. shall apply mutatis mutandis to the confiscation and collection of equivalent value, and international cooperation pursuant to this Act.

Act on Special Cases Concerning the Prevention of Illegal Trafficking in Narcotics, Etc.

Article 64 (Providing Cooperation)

(1) Where a foreign country requests cooperation concerning a foreign criminal case against an act that falls under narcotics crimes in the execution of a final and conclusive judgement of confiscation or collection or in the preservation of a property for confiscation or collection purposes under a treaty, cooperation may be provided in response to the request except as provided for in the following subparagraphs:

1. Where it is deemed impossible to penalize a cooperation crime (referring to a crime that is the object of a request for cooperation; hereinafter the same shall apply) under the statutes of the Republic of Korea;

2. Where a trial on a case regarding a cooperation crime is in progress in a court of the Republic of Korea or a judgement thereon has already become final and conclusive or where an order of preservation for confiscation or collection has already been issued for a property subject to the cooperation;

3. Where a property relating to a request for cooperation in the execution of a final and conclusive judgement of confiscation or for cooperation in the preservation of property for confiscation purposes does not fall under the category of property that may be brought to a confiscation trial or become subject to the preservation for confiscation under the statutes of the Republic of Korea;

4. Where it is deemed impossible to make a judgment of collection or to preserve property for collection under the statutes of the Republic of Korea, in regard to a cooperation crime related to a request for cooperation in the execution of a final and conclusive judgement of collection or for cooperation in the preservation of property for collection purposes;

5. Where it is deemed that a third party who has a reasonable ground to be recognized as the owner of the property related to a request for cooperation in the execution of a final and conclusive judgement of confiscation or has any surface rights, mortgage, or other rights over the property was unable to claim such right at the relevant trial through no fault of such third party;

6. Where it is deemed that no grounds exist under Article 33 (1) or 52 (1) for cooperation in the preservation of property for confiscation or collection purposes: Provided, That this shall not apply if a request for cooperation in the preservation of property is based on a judgement executed by a court or judge of the foreign country making the request for the preservation of property for confiscation or collection purposes or if a request is made after a judgement of confiscation or collection becomes final and conclusive.

(2) When a property on which surface rights, mortgage, or other rights exist is confiscated for the cooperation of the execution of a final and conclusive judgement of confiscation, if necessary under the statutes of the Republic of Korea, such rights shall continue to exist.

Article 66 (Receipt of Request)

A request for cooperation shall be received by the Minister of Foreign Affairs: Provided that in cases of emergency or special circumstances, the Minister of Justice may receive a request for cooperation with the consent of the Minister of Foreign Affairs.

Article 67 (Review by Court)

(1) Where a request for cooperation concerns the execution of a final and conclusive judgement of confiscation or collection, a prosecutor shall request a court to review whether it is a case which allows cooperation.

(2) The court shall dismiss the prosecutor's request after review thereof where it deems the request for review to be unlawful, shall decide to allow a whole or partial cooperation where it deems the cooperation to be acceptable in all or in part of the final and conclusive judgement for which cooperation is requested, or shall decide to refuse to cooperate where it deems the request for cooperation to be totally unacceptable.

[...]

Article 69 (Effect of Decision)

Where a decision to allow cooperation in the execution of a final and conclusive judgement of confiscation or collection becomes final and conclusive, such judgment of confiscation or collection shall be deemed a final and conclusive judgement of confiscation or collection made by the court of the Republic of Korea in the provision of cooperation.

Act on Special Cases Concerning the Confiscation and Return of Property Acquired Through Corrupt Practices

Article 7 (Facilitation of International Cooperation)

Whenever a foreign state requests the return of property subject to execution, etc. in relation to a criminal case of an act constituting a corruption offense in the foreign state, cooperation may be provided for such request, except for those cases falling under any of the following subparagraphs:

1. Where an act involved in the offense for which cooperation is requested was committed within the territories of the Republic of Korea and it is held that the act does not constitute a corruption offense under relevant Acts and subordinate statutes of the Republic of Korea;

2. Where the requesting State has not made a guaranty to the extent that it will accept and respond to a request for cooperation of the same kind if the Republic of Korea makes such a request;

3. Where the requesting State has not made a guaranty that the property subject to execution, etc. will be conveyed to the original owner of the property subject to execution, etc., the victim of the offense, or any other person who has a legitimate right;

4. Where a case falls under any subparagraph of Article 64 (1) of the Act on Special Cases Concerning the Prevention of Illegal Trafficking in Narcotics, etc.

Article 8 (Application Mutatis Mutandis of Act on Special Cases Concerning the Prevention of Illegal Trafficking in Narcotics, etc.)

As to the confiscation, collection of an equivalent value, and international cooperation under this Act, Articles 19 through 63, 64 (2) and 65 through 78 of the Act on Special Cases concerning the Prevention of Illegal Trafficking in Narcotics, etc. shall apply mutatis mutandis.

RUSSIAN FEDERATION

Criminal Procedure Code

Chapter 55.1.
Procedure for Consideration and Resolution of Issues Related to the Recognition and Enforcement of the Verdict, Foreign Court Order in Part of Confiscation on the Territory of the Russian Federation of the Proceeds of Crime

Article 473.1. Recognition and enforcement of the verdict, foreign court order in part of confiscation on the territory of the Russian Federation of the proceeds of crime

1. The verdict, foreign court order in part of confiscation on the territory of the Russian Federation of the proceeds of crime shall be recognized and enforced in the Russian Federation if this is stipulated by an international treaty of the Russian Federation. In the absence of a relevant international treaty, the issue of recognition of the verdict, foreign court order can be solved on the basis of the principle of reciprocity, confirmed by a written obligation of the foreign state and received by the Ministry of Justice of the Russian Federation in accordance with Part 1 of Article 457 of this Code.

2. The basis of enforcement of the verdict, foreign court order in part of confiscation on the territory of the Russian Federation of the proceeds of crime is the court order of the Russian Federation on the recognition and enforcement of the verdict, foreign court order, delivered in accordance with the international treaty of the Russian Federation or on the basis of reciprocity upon consideration of request sent in the prescribed manner to the competent authority of the foreign state and the relevant foreign court order.

3. For the purposes of this Chapter, the proceeds of crime mean the property specified in Article 104.1 of the Criminal Code of the Russian Federation.

Article 473.2. Content of the request for recognition and enforcement of the verdict, foreign court order in part of confiscation on the territory of the Russian Federation of the proceeds of crime

1. The request of the competent authority of the foreign state for recognition and enforcement of the verdict, foreign court order in part of confiscation on the territory of the Russian Federation of the proceeds of crime shall contain:
   1) name of the competent authority of the foreign state which sent the request;
   2) name of the criminal case and information on the court of the foreign state which ruled the verdict or the order;
   3) information on the property, which is located on the territory of the Russian Federation and is subject to forfeiture as the proceeds of crime, as well as information on the proprietor, owner of the property, including date and place of birth, citizenship, occupation, place of residence or location, and for legal entities—name and location;
   4) request of the competent authority of the foreign state on recognition of the verdict, foreign court order in part of confiscation of the proceeds of crime and enforcement of the decision regarding confiscation of the proceeds of crime in accordance with the verdict or the order.

2. The request of the competent authority of the foreign state can specify other information, including phone numbers, fax numbers, E-mail addresses, if they are necessary for the proper and timely consideration of the case.

3. The request of the competent authority of the foreign state shall include documents provided by the international treaty of the Russian Federation,

and if this is not stipulated by the international treaty of the Russian Federation the following documents shall be attached:

1) certified by the foreign court copy of the verdict, foreign court order, which provides for the confiscation on the territory of the Russian Federation of the proceeds of crime;

2) document that the verdict, foreign court order entered into legal force;

3) document on the execution of the verdict, foreign court order if they had been previously executed on the territory of the respective foreign state;

4) document confirming that the property subject to forfeiture is located on the territory of the Russian Federation;

5) document from which it follows that the person, against whom the default judgment was made on confiscation on the territory of the Russian Federation of the proceeds of crime, did not participate in the proceedings, despite the fact that he/she was timely and duly notified of the place, date and time of the hearing of the case;

6) certified translation of documents referred to in paragraphs 1-5 of this Part to the Russian language.

Article 473.3. Court considering the request for recognition and enforcement of the verdict, foreign court order in part of confiscation on the territory of the Russian Federation of the proceeds of crime

The request of the competent authority of the foreign state on recognition and enforcement of the verdict, foreign court order in part of confiscation on the territory of the Russian Federation of the proceeds of crime, addressed in the prescribed manner, shall be sent by the Ministry of Justice of the Russian Federation for the consideration to the Republic Court, krai or regional court, court of the city with federal status, court of the autonomous region or court of the autonomous district at the place of residence or location in the Russian Federation of the person in respect of whose property, by the verdict, foreign court order, the decision on confiscation was made, and in the case if such person has no place of residence or location in the Russian Federation or his/her domicile is unknown—at location in the Russian Federation of his/her property subject to forfeiture.

Article 473.4. Procedure for considering the request for recognition and enforcement of the verdict, foreign court order in part of confiscation on the territory of the Russian Federation of the proceeds of crime

1. The request of the competent authority of the foreign state for recognition and enforcement of the verdict, foreign court order in part of confiscation on the territory of the Russian Federation of the proceeds of crime shall be considered by a single judge in open court with a notice about the place, date and time of request consideration of the person in respect of whose property, by the verdict, foreign court order, the decision on confiscation was made, other interested parties in whose ownership, possession, use or disposal of the property subject to forfeiture is, and (or) their representatives, the competent authority of the foreign state and the attorney.

2. Persons referred to in paragraph 1 of this Article, living or staying on the territory of the Russian Federation, shall be notified of the place, date and

time of the hearing no later than 30 days prior to the day of the hearing. Notice to persons, living or staying outside the Russian Federation, and the competent authority of the foreign state shall be sent in the prescribed manner, according to Part 3 of Article 453 of this Code, not later than 6 months prior to the day of the hearing.

3.   The person, in respect of whose property, by the verdict, foreign court order, the decision on confiscation was made, held in custody and declared his/her desire to participate in the consideration of the request from the competent authority of the foreign state, shall be given by the court the right to participate in the hearing directly or via video conference, as well as the right to inform the court of his/her position with the help of his/her representative on his/her behalf or in writing.

4.   Other interested parties in whose ownership, possession, use or disposal the property subject to forfeiture is, and (or) their representatives can participate in the hearing.

5.   The failure to appear in the court of persons, timely notified of the place, date and time of the hearing, except persons whose participation in the hearing is recognized by the court as compulsory, shall not preclude the consideration of the request from the competent authority of the foreign state.

6.   The consideration of the request from the competent authority of the foreign country shall start with the hearing of explanations of the person, in respect of whose property, by the verdict, foreign court order, the decision on confiscation was made, the representative of the competent authority of the foreign state, interested parties, if they participate in the hearing, as well as conclusions of the Prosecutor. Upon the consideration of the request, the court shall decide on recognition and enforcement of the verdict, foreign court order in part of confiscation on the territory of the Russian Federation of the proceeds of crime, refusal to do so or recognition and partial enforcement of the verdict, foreign court order.

7.   If the court has any doubts in connection with the incompleteness or absence of required information, the judge may request in the prescribed manner the competent authority of the foreign state, submitting the said request, as well as other persons participating in the consideration of the request, additional clarifications, additional information and materials.

Article 473.5. Grounds for refusing recognition and enforcement of the verdict, foreign court order in part of confiscation on the territory of the Russian Federation of the proceeds of crime

Recognition and enforcement of the verdict, foreign court order in part of confiscation on the territory of the Russian Federation of the proceeds of crime shall not be permitted if:

1)   execution of the verdict, foreign court order in part of confiscation of the property contradicts to the Constitution of the Russian Federation, generally recognized principles and norms of international law, international treaties of the Russian Federation, the legislation of the Russian Federation;

2)   execution of the verdict, foreign court order in part of confiscation of the property may cause damage to the sovereignty or security or other essential interests of the Russian Federation;

3) the verdict, foreign court order, providing for the confiscation of the property, did not enter into legal force;

4) property subject to confiscation is located on the territory that is not under the jurisdiction of the Russian Federation;

5) the act, in respect of which the verdict, foreign court order provides for the confiscation of the property, was committed on the territory of the Russian Federation and (or) the act is not recognized by the legislation of the Russian Federation as a crime;

6) the legislation of the Russian Federation does not provide for the confiscation of the property for the act, similar to the act in respect of which the verdict, foreign court order decided on confiscation;

7) in regard to the person referred to in the request of the competent authority of the foreign state, the court of the Russian Federation ruled the legally effective verdict in respect of the act, criminal proceedings were terminated, as well as there is an irreversible decision on the termination of the preliminary investigation on the criminal case or refusal of the initiation of the criminal case;

8) the verdict, foreign court order, providing for the confiscation of the property, cannot be enforced due to the lapse or other grounds envisaged by the Constitution of the Russian Federation, international treaties of the Russian Federation, the legislation of the Russian Federation;

9) the request of the competent authority of the foreign state and the accompanying verdict, foreign court order, providing for the confiscation of the property, have no evidence that the property subject to the confiscation is the proceeds of the crime or is the income received from criminal activities, as well as used to commit the crime;

10) in the Russian Federation in connection with the same act, there is the criminal prosecution of the person regarding whose property the request on confiscation is sent to the competent authority of the foreign state;

11) the property, the confiscation of which was requested by the competent authority of the foreign state, was charged by the verdict or decision of the court of the Russian Federation in criminal, civil or administrative proceedings;

12) the property, specified in the verdict, foreign court order, is not subject to confiscation in accordance with the legislation of the Russian Federation.

Article 473.6. Court decision upon the consideration of the request from the competent authority of the foreign state on recognition and enforcement of the verdict, foreign court order in part of confiscation on the territory of the Russian Federation of the proceeds of crime

1. When considering the request from the competent authority of the foreign state on recognition and enforcement of the verdict, foreign court order in part of confiscation on the territory of the Russian Federation of the proceeds of crime, the court shall conclude on the presence of grounds under Article 473.5 of the Code for the refusal of recognition and enforcement of the verdict, foreign court order in part of confiscation on the territory of the

Russian Federation of the proceeds of crime, shall rule on the refusal of recognition of the verdict, foreign court order and their enforcement.

2. In all other cases, the court shall decide on recognition of the verdict, foreign court order in part of confiscation of the proceeds of crime and their enforcement completely or partially, with the relevant order which specifies:

    1) name of the court of the foreign state, place and date of the verdict, foreign court order;

    2) information on the last place of residence, place of work and occupation in the Russian Federation of the person convicted by the court of the foreign state;

    3) description of the crime for which the convicted person was found guilty, and the criminal law of the foreign state under which he/she was convicted and the decision on confiscation of the property was made;

    4) article of the Criminal Code of the Russian Federation providing responsibility for the crime committed by the convicted person and the application of confiscation of the property;

    5) information on the property located on the territory of the Russian Federation and subject to confiscation;

    6) appeal procedure established by Chapters 45.1, 47.1 and 48.1 of this Code.

3. If the confiscation of a specific item, included in the property subject to forfeiture, at the time of the court's decision on recognition of the verdict, foreign court order in part of confiscation of the proceeds of crime and their enforcement fully or partially, is impossible due to its use, sale, or other reason, the court in accordance with Article 104.2 of the Criminal Code of the Russian Federation shall determine the amount subject to confiscation that equals the value of this item, or shall determine a different property the value of which corresponds to the value of the item subject to confiscation or comparable to its cost.

4. Copies of the order within 3 days from the date of the verdict shall be sent by the court to the competent authority of the foreign state, the person in respect of whose property, by the verdict, foreign court order, the decision on confiscation was made, the Prosecutor, as well as other interested parties in whose ownership, possession, use or disposal the property subject to forfeiture is.

Article 473.7. Issue of the writ of execution and its enforcement

1. On the basis of the enforceable court decision on recognition and enforcement of the verdict, foreign court order in part of confiscation on the territory of the Russian Federation of the proceeds of crime, the court shall issue the writ, which shall contain the operative part of the verdict, foreign court order, as well as the operative part of the court decision on recognition of the verdict, foreign court order and their enforcement fully or partially.

2. The writ with copies of the verdict, foreign court order and the copy of the court decision on recognition and enforcement of judgment the verdict, foreign court order shall be sent to a bailiff for execution in accordance with the legislation of the Russian Federation on proceedings.

SEYCHELLES

Mutual Assistance in Criminal Matters Act

Division 2—Requests by Foreign Countries
Request by a foreign country for enforcement of orders

27. (1) Where—

    (a)   a foreign country requests the Central Authority to make arrangements for the enforcement of—

        (i)   a foreign forfeiture order, made in respect of a serious offence, against property that is believed to be located in Seychelles; or

        (ii)   a foreign pecuniary penalty order, made in respect of a serious offence, where some or all of the property available to satisfy the order is believed to be located in Seychelles; and

    (b)   the Central Authority is satisfied that

        (i)   a person has been convicted of the offence; and

        (ii)   the conviction and the order are not subject to further appeal in the foreign country, the Central Authority may authorise in writing the making of an application for the registration of the order in the Supreme Court.

(2) Where a foreign country requests the Central Authority to make arrangements for the enforcement of a foreign restraining order, made in respect of a serious offence, against property that is believed to be located in Seychelles, the Central Authority may authorise the making of the arrangements for the registration of the order in the Supreme Court.

(3) Where an application for the registration of a foreign order in accordance with an authorisation is made under subsection (1) or subsection (2), the Supreme Court shall, notwithstanding any other written law, register the order accordingly.

(4) A foreign forfeiture order registered in the Supreme Court in accordance with this section has effect and may be enforced as if it were a forfeiture order made by the Supreme Court under a written law relating to the tracing, confiscation or forfeiture of proceeds of a crime at the time of registration.

(5) A foreign pecuniary penalty order registered in the Supreme Court in accordance with this section has effect, and may be enforced, as if it were a pecuniary penalty order made by the Supreme Court under a written law relating to the tracing, confiscation or forfeiture of the proceeds of a crime at the time of registration and requiring the payment to the Republic of the amount payable under the order.

Note: There is no subsection 27(6) in the last official (1996) revised edition.

(7) A foreign restraining order registered in the Supreme Court in accordance with this section has effect, and may be enforced, as if it were a restraining order made by the Supreme Court under any written law of Seychelles relating to the tracing, seizure, confiscation or forfeiture of the proceeds of a crime at the time of registration.

(8) Where an order is registered in the Supreme Court in accordance with this section, a copy of any amendment made to the order (whether before or after registration) may be registered in the same way as the order and the amendment does not, for the purposes of this Act and a written law relating to the tracing, confiscation or the forfeiture of the proceeds of a crime, have effect until they are registered.

(9) An order or an amendment of an order shall be registered in the Supreme Court by the registration, in accordance with the rules of the Court, of—

(a) a copy of the appropriate order or amendment sealed by the court or other authority making that order or amendment; or

(b) a copy of that order or amendment duly authenticated in accordance with section 34.

(10) A facsimile copy of a sealed or authenticated copy of an order or an amendment of an order shall be regarded for the purposes of this Act as the same as the sealed or authenticated copy but registration effected by means of the facsimile copy ceases to have effect at the end of 21 days unless the sealed or authenticated copy has been registered by then.

(11) The Central Authority may cause an application for the cancellation of—

(a) a foreign forfeiture order;

(b) a foreign pecuniary penalty order; or

(c) a foreign restraining order, under this Act.

(12) Without limiting the generality of subsection (11), the Central authority may, give a direction under that subsection in relation to an order if the Central Authority is satisfied that—

(a) the order has ceased to have effect in the foreign country in which the order was made; or

(b) cancellation of the order is appropriate having regard to the arrangements entered into between Seychelles and the foreign country in relation to the enforcement of orders of that kind.

(13) Where an application is made to the Supreme Court for cancellation of a registration under subsection (11), the Court shall cancel the registration accordingly.

Request by a foreign country for search and seizure warrants in respect of illegal property

28. Where—

(a) a criminal proceeding or criminal investigation has commenced in a foreign country in respect of a serious offence;

(b) there are reasonable grounds to believe that illegal property in relation to the offence is located in Seychelles; and

(c) the foreign country requests the Central Authority to obtain the issue of a search warrant under a written law relating to the tracing, seizure, confiscation or forfeiture of the proceeds of a crime in relation to the illegal property, the Central Authority may authorise a police officer to apply to a judicial officer for the search warrant requested by the foreign country.

Request by a foreign country for restraining orders

29. Where—

  (a) a criminal proceeding has commenced in a foreign country in respect of a serious offence;

  (b) there are reasonable grounds to believe that property that may be made or is about to be made the subject of a foreign restraining order is located in Seychelles; and

  (c) the foreign country requests the Central Authority to obtain the issue of a restraining order under a written law relating to tracing, seizure, confiscation or forfeiture of the proceeds of a crime against the property, the Central Authority may cause an application to be made to the Supreme Court for the restraining order requested by the foreign country.

Request by a foreign country for information gathering orders

30. (1) Where—

  (a) a criminal proceeding or criminal investigation has commenced in a foreign country in respect of a serious offence;

  (b) a property-tracing document in relation to the offence is reasonably believed to be located in Seychelles; and

  (c) the foreign country requests the Central Authority to obtain the issue of —

   (i) a production order under a written law relating to the tracing, seizure, confiscation or forfeiture of the proceed of a crime in respect of the document; or

   (ii) a search warrant under a written law referred to in subparagraph (i) in respect of the document, the Central Authority may cause an application to be made to the Supreme Court for the order requested by the foreign country.

Note: There is no subsection 30(2) in the last official (1996) revised edition.

(3) Where—

  (a) a criminal proceeding or criminal investigation has commenced in a foreign country in respect of a serious offence that is—

   (i) a drug trafficking offence;

   (ii) a money laundering offence in respect of proceeds of a drug trafficking offence; or

   (iii) an ancillary offence in relation to an offence of a kind referred to in subparagraph (i) or (ii);

  (b) information about transactions conducted through an account with a financial institution in Seychelles is reasonably believed to be relevant to the proceeding or investigation; and

  (c) the foreign country requests the Central Authority to obtain the issue of an order under the Misuse of Drugs [Cap. 133] Act, directing the financial institution to give information to the police about transactions conducted through the account, the Central Authority may cause an application to be made to the Supreme Court for the order requested by the foreign country.

SINGAPORE

Mutual Assistance in Criminal Matters Act (MACMA)

Part III Requests to Singapore
Division 5—Enforcement of Foreign Confiscation Order, etc.

Requests for enforcement of foreign confiscation order

29.—(1) The appropriate authority of a prescribed foreign country may request the Attorney-General to assist in—

(a) the enforcement and satisfaction of a foreign confiscation order, made in any judicial proceedings instituted in that country, against property that is reasonably believed to be located in Singapore; or

(b) where a foreign confiscation order may be made in judicial proceedings which have been or are to be instituted in that country, the restraining of dealing in any property that is reasonably believed to be located in Singapore and against which the order may be enforced or which may be available to satisfy the order.

(2) On receipt of a request referred to in subsection (1), the Attorney-General may—

(a) in the case of subsection (1)(a), act or authorise the taking of action under section 30 and the provisions of the Third Schedule; or

(b) in the case of subsection (1)(b), act or authorise the taking of action under the provisions of the Third Schedule, and in that event the provisions of the Third Schedule shall apply accordingly.

(3) For the purposes of this section and the provisions of the Third Schedule, judicial proceedings that are criminal proceedings are instituted in a prescribed foreign country when a person is produced and charged in court with a foreign offence.

Registration of foreign confiscation order

30.—(1) The Attorney-General or a person authorised by him may apply to the High Court for the registration of a foreign confiscation order.

(2) The General Division of the High Court may, on an application referred to in subsection (1), register the foreign confiscation order if it is satisfied—

(a) that the order is in force and not subject to further appeal in the foreign country;

(b) where a person affected by the order did not appear in the proceedings, that the person received notice of the proceedings in sufficient time to enable him to defend them; and

(c) that enforcing the order in Singapore would not be contrary to the interests of justice.

(3) For the purposes of subsection (2), "appeal" includes—

(a) any proceedings by way of discharging or setting aside a judgment; and

(b) an application for a new trial or a stay of execution.

(4) The General Division of the High Court shall cancel the registration of a foreign confiscation order if it appears to the General Division of the High

Court that the order has been satisfied by payment of the amount due under it or by the person against whom it was made serving imprisonment in default of payment or other means.

(5) Where an amount of money (if any) payable or remaining to be paid under a foreign confiscation order registered in the General Division of the High Court under this section is expressed in a currency other than that of Singapore, the amount shall, for the purpose of any action taken in relation to that order, be converted into the currency of Singapore on the basis of the exchange rate prevailing on the date of registration of the order.

(6) For the purposes of subsection (5), a certificate issued by the Monetary Authority of Singapore and stating the exchange rate prevailing on a specified date shall be admissible in any judicial proceedings as evidence of the facts so stated.

Proof of orders, etc., of prescribed foreign country

31.—(1) For the purposes of sections 29 and 30 and the Third Schedule—

(a) any order made or judgment given by a court of a prescribed foreign country purporting to bear the seal of that court or to be signed by any person in his capacity as a judge, magistrate or officer of the court, shall be deemed without further proof to have been duly sealed or, as the case may be, to have been signed by that person; and

(b) a document, duly authenticated, that purports to be a copy of any order made or judgment given by a court of a prescribed foreign country shall be deemed without further proof to be a true copy.

(2) A document is duly authenticated for the purpose of subsection (1)(b) if it purports to be certified by any person in his capacity as a judge, magistrate or officer of the court in question or by or on behalf of the appropriate authority of that country.

Evidence in relation to proceedings and orders in prescribed foreign country

32.—(1) For the purposes of sections 29 and 30 and the Third Schedule, a certificate purporting to be issued by or on behalf of the appropriate authority of a prescribed foreign country stating that—

(a) judicial proceedings have been instituted and have not been concluded, or that judicial proceedings are to be instituted, in that country;

(b) a foreign confiscation order is in force and is not subject to appeal;

(c) all or a certain amount of the sum payable under a foreign confiscation order remains unpaid in that country, or that other property recoverable under a foreign confiscation order remains unrecovered in that country;

(d) a person has been notified of any judicial proceedings in accordance with the law of that country; or

(e) an order (however described) made by a court of that country has the purpose of—

(i) recovering, forfeiting or confiscating—

(A) any payment or other reward received in connection with an offence against the law of that country, or the value of any such payment or reward; or

(B) any property derived or realised, directly or indirectly, from any payment or other reward referred to in sub-paragraph (A), or the value of any such property; or

(ii) forfeiting, and destroying or otherwise disposing of—

(A) any drug or other substance in respect of which an offence against the corresponding drug law of that country has been committed; or

(B) any property which was used in connection with the commission of any offence against the law of that country, shall, in any proceedings in a court, be admissible as evidence of the facts so stated.

(2) In any such proceedings, a statement contained in a duly authenticated document, which purports to have been received in evidence or to be a copy of a document so received, or to set out or summarise evidence given in proceedings in a court in a prescribed foreign country, shall be admissible as evidence of any fact stated therein.

(3) A document is duly authenticated for the purposes of subsection (2) if it purports to be certified by any person in his capacity as a judge, magistrate or officer of the court in the prescribed foreign country, or by or on behalf of an appropriate authority of that country.

(4) Nothing in this section shall prejudice the admissibility of any evidence, whether contained in any document or otherwise, which is admissible apart from this section.

Third Schedule
Enforcement of Foreign Confiscation Orders
Part I
Preliminary

Interpretation

1. —(1) In this Schedule, unless the context otherwise requires—

[...]

"realisable property" means—

(a) where a foreign confiscation order (not being an instrumentality forfeiture order) has been made, any property in respect of which the order was made; or

(b) where a foreign confiscation order (not being an instrumentality forfeiture order) may be made in proceedings which have been, or are to be, instituted in the prescribed foreign country concerned, any property in respect of which such an order could be made.

[...]

(4) For the purposes of this Schedule, judicial proceedings instituted in a prescribed foreign country that are criminal proceedings are concluded on the occurrence of one of the following events:

(a) the discontinuance of the proceedings;

(b) the acquittal of the defendant;

(c) the quashing of the defendant's conviction for the offence;

(d) the grant of a pardon in respect of the defendant's conviction for the offence;

(e) the court sentencing or otherwise dealing with the defendant in respect of his conviction for the offence without having made a foreign confiscation order;

(f) the satisfaction of a foreign confiscation order made in the proceedings, whether by payment of the amount due under the order, by the defendant serving imprisonment in default, by the recovery of all property liable to be recovered, or otherwise.

(5) For the purposes of this Schedule, a foreign confiscation order is subject to appeal as long as an appeal or further appeal is pending against the order or (if it was made on a conviction) against the conviction; and for this purpose, an appeal or further appeal shall be treated as pending (where one is competent but has not been brought) until the expiration of the time for bringing the appeal.

Application

2. This Schedule shall only apply to any matter which is the subject of a request under section 29, and in relation to which the Attorney-General has decided to act, or has authorised that action be taken, under the provisions of this Schedule.

SOUTH AFRICA

International Co-operation in Criminal Matters Act
Chapter 4
Confiscation and transfer of proceeds of crime

Registration of foreign confiscation order

20. (1) When the Director-General receives a request for assistance in executing a foreign confiscation order in the Republic, he or she shall, if satisfied—

(a) that the order is final and not subject to review or appeal;

(b) that the court which made the order had jurisdiction;

(c) that the person against whom the order was made, had the opportunity of defending himself or herself;

(d) that the order cannot be satisfied in full in the country in which it was imposed;

(e) that the order is enforceable in the requesting State; and

(f) that the person concerned holds property in the Republic, submit such request to the Minister for approval.

(2) Upon receiving the Minister's approval of the request contemplated in sub-section (1), the Director-General shall lodge with the clerk of a magistrate's court in the Republic a certified copy of such foreign confiscation order.

(3) When a certified copy of a foreign confiscation order is lodged with a clerk of a magistrate's court in the Republic, that clerk of the court shall register the foreign confiscation order—

 (a) where the order was made for the payment of money, in respect of the balance of the amount payable thereunder; or

 (b) where the order was made for the recovery of particular property, in respect of the property which is specified therein.

(4) The clerk of the court registering a foreign confiscation order shall forth-with issue a notice in writing addressed to the person against whom the order has been made—

 (a) that the order has been registered at the court concerned; and

 (b) that the said person may, within the prescribed period and in the pre-scribed manner, apply to that court for the setting aside of the registra-tion of the order.

(5) (a) Where the person against whom the foreign confiscation order has been made is present in the Republic, the notice contemplated in sub-section (4) shall be served on such person in the prescribed manner.

 (b) Where the said person is not present in the Republic, he or she shall in the prescribed manner be informed of the registration of the foreign confiscation order.

Effect of registration of foreign confiscation order

21. (1) When any foreign confiscation order has been registered in terms of sec-tion 20, such order shall have the effect of a civil judgment of the court at which it has been registered in favour of the Republic as represented by the Minister.

(2) A foreign confiscation order registered in terms of section 20 shall not be executed before the expiration of the period within which an application in terms of section 20(4)(b) for the setting aside of the registration may be made, or if such application has been made, before the application has been finally decided.

(3) The Director-General shall, subject to any agreement or arrangement between the requesting State and the Republic, pay over to the requesting State any amount recovered in terms of a foreign confiscation order, less all expenses incurred in connection with the execution of such order.

Setting aside of registration of foreign confiscation order

22. (1) The registration of a foreign confiscation order in terms of section 20 shall, on the application of any person against whom the order has been made, be set aside if the court at which it was registered is satisfied—

 (a) that the order was registered contrary to a provision of this Act;

 (b) that the court of the requesting State had no jurisdiction in the matter;

 (c) that the order is subject to review or appeal;

(d) that the person against whom the order was made did not appear at the proceedings concerned or did not receive notice of the said proceedings as prescribed by the law of the requesting State or, if no such notice has been prescribed, that he or she did not receive reasonable notice of such proceedings so as to enable him or her to defend him or her at the proceedings;

(e) that the enforcement of the order would be contrary to the interests of justice; or

(f) that the order has already been satisfied.

(2) The court hearing an application referred to in subsection (1) may at any time postpone the hearing of the application to such date as it may determine.

Registration of foreign restraint order

24. (1) When the Director-General receives a request for assistance in enforcing a foreign restraint order in the Republic, he or she may lodge with the registrar of a division of the Supreme Court a certified copy of such order if he or she is satisfied that the order is not subject to any review or appeal.

(2) The registrar with whom a certified copy of a foreign restraint order is lodged in terms of subsection (1), shall register such order in respect of the property which is specified therein.

(3) The registrar registering a foreign restraint order shall forthwith give notice in writing to the person against whom the order has been made—

(a) that the order has been registered at the division of the Supreme Court concerned; and

(b) that the said person may within the prescribed period and in terms of the rules of the court apply to that court for the setting aside of the registration of the order.

(4) (a) Where the person against whom the foreign restraint order has been made is present in the Republic, the notice contemplated in subsection (3) shall be served on such person in the prescribed manner.

(b) Where the said person is not present in the Republic, he or she shall in the prescribed manner be informed of the registration of the foreign restraint order.

Effect of registration of foreign restraint order

25. When any foreign restraint order has been registered in terms of section 24, that order shall have the effect of a restraint order made by the division of the Supreme Court at which it has been registered.

Setting aside of registration of foreign restraint order

26. (1) The registration of a foreign restraint order in terms of section 24 shall, on the application of the person against whom the order has been made, be set aside if the court at which the order was registered is satisfied—

(a) that the order was registered contrary to a provision of this Act;

(b) that the court of the requesting State had no jurisdiction in the matter;

(c) that the order is subject to review or appeal;

(d) that the enforcement of the order would be contrary to the interests of justice; or

(e) that the sentence or order in support of which the foreign restraint order was made, has been satisfied in full.

(2) The court hearing an application referred to in subsection (1) may at any time postpone the hearing of the application to such date as it may determine.

Admissibility of foreign documents

30. Any deposition, affidavit, record of any conviction or any document evidencing any order of a court, issued in a foreign State, or any copy or sworn translation thereof, may be received in evidence at any proceedings in terms of a provision of this Act if it is—

(a) authenticated in the manner in which foreign documents are authenticated to enable them to be produced in any court in the Republic; or

(b) authenticated in the manner provided for in any agreement with the foreign State concerned.

Regulations under the International Co-Operation in Criminal Matters Act, 1996

Chapter 4
Foreign Confiscation Orders

Registration of foreign confiscation order

10. Whenever a certified copy of a foreign confiscation order is lodged with the clerk of the court in terms of section 20(2) of the Act, such clerk of the court shall register that order by—

(a) numbering the foreign confiscation order with a consecutive case number for the year during which it is lodged; and

(b) recording—

(i) where the order was made for the payment of money, the balance in the currency of the Republic of the amount payable thereunder; and

(ii) where the order was made for the recovery of particular property, full particulars of that property, in so far as such particulars are available, in favour of the Republic as represented by the Minister, on the case cover in which the certified copy of the foreign confiscation order is filed.

Notice of registration of foreign confiscation order

11. (1) The written notice of registration of a foreign confiscation order contemplated in section 20(4) of the Act shall correspond substantially with Form 3 of the Annexure, and shall contain—

(a) the consecutive case number referred to in regulation 10(a);

(b) the date on which the foreign confiscation order was registered;

(c) in the case of the payment of money, the balance in the currency of the Republic of the amount payable under the foreign confiscation order;

(d) in the case of the recovery of particular property, full particulars of the property specified in the foreign confiscation order in so far as such particulars are available; and

(e) a reference to the provisions of section 20(4)(b) of the Act and regulations 12 and 13.

(2) (a) Where the person against whom the order has been made is present in the Republic, the written notice of registration, together with a copy thereof, is delivered to a sheriff who shall serve such notice on that person in accordance with the manner provided for in regulation 7(2) to (6), and the provisions of regulation 7(7) to (10) shall, read with the changes required by the context, apply to such service.

(b) Where the person against whom the foreign confiscation order has been made is not present in the Republic that person shall-

(i) be informed of the registration of the order in the manner provided for in an agreement contemplated in section 27 of the Act or any other agreement concluded with the foreign State where that person is present; or

(ii) in the absence of an agreement referred to in subparagraph (i), be informed of such registration by sending a copy of the written notice of registration to that person by registered mail.

(c) The clerk of the court sending a copy of the notice in terms of paragraph (b)(ii) to the person against whom the foreign confiscation order has been made, shall require that proof of receipt thereof be returned to him or her by the relevant postal authority.

Period within which a person may apply for setting aside of registration of foreign confiscation order

12. (1) An application for the setting aside of the registration of a foreign confiscation order in terms of section 20(4)(b) of the Act shall be made within 20 court days from the date on which such registration came to the knowledge of the applicant.

(2) Unless the applicant proves the contrary, it shall be presumed that where—

(a) the written notice of registration was served on that applicant personally, he or she had knowledge of such registration on the date of service of the notice;

(b) the written notice of registration was not served on that applicant personally, he or she had knowledge of such registration within 10 days after the date of service of the notice;

(c) the written notice of registration was sent to that applicant by registered mail, he or she had knowledge of such registration on the date of receipt thereof indicated in the proof of receipt contemplated in regulation 11(2)(c); or

(d) that applicant was informed of such registration in any other manner, he or she had knowledge of such registration on the date on which he or she was so informed.

Manner in which a person may apply for setting aside of registration of foreign confiscation order

13. (1) An application for the setting aside the registration of a foreign confiscation order shall be made to the court where that order was registered.

(2) Such an application shall be on notice which shall state—

   (a) that an order for the setting aside of the registration of a foreign confiscation order is applied for;

   (b) the grounds contemplated in section 22(1) of the Act on which the application is based; and

   (c) the date and time when the application will be made to the court, and shall be accompanied by an affidavit, made by the applicant or a person who can swear positively to the facts, in support of the grounds referred to in paragraph (b).

(3) Delivery of such notice shall be effected to the Office of the State Attorney in Pretoria, or a branch of that Office nearest to the court to which such an application is made, not later than 20 court days before the day appointed for the hearing of the application.

Chapter 5
Foreign Restraint Orders

Registration of foreign restraint order

14. Whenever a certified copy of a foreign restraint order is lodged with a registrar of a division of the High Court in terms of section 24(1) of the Act, such registrar shall register that order by—

   (a) numbering the foreign restraint order with a consecutive case number for the year during which it is lodged; and

   (b) recording the restraint in respect of the property specified in the order and full particulars of that property, in so far as such particulars are available, on the case cover in which the certified copy of the foreign restraint order is filed.

Notice of registration of foreign restraint order

15. (1) The written notice of registration of a foreign restraint order contemplated in section 24(3) of the Act shall correspond substantially with Form 4 of the Annexure, and shall contain—

   (a) the consecutive case number referred to in regulation 14(a);

   (b) the date on which the foreign restraint order was registered;

   (c) the restraint in respect of the property specified in the order and full particulars of that property in so far as such particulars are available; and

   (d) a reference to the provisions of section 24(3)(b) of the Act and regulation 16.

(2) (a) Where the person against whom the foreign restraint order has been made is present in the Republic, the written notice of registration, together with a copy thereof, shall be delivered to a sheriff who shall serve such notice on that person in accordance with the manner provided for in regulation 7(2) to (6), and the provisions of regulation 7(7) to (10) shall, read with the changes required by the context, apply to such service: Provided that the endorsement of the manner in

which a copy of the notice was served, shall be returned to the registrar of the High Court from whom the notice was received.

(b) Where the person against whom the foreign restraint order has been made is not present in the Republic that person shall—

(i) be informed of the registration of the order in the manner provided for in an agreement contemplated in section 27 of the Act or any other agreement concluded with the foreign State where that person is present; or

(ii) in the absence of an agreement referred to in subparagraph (i), be informed of such registration by sending a copy of the written notice of registration to that person by registered mail.

(c) The registrar of the High Court sending a copy of the notice in terms of paragraph (b)(ii) to the person against whom the foreign restraint order has been made, shall require that proof of receipt thereof be returned to him or her by the relevant postal authority.

Period within which a person may apply for setting aside of registration of foreign restraint order

16. (1) An application for the setting aside of the registration of a foreign restraint order contemplated in section 24(3)(b) of the Act shall be made within 20 court days from the date on which such registration came to the knowledge of the applicant.

(2) Unless the applicant proves the contrary, it shall be presumed that where—

(a) the written notice of registration was served on that applicant personally, he or she had knowledge of such registration on the date of service of the notice;

(b) the written notice of registration was not served on that applicant personally, he or she had knowledge of such registration within 10 days after the date of service of the notice;

(c) the written notice of registration was sent to that applicant by registered mail, he or she had knowledge of such registration on the date of receipt thereof indicated in the proof of receipt contemplated in regulation 15(2)(c); or

(d) that applicant was informed of such registration in any other manner, he or she had knowledge of such registration on the date which he or she was so informed.

SWITZERLAND

Federal Act on International Mutual Assistance in Criminal Matters (Mutual Assistance Act, IMAC)

Section 2: Specific Mutual Assistance Measures

Art. 74a Handing over of objects or assets for the purpose of forfeiture or return

1. On request, objects or assets subject to a precautionary seizure may be handed over to the competent foreign authority after conclusion of the mutual assistance proceedings (Art. 80d) for the purpose of forfeiture or return to the person entitled.

2. The objects or assets referred to in paragraph 1 include:

    a. instruments which were used to commit the offence;

    b. products of or profits from the offence, their replacement value and any unlawful advantage;

    c. gifts and other contributions which served to instigate the offence or recompense the offender, as well as their replacement value.

3. The handing over may take place at any stage of the foreign proceedings, normally based on a final and executable decision from the requesting State.

4. However, the objects or assets may be retained in Switzerland if:

    a. the victim is habitually resident in Switzerland and they have to be returned to him;

    b. an authority asserts rights over them;

    c. a person not involved in the offence and whose claims are not guaranteed by the requesting State shows probable cause that he has acquired rights over these objects and assets in good faith in Switzerland, or if he is habitually resident in Switzerland, in a foreign country; or

    d. the objects or assets are necessary for pending criminal proceedings in Switzerland or appear, because of their nature, to be subject to forfeiture in Switzerland.

5. Whenever a person claims to have rights over the objects or assets under paragraph 4, its handing over to the requesting State shall be postponed until the legal situation is clear. The objects or assets claimed may be handed over to the person entitled if:

    a. the requesting State agrees;

    b. in the case of paragraph 4 letter b, the authority gives its consent; or

    c. the claim has been recognised by a Swiss court.

6. Article 60 applies to fiscal liens.

7. Objects and assets to which Switzerland is entitled according to an asset sharing agreement based on the Federal Act of 19 March 2004 on the Division of Forfeited Assets 112 shall not be handed over in accordance with paragraph 1.1.

UNITED ARAB EMIRATES

Federal Decree-law No. (20) of 2018 on Anti-Money Laundering and Combating the Financing of Terrorism and Financing of Illegal Organisations

Article (20)

Any court injunction or court decision providing for the confiscation of funds, proceeds or instrumentalities relating to money-laundering, terrorist financing or financing of illegal organisations may be recognized if issued by a court or judicial authority of another State with which the State has entered into a ratified Convention.

UNITED KINGDOM

The Proceeds of Crime Act 2002 (External Requests and Orders) Order 2005

Part 2
Giving Effect in England and Wales to External Requests in Connection with Criminal Investigations or Proceedings and to External Orders Arising from Such Proceedings

Chapter 2
External Orders

Applications to give effect to external orders

20.—(1) An application may be made by the relevant Director to the Crown Court to give effect to an external order.

(2) No application to give effect to such an order may be made otherwise than under paragraph (1).

(3) An application under paragraph (1)—

 (a) shall include a request to appoint the relevant Director as the enforcement authority for the order;

 (b) may be made on an ex parte application to a judge in chambers.

Conditions for Crown Court to give effect to external orders

21.—(1) The Crown Court must decide to give effect to an external order by registering it where all of the following conditions are satisfied.

(2) The first condition is that the external order was made consequent on the conviction of the person named in the order and no appeal is outstanding in respect of that conviction.

(3) The second condition is that the external order is in force and no appeal is outstanding in respect of it.

(4) The third condition is that giving effect to the external order would not be incompatible with any of the Convention rights (within the meaning of the Human Rights Act 1998(a)) of any person affected by it.

(5) The fourth condition applies only in respect of an external order which authorises the confiscation of property other than money that is specified in the order.

(6) That condition is that the specified property must not be subject to a charge under any of the following provisions—

 (a) section 9 of the Drug Trafficking Offences Act 1986(b);

 (b) section 78 of the Criminal Justice Act 1988(c);

 (c) Article 14 of the Criminal Justice (Confiscation) (Northern Ireland) Order 1990(d);

 (d) section 27 of the Drug Trafficking Act 1994(e);

(7) In determining whether the order is an external order within the meaning of the Act, the Court must have regard to the definitions in subsections (2), (4), (5), (6), (8) and (10) of section 447 of the Act.

(8) In paragraph (3) "appeal" includes—

    (a) any proceedings by way of discharging or setting aside the order; and

    (b) an application for a new trial or stay of execution.

Registration of external orders

22.—(1) Where the Crown Court decides to give effect to an external order, it must—

    (a) register the order in that court;

    (b) provide for notice of the registration to be given to any person affected by it; and

    (c) appoint the relevant Director as the enforcement authority for the order.

(2) Only an external order registered by the Crown Court may be implemented under this Chapter.

(3) The Crown Court may cancel the registration of the external order, or vary the property to which it applies, on an application by the relevant Director or any person affected by it if, or to the extent that, the court is of the opinion that any of the conditions in article 21 is not satisfied.

(4) The Crown Court must cancel the registration of the external order, on an application by the relevant Director or any person affected by it, if it appears to the court that the order has been satisfied—

    (a) in the case of an order for the recovery of a sum of money specified in it, by payment of the amount due under it, or

    (b) in the case of an order for the recovery of specified property, by the surrender of the property, or

    (c) by any other means.

(5) Where the registration of an external order is cancelled or varied under paragraph (3) or (4), the Crown Court must provide for notice of this to be given to the relevant Director and any person affected by it.

Appeal to Court of Appeal about external orders

23.—(1) If on an application for the Crown Court to give effect to an external order by registering it, the court decides not to do so, the relevant Director may appeal to the Court of Appeal against the decision.

(2) If an application is made under article 22(3) or (4) in relation to the registration of an external order, the following persons may appeal to the Court of Appeal in respect of the Crown Court's decision on the application—

    (a) the relevant Director;

    (b) any person affected by the registration.

(3) On an appeal under paragraph (1) or (2) the Court of Appeal may—

    (a) confirm or set aside the decision to register; or

    (b) direct the Crown Court to register the external order (or so much of it as relates to property other than to which article 21(6) applies).

Appeal to House of Lords about external orders

24.—(1) An appeal lies to the House of Lords from a decision of the Court of Appeal on an appeal under article 23.

(2) An appeal under this article lies at the instance of any person who was a party to the proceedings before the Court of Appeal.

(3) On an appeal under this article the House of Lords may—

(a) confirm or set aside the decision of the Court of Appeal, or

(b) direct the Crown Court to register the external order (or so much of it as relates to property other than property to which article 21(6) applies).

Sums in currency other than sterling

25.—(1) This article applies where the external order which is registered under article 22 specifies a sum of money.

(2) If the sum of money which is specified is expressed in a currency other than sterling, the sum of money to be recovered is to be taken to be the sterling equivalent calculated in accordance with the rate of exchange prevailing at the end of the working day immediately preceding the day when the Crown Court registered the external order under article 22.

(3) The sterling equivalent must be calculated by the relevant Director.

(4) The notice referred to in article 22(1)(b) and (5) must set out the amount in sterling which is to be paid.

[...]

Time for payment

26.—(1) This article applies where the external order is for the recovery of a specified sum of money.

(2) Subject to paragraphs (3) to (6), the amount ordered to be paid under—

(a) an external order that has been registered under article 22, or

(b) where article 25(2) applies, the notice under article 22(1)(b), must be paid on the date on which the notice under article 22(1)(b) is delivered to the person affected by it.

(3) Where there is an appeal under article 23 or 24 and a sum fails to be paid when the appeal has been determined or withdrawn, the duty to pay is delayed until the day on which the appeal is determined or withdrawn.

(4) If the person affected by an external order which has been registered shows that he needs time to pay the amount ordered to be paid, the Crown Court which registered the order may make an order allowing payment to be made in a specified period.

(5) The specified period—

(a) must start with the day on which the notice under article 22(1)(b) was delivered to the person affected by the order or the day referred to in paragraph (3), as the case may be, and

(b) must not exceed six months.

(6) If within the specified period the person affected by an external order applies to the Crown Court which registered the order for the period to be extended and the court believes that there are exceptional circumstances, it may make an order extending the period.

(7) The extended period—

(a) must start with the day on which the notice under article 22(1)(b) was delivered to the person affected by it or the day referred to in paragraph (3), as the case may be, and

(b) must not exceed 12 months.

(8) An order under paragraph (6)—

(a) may be made after the end of the specified period, but

(b) must not be made after the end of the extended period.

(9) The court must not make an order under paragraph (4) or (6) unless it gives the relevant Director an opportunity to make representations.

Appointment of enforcement receivers

27.—(1) This article applies if—

(a) an external order is registered,

(b) it is not satisfied, and

(c) in the case of an external order for the recovery of a specified sum of money, any period specified by order under article 26 has expired.

(2) On the application of the relevant Director, other than the Director of the Agency, the Crown Court may by order appoint a receiver in respect of—

(a) where the external order is for the recovery of a specified sum of money, realizable property;

(b) where the external order is for the recovery of specified property, that property.

Part 5
Giving Effect in the United Kingdom to External Orders by Means of Civil Recovery

Chapter 1
Introduction

Action to give effect to an order

142.—(1) The Secretary of State may forward an external order to the enforcement authority.

(2) This Part has effect for the purpose of enabling the enforcement authority to realise recoverable property (within the meaning of article 202) in civil proceedings before the High Court or Court of Session for the purpose of giving effect to an external order.

(3) The powers conferred by this Part are exercisable in relation to any property whether or not proceedings have been brought in the country from which the external order was sent for criminal conduct (within the meaning of section 447(8) of the Act) in connection with the property.

UNITED STATES

28 U.S. Code § 2467—Enforcement of foreign judgment

(a) Definitions.—In this section—

    (1) the term "foreign nation" means a country that has become a party to the United Nations Convention Against Illicit Traffic in Narcotic Drugs and Psychotropic Substances (referred to in this section as the "United Nations Convention") or a foreign jurisdiction with which the United States has a treaty or other formal international agreement in effect providing for mutual forfeiture assistance; and

    (2) the term "forfeiture or confiscation judgment" means a final order of a foreign nation compelling a person or entity—

        (A) to pay a sum of money representing the proceeds of an offense described in Article 3, Paragraph 1, of the United Nations Convention, any violation of foreign law that would constitute a violation or an offense for which property could be forfeited under Federal law if the offense were committed in the United States, or any foreign offense described in section 1956(c)(7)(B) of title 18, or property the value of which corresponds to such proceeds; or

        (B) to forfeit property involved in or traceable to the commission of such offense.

(b) Review by Attorney General.—

    (1) In general.—A foreign nation seeking to have a forfeiture or confiscation judgment registered and enforced by a district court of the United States under this section shall first submit a request to the Attorney General or the designee of the Attorney General, which request shall include—

        (A) a summary of the facts of the case and a description of the proceedings that resulted in the forfeiture or confiscation judgment;

        (B) certified [1] copy of the forfeiture or confiscation judgment;

        (C) an affidavit or sworn declaration establishing that the foreign nation took steps, in accordance with the principles of due process, to give notice of the proceedings to all persons with an interest in the property in sufficient time to enable such persons to defend against the charges and that the judgment rendered is in force and is not subject to appeal; and

        (D) such additional information and evidence as may be required by the Attorney General or the designee of the Attorney General.

    (2) Certification of request.—

    The Attorney General or the designee of the Attorney General shall determine whether, in the interest of justice, to certify the request, and such decision shall be final and not subject to either judicial review or review under subchapter II of chapter 5, or chapter 7, of title 5 (commonly known as the "Administrative Procedure Act").

(c) Jurisdiction and Venue.—

    (1) In general.—

    If the Attorney General or the designee of the Attorney General certifies a request under subsection (b), the United States may file an application on behalf of a foreign nation in district court of the United States seeking to enforce the foreign forfeiture or confiscation judgment as if the judgment had been entered by a court in the United States.

(2) Proceedings.—In a proceeding filed under paragraph (1)—

   (A) the United States shall be the applicant and the defendant or another person or entity affected by the forfeiture or confiscation judgment shall be the respondent;

   (B) venue shall lie in the district court for the District of Columbia or in any other district in which the defendant or the property that may be the basis for satisfaction of a judgment under this section may be found; and

   (C) the district court shall have personal jurisdiction over a defendant residing outside of the United States if the defendant is served with process in accordance with rule 4 of the Federal Rules of Civil Procedure.

(d) Entry and Enforcement of Judgment.—

   (1) In general.—The district court shall enter such orders as may be necessary to enforce the judgment on behalf of the foreign nation unless the court finds that—

   (A) the judgment was rendered under a system that provides tribunals or procedures incompatible with the requirements of due process of law;

   (B) the foreign court lacked personal jurisdiction over the defendant;

   (C) the foreign court lacked jurisdiction over the subject matter;

   (D) the foreign nation did not take steps, in accordance with the principles of due process, to give notice of the proceedings to a person with an interest in the property of the proceedings [2] in sufficient time to enable him or her to defend; or

   (E) the judgment was obtained by fraud.

   (2) Process.—
   Process to enforce a judgment under this section shall be in accordance with rule 69(a) of the Federal Rules of Civil Procedure.

   (3) Preservation of property.—

   (A) Restraining orders.—

      (i) In general.—

         To preserve the availability of property subject to civil or criminal forfeiture under foreign law, the Government may apply for, and the court may issue, a restraining order at any time before or after the initiation of forfeiture proceedings by a foreign nation.

      (ii) Procedures.—

         (I) In general.—

            A restraining order under this subparagraph shall be issued in a manner consistent with subparagraphs (A), (C), and (E) of paragraph (1) and the procedural due process protections for a restraining order under section 983(j) of title 18.

(II) Application.—For purposes of applying such section 983(j)—

aa) references in such section 983(j) to civil forfeiture or the filing of a complaint shall be deemed to refer to the applicable foreign criminal or forfeiture proceedings; and

(bb) the reference in paragraph (1)(B)(i) of such section 983(j) to the United States shall be deemed to refer to the foreign nation.

(B) Evidence.—The court, in issuing a restraining order under subparagraph (A)—

(i) may rely on information set forth in an affidavit describing the nature of the proceeding or investigation underway in the foreign country, and setting forth a reasonable basis to believe that the property to be restrained will be named in a judgment of forfeiture at the conclusion of such proceeding; or

(ii) may register and enforce a restraining order that has been issued by a court of competent jurisdiction in the foreign country and certified by the Attorney General pursuant to subsection (b)(2).

(C) Limit on grounds for objection.—

No person may object to a restraining order under subparagraph (A) on any ground that is the subject of parallel litigation involving the same property that is pending in a foreign court.

(e) Finality of Foreign Findings.—

In entering orders to enforce the judgment, the court shall be bound by the findings of fact to the extent that they are stated in the foreign forfeiture or confiscation judgment.

(f) Currency Conversion.—

The rate of exchange in effect at the time the suit to enforce is filed by the foreign nation shall be used in calculating the amount stated in any forfeiture or confiscation judgment requiring the payment of a sum of money submitted for registration.